RECORDING
ORAL
HISTORY

In memory of my father, Fletcher Raleigh Yow,
who showed me the power of words.
And for my mother, Mae Moore Wyatt,
who revealed to me the power of imagination.

RECORDING
ORAL
HISTORY

A PRACTICAL GUIDE
FOR SOCIAL SCIENTISTS

VALERIE RALEIGH YOW

SAGE Publications
International Educational and Professional Publisher
Thousand Oaks   London   New Delhi

For information address:

SAGE Publications, Inc.
2455 Teller Road
Thousand Oaks, California 91320
E-mail: order@sagepub.com

SAGE Publications Ltd.
6 Bonhill Street
London EC2A 4PU
United Kingdom

SAGE Publications India Pvt. Ltd.
M-32 Market
Greater Kailash I
New Delhi 110 048 India

Printed in the United States of America

Library of Congress Cataloging-in-Publication Data

Yow, Valerie Raleigh.
　　Recording oral history : a practical guide for social scientists /
Valerie Raleigh Yow.
　　　　p.　cm.
　　Includes bibliographical references and index.
　　ISBN 0-8039-5578-2 (cloth).　—　ISBN 0-8039-5579-0 (pbk.)
　　1. Oral history—Methodology.　I. Title.
D14.Y69　1994
907.2—dc20　　　　　　　　　　　　　　　　　93-41635

03　04　10　9

Sage Production Editor: Yvonne Könneker

Contents

Preface

This book is intended for use by researchers who want information on carrying out the recorded in-depth interview. Ethical issues, questions about interpersonal relationships, and techniques for interviewing will be of interest to scholars in the social sciences and also to those who use the in-depth interview to enrich their knowledge of their own history. Because I am a historian, I often take a historian's point of view and discuss specific issues of concern to those researching contemporary history by means of oral history methodology. But I also address concerns of scholars in other disciplines when they differ from the historian's approach.

This is not a guide for conducting a diagnostic interview, although some aspects—such as building rapport—are similar to the work done in an oral history interview. And although it is not a book intended for researchers doing focused interviews, the chapters on interviewing skills, ethics, and interpersonal relationships may be helpful to them as well.

The in-depth interview is a research methodology with standards of excellence and guidelines for achieving these, and I present them here. Hard and fast rules, however, are not always appropriate in approaching the in-depth interview. Often problems arise that require considering the consequences of several strategies and then making a judgment. Nevertheless, a thorough knowledge of ethics, legalities, and techniques helps in this process of deciding what to do. And an awareness of what is happening in the interpersonal relationship during the interview situation can make the difference between a productive interview and a superficial, truncated interview.

Because almost no empirical research has been done on the efficacy of specific interviewing techniques, I must of necessity rely on the consensus (when there is one) of experienced interviewers on a solution for a particular problem. I give examples to illustrate what I mean with the attitude that we are all in this together and that we learn from one another. I hope my readers will forgive the prescriptive tone: It stems from an earnest desire to help the individual beginning to do this kind of research and also from the conviction that this is serious business—this dealing with living persons. On the other hand, I have tried not to be formal because I wanted the manual to be "user friendly." I do not disguise the speaker's "I": This is congruent with my belief that the writer of this kind of manual is a guide, not an unquestionable authority. And although it is impossible to pinpoint the absolute truth, I can strive to be honest with my reader, indicating how I arrived—in terms of my own values and experiences—at a conclusion.

Oral historians are a helpful group of people, perhaps the most helpful of my colleagues in history. I am grateful for help given me by Sally Smith Hughes at the Regional Oral History Office, Bancroft Library, University of California, Berkeley, California; Paul Buhle, director of the Oral History of the American Left, Tamiment Library, New York University; Jane Adams, Department of Anthropology, Southern Illinois University at Carbondale; and Linda Shopes of the Pennsylvania Historical and Museum Commission, Harrisburg, Pennsylvania. Each of these generous scholars has read several chapters and given me perceptive criticisms. Ronald Grele, director of the Oral History Research Office at Columbia University, critiqued the first chapter. Carl Ryant, of the Oral History Program at the University of Louisville, read the chapter on public history; James Findlay, director of the State Oral History Project at the University of Rhode Island, read the chapter on ethics. They have all given me the benefit of their reflections. Especially enthusiastic thanks go to Charles Morrissey, director of the Oral History and Archives Office of the Baylor College of Medicine, for reading the entire manuscript. With his usual good humor and sharp critic's eye, he has made invaluable suggestions. I must, of course, accept responsibility for this book's shortcomings, but without these scholars' help, there would have been even more deficiencies. And I wish to take this opportunity also to thank my students at the University of Rhode Island and Northern Illinois University for their enthusiasm and interest and for good times in our class oral history projects.

1

Introduction to the In-Depth Interview

Recently a development has been going on in the fields of education, anthropology, oral history, folklore, biographical literature, psychology, and humanistic sociology. This has been spurred in part by feminist psychologists, historians, and anthropologists, in part by men and women writing literary biography, humanistic sociology, and ethnography. This development is centered on a concern about the process of meaning making. Many of us who use the in-depth interview are interested in how the respondents interpret experience and how we, the questioners, interject ourselves into this process. We try to be conscious of the effects of the research process on both interviewer and narrator. Sociologist Judith Stacey described this as the realization that "ethnographic writing is not cultural reportage, but cultural construction, and always a construction of self as well as of the other."[1]

1

We are also concerned about the ways power relationships based on knowledge, gender, race, class, status, age, and ethnicity impinge on the interview situation. We strive to be aware of when and how these conditions affect the narrator and interviewer as they interact and how this influences the testimony recorded.

In ethnographic research in general and in oral history research specifically, there has been a shift in the relationship of interviewer to narrator. Formerly, the relationship of researcher (who plays the role of authoritative scholar) to narrator (who is the passive yielder of data) was one of subject to object. In this new view, power may be unequal, but both interviewer and narrator are seen as having knowledge of the situation as well as deficits in understanding. Although the interviewer brings to the interviewing situation a perspective based on research in a discipline, the narrator brings intimate knowledge of his or her own culture and often a different perspective—one just as valid as the interviewer's. Now the relationship is one of subject to subject. The interviewer thus sees the work as a collaboration and values the narrator's contribution as being as important as his or her own, if not more so.[2] This is an underlying assumption in this book.

In striving to see the world as the narrator sees it, we realize this stance compels some degree of compassion for the narrator. We cannot—and do not wish to—pretend to complete objectivity.

The guide is intended for all who use the recorded in-depth interview in their fieldwork and are open to reflecting on ethics and interpersonal relationships as well as on gaining information about interviewing techniques. Admittedly there is an emphasis on historical research because my own work has been centered on historical issues. For example, I emphasize the life history approach rather than the present-centered interview. However, my thinking has been enriched by research and debates in other disciplines, and I draw examples from the experience of scholars in anthropology, sociology, psychology, education, and folklore. I discuss specifically issues in in-depth interviewing that concern scholars in other disciplines when they diverge from those of historians.

This first chapter contains an explanation of terms used in referring to the recorded in-depth interview. There is a brief discussion about differences between qualitative and quantitative research methods; and the in-depth interview, or oral history, is presented in the context of the general field of qualitative research. Appropriate uses of the in-depth interview and its limitations as well as ways to deal with limitations are suggested.

Brief History of the Use of Oral History

Most writers begin books on oral history by reminding readers that the first oral historian was Thucydides, who sought out people to interview and used their information in writing the *History of the Peloponnesian War.* Use of personal testimony in the investigation of society has never ceased. However, the tape-recorded interview was possible only after World War II when portable recording machines became available. So, although the use of data from individual memory is at least as old as the fifth century B.C., the mechanical recording of the in-depth interview is not so old—less than 50 years, in fact.

In 1948 Alan Nevins, at Columbia University, began to tape-record the spoken memories of white male elites: This was the first organized oral history project.[3] At that time, heavy, cumbersome reel-to-reel recording machines were used. Soon lighter machines came into use, and by the 1960s the easy-to-carry tape recorder using cassettes became the standard equipment. Also in the 1960s, an interest in recording the memories of people other than elites became paramount among academics. Because of this interest and technical improvements in recorders, by 1965 there were 89 oral history projects ongoing in this country, and the number of projects has grown in each year since then.[4]

At the same time, the easy portability of cassette recorders enhanced the quantity and quality of interviews by folklorists, ethnographers, sociologists, and psychologists whose research was based on qualitative methodology. Although each discipline uses the in-depth interview in somewhat different ways, the practical and theoretical problems tend to cut across disciplinary boundaries. The question "What is oral history anyway?" has stymied nearly all of us at one point or another.

Definition of Oral History

Oral historians have probably devoted more energy to definitional issues and problems of application than other disciplines. Charles

Morrissey, an oral historian, searched for the origin of the term *oral history* and traced it to a New York citizen of the 19th century.[5] Nevins called what he was doing "oral history."[6] But what is oral history? Is it the taped memoir? Is it the typewritten transcript? Is it the research method that involves in-depth interviewing? The term refers to all three. Lamentations have been heard about the inadequacy, the imprecision, the misleading characteristic of the term, but is it possible to find a better one? In this book, I use several terms interchangeably with *oral history.* James Bennett mentioned a string of them in his speech to the annual meeting of the Oral History Association in 1982: among them, *life history, self-report, personal narrative, life story, oral biography, memoir, testament.*[7] The terms used here—such as *in-depth interview, recorded memoir, life history, the recorded narrative, taped memories, life review*—imply that there is someone else involved who inspires the narrator to begin the act of remembering, jogs memory, and records and presents the narrator's words.

Most of these terms also have been used in cognate disciplines. Although theorists have proposed a set of more technically specific meanings for each term, these meanings seem not to have caught on, and the terms remain interchangeable. *Oral history* seems lately to be the one most frequently used to refer to the recorded in-depth interview, although *life history* is also frequently used.

Oral History: Still a New Kid on the Block

Social scientists, in general, are trained to view manufacturing the evidence as the worst thing one can do. True, evidence can be "massaged" and "manipulated," but not made. The recorded in-depth interview is a research method that is based on direct intervention by the observer and on the evocation of evidence. In the sense that the evidence was not tangible until the interviewer recorded it, and that the evidence is the result of the interviewer's questioning, this is the making of evidence. This is the worst sin one can commit, according to traditional methodologists in history.

But return to the first historians who wrote history, the Greeks: They, too, questioned and listened to the witnesses of events and used the accounts related *for them* as the evidence for their histories. The seeking and recording in some manner of answers to questions in an effort to understand is the oldest kind of research. The subjectivity of the process did not bother the Greeks: They knew that their witnesses and they themselves were human beings involved in the process of living, of history, even as they searched for its meanings.

Nevertheless, many historians trained in research methods rooted in the Germanic "scientific school" of the 19th century cast a suspicious glance on oral history. They rely mainly on written records and on a critical examination of them. In the latter part of this chapter I will suggest ways of subjecting the orally transmitted document to the same critical examination with which written records are evaluated.

Many sociologists and other social scientists today still hold the view that quantitative research is the only real way to be certain about evidence. They have grave reservations about qualitative research because they view it as uncontrolled and lacking in the rigorous procedures followed by quantitative researchers. Qualitative methodology has its own body of strict standards for procedure and evaluation. Standards for the recorded in-depth interview as a research method and a critical evaluation of procedures are the subjects discussed in the chapters that follow.

Qualitative Research and Quantitative Research: Comparisons

Sharan Merriam, in the book *Case Study Research in Education: A Qualitative Approach*, explained that the quantitative researcher assesses a limited number of variables by examining a number of researcher-controlled answers, trying to find out if a preconceived hypothesis is operating, if the prediction that certain variables cause certain effects will hold true.[8] By using a questionnaire requiring short answers, a large number of subjects can be queried. The subjects are selected in such a way that they are representative of the population studied. Therefore researchers can make generalizations with a degree of confidence.

Qualitative research does not involve manipulation of a few variables. Rather, Merriam argued, this kind of research is inductive, and a multiplicity of variables and their relationships are considered not in isolation but as being interrelated in the life context.[9] The in-depth interview enables the researcher to give the subject leeway to answer as he or she chooses, to attribute meanings to the experiences under discussion, and to interject topics. In this way, new hypotheses may be generated.

The origins of the data used in these two ways of finding answers to questions about human society are at their foundations similar: observations of human behavior. British oral historian Paul Thompson reminded readers that the basic information that statisticians use—census data, registrations of birth, marriage, and death—is suspect. Marriage registers, for example, contain false information about age because often couples did not want the official to know they were still of the age that required parental consent.[10] Birthdates are falsified to present a nine-month interval between marriage and birth of the first child. People give census takers false information, sometimes because they do not understand what the census taker means. People answer questionnaires in a slapdash way because they are in a hurry. British historian Trevor Lummis summed up this idea: "So even 'hard' contemporary statistical data is only what somebody told somebody and if they have good reason and the opportunity to conceal the truth, then the 'facts' will be erroneous."[11] All of us who study humans—whether with quantitative or qualitative methods—know that we cannot hold our conclusions with absolute certainty.

One advantage in using qualitative methodology is that, because the researcher does not use an unchangeable testing instrument, he or she is open to observing the informants' choice of behaviors. In this way, the researcher learns new things not in an original hypothesis—in fact, many qualitative researchers do not form hypotheses at the beginning of the research.

An example of finding something outside the researcher's thinking comes from sociologist Arlene Daniels, who studies organization of work, especially unwritten codes of behavior. In a project on military psychiatrists, if she had used a questionnaire whose data she could then easily quantify, she would not have asked a question about sexuality. Earlier information would not have suggested that she do so unless the subject was sexual dysfunction, which the psychiatrist would treat clinically. Instead, in the in-depth interviews she conducted, she found that sexual practice was an important topic. When wives of high-ranking officers began affairs with lower-ranking officers, the local military psychiatrist would send the offender to a hospital for evaluation and possible treatment. Thus the psychiatrist provided a short-term but effective solution to a nonpsychiatric problem. By listening and allowing her narrators to teach her, Daniels discovered an aspect of behavior connected to sexuality in the military that was not previously in her thinking.[12]

This possibility of discovering something not even thought of before is an advantage of the method. However, in-depth interviews are time-consuming, and so the qualitative researcher cannot examine the number of cases that the quantitative researcher can. Generalizations about a wider population have to be held even more tentatively.

One aim in quantitative research is to reduce as much as possible the influence of the researcher's bias. However, because it is the researcher who forms the research questions, the bias is present from the beginning. The researcher interprets the mathematical results: The probability of bias is there as well. Nevertheless, subjectivity is undoubtedly more intrusive in qualitative research because the researcher is constantly interacting with the people being studied. Sociologist Jack Douglas described the way the qualitative researcher acknowledges and uses his or her bias: "Rather than trying to eliminate the subjective effects, the goal must be to try to understand how they are interdependent, how different forms of subjective interaction with the people we are studying affect our conclusions about them, and so on."[13] Qualitative researchers therefore must constantly reflect on the ways their own assumptions and biases impinge on the research process.

The qualitative researcher learns about a way of life by studying the people who live it and asking them how they think about their experiences. The many examples they offer in their testimony are carefully studied. The term used to describe the close examination of examples that yields the hypothesis is *grounded theory,* an approach originated by sociologists Anselm Strauss and Barney Glaser.[14] *Thick description,* a term used by ethnographer Clifford Geertz, is the goal: not a single view of the experience, but a larger number of testimonies that give great variety in detail.[15]

Quantification has its appropriate usage, as does qualitative research. The kind of question asked leads to the choice of research method. For example, oral historian Fern Ingersoll and anthropologist Jasper Ingersoll worked together on a project in southern Thailand, using field techniques from anthropology and oral history as well as population data gathered by sociologists. By observing behaviors and conducting in-depth interviews and focused group interviews, they sought an understanding of the way income was experienced in the total life of the families.[16] If they had chosen to do so, they could have studied quantitative data and arrived at two dimensions of the society they studied—actual level of income as well as perceived level.

Qualitative methods and quantitative methods may also be profitably used together when data from several in-depth interviews are coded and expressed mathematically. In the example given above, the Ingersolls could have analyzed the content of all the individual interviews in terms of answers to particular questions, assigning each answer to a category, which was given a number. Statistical analysis could have then been feasible. Researchers may also use an in-depth interviewing project to suggest hypotheses that may be tested by using a questionnaire with a larger sample drawn from the population being studied.

The In-Depth Interview
as a Qualitative Research Method

The *recorded in-depth interview,* or *oral history,* is a specific research method within the general designation of qualitative methodology and is close to the basic principle of grounded theory. The difference lies in the emphasis placed on the formation of questions that guide the research. Also *grounded theory* refers to other kinds observations of behaviors besides the interview. Proponents of grounded theory insist on approaching research without preconceptions—that is, hypotheses. Social scientists such as Leonard Schatzman and Anselm Strauss warn against having any preconceived notions before beginning the research.[17] For others, there is acceptance of the researcher starting with articulated problems or questions that guide the interview process. This may or may not result in the formulation of specific hypotheses during the research or at its completion. Ethnographer Renato Rosaldo described this approach:

> Ethnographers begin research with a set of questions, revise them throughout the course of inquiry, and in the end emerge with different questions than they started with. One's surprise at the answer to a question, in other words, requires one to revise the question until lessening surprises or diminishing returns indicate a stopping point.[18]

Some historians as well as other social scientists use hypotheses based on previous knowledge that are tested and discarded as the evidence suggests other explanations. Other historians do not test hypotheses but have in mind some questions that they pursue with the aim of finding answers so they can construct a narrative that makes sense. British historian and philosopher R. G. Collingwood stressed that the historian does not collect data without questions to guide the search: "It is only when he has a problem in his mind that he can begin to search for data bearing on it."[19]

It is important to acknowledge that there are at least assumptions— if not hypotheses or questions—that direct the researcher's attention to some aspects of behavior or discourse and not to others. If assumptions are not acknowledged, how can they be examined? The qualitative researcher must be conscious of assumptions and interests that inform the work and be aware of how and why these change during the research process.

Differences in Ways That Disciplines Approach the In-Depth Interview

Researchers from different disciplines use the in-depth interview differently, although interviewing techniques may be the same. According to your discipline, you will no doubt combine it with other methods. For historians, this will mean a thorough search for other primary sources. For anthropologists, it will be close observation of behaviors over a long period of living in the field. For sociologists, it will probably be fieldwork as well as manipulation of aggregate data such as census reports or survey research results. But these methods may be used by all three: The strict boundaries between disciplines are artificial. Often a more helpful question is simply, "Given my research question, what do I need to do to find the answer?"

The kind of general research question you ask, however, is often the result of the discourse you have studied in a particular discipline, and I do not wish to obscure differences. Ethnography—that is, participant-observation research whether practiced by anthropologists or sociologists—and history ask somewhat different questions of narrators. For example, historians cannot stop with asking questions about how things are but must also ask the question, "How did things get to be the way they are?" This catapults them into an examination of sources of information about the past. There is often a difference in the way the document (tape or transcript) is handled regarding the narrator's identity. There are differences in approaches to interpretation of the document. However, in practice the lines between disciplines are often blurred as scholars in one discipline use concepts or approaches from another. In all of these disciplines, researchers who are using the recorded in-depth interview are seeking to understand the ways that the narrator attributes meanings to experience.

Uses of the Recorded In-Depth Interview

Whatever the particular approach or discipline, the recorded in-depth interview can offer answers to questions that no other methodology can provide. Consider here its appropriate uses.

The interview method permits questioning of the witness. In his book *Listening to History,* Trevor Lummis explained, "One precise advantage of oral evidence is that it is interactive and one is not left alone, as with documentary evidence, to divine its significance; the 'source' can reflect upon the content and offer interpretation as well as facts."[20]

This is especially important when we need to know underlying reasons for a decision. The official records state the decision blandly and in the most general terms. We might read that "the motion was made, seconded, and voted," but we have no way of knowing what the participants intended when they voted a certain way because the real motivation rarely appears in official written records. An ostensible reason may be given for public consumption. The in-depth interview is indispensable for probing behind the public-oriented statement. Once, when reading the minutes of a hospital board, I saw that a brilliant physician and creative administrator had handed in his resignation and that it had been accepted. As soon as I could interview the head of the hospital's board at the time, I asked him what happened those 30 years ago. He gave me a blow-by-blow description, explaining the underlying antithetical views of hospital administration held by the physician and the board members and the ways these views were played out and antagonism escalated— none of which was in the hospital board's minutes.[21]

In oral history questioning with individuals, the "closed door" of the written record gives way to the "open door" of the interview.

Even the spoken words by which the motive is phrased by the individual is significant, and the interviewer can find out who the narrator thought was listening over his or her shoulder. The influence of the formerly unnamed can be revealed.

The reasons why ordinary people made decisions that in the aggregate influenced history but are nowhere written down can also be ascertained. For example, why did parents in farm families continue to limit family size from the 19th into the 20th centuries? Were there material reasons? Were there psychological reasons? Sociologists and other social scientists seek answers to these questions in the present. Asking questions that involve this kind of personal, complex decision can best be done in the in-depth interview.

The life review reveals other kinds of information that do not get into the public record. People would rather not admit some things to the census taker—such as, who is living with whom. Nearly everyone underestimates the value of renovations to property when they fill out forms for the county tax office. And underlying the official accounts of "accidental death" are stories of despair on both the personal and societal level. If the interviewer presents no danger and is an empathic listener, this information may be articulated.

In the 20th century, much business is transacted orally. It is not a matter of supplementing the written record or explaining the written record because there are no written records for some decisions. For example, important decisions are arrived at over the telephone: There may not be written records. (The technology of faxing documents may be changing this situation.) Business deals of importance for thousands of workers are discussed over lunch. A final decision on policy is settled while two people are riding up on the elevator. Out on the course, while carefully choosing the right golf club, an executive fires his subordinate who had come along anticipating a relaxing round. There is no record of the firing: Indeed, the only written record is the positive portrayal in the recommendation the executive writes for him.

Certainly an obvious (but not intrinsic) use of oral history projects is that they often involve recording life histories among all socioeconomic levels of the population. In the past, only the well-to-do documented their lives. They not only had a sense of their own importance and were literate, but they also had the leisure and staff support to write. Because they were the ones who held power, their accounts of their lives were usually consonant with accounts in official documents. Through oral history, the viewpoints of the non-elite who do not leave memoirs or have biographers are presented.

This was the situation British oral historian Bill Williams encountered when he began research on Jewish immigrants in Manchester, England. There were plenty of written records, but these had a particular slant:

> In so far as the immigrants survive in the written record they do so chiefly in accounts composed by an older-established Anglo-Jewish elite, with a vested interest in rapid assimilation, or of the majority society, where they appear most frequently either as the "foreign refuse" of anti-alienism or as the pale reflection of middle-class liberalism. Written accounts by immigrants of their own experience are rare, and in the case of Manchester Jewry, all but non-existent.[22]

Paul Thompson commented on the paucity of written evidence for the history of working men and women: "The more personal, local, and unofficial a document, the less likely it was to survive." He listed the official documents that were deliberately saved to shape a view of the past wanted by those in power: legal documents, correspondence of landowners, account books from private firms. He concluded, "But of the innumerable postcards, letters, diaries, and ephemera of working-class men and women, or the papers of small businesses like corner shops or hill farmers, for example, very little has been preserved anywhere."[23]

On the other hand, sometimes in researching contemporary history, we are overwhelmed by the abundance of written documents. Much depends on the topic. Government requirements, such as documentation for the Equal Employment Opportunity Commission, result in a flood of paper. Oral history testimony can help us understand what was significant to the people who made the documents or lived through the times when the documents had power. Such testimony can reveal which documents are important enough to net from the waves of paper.

Oral history testimony is the kind of information that makes other public documents understandable. For example, we may know the average wage of unskilled male workers from looking at government data. What we cannot know unless we ask is how the man supplemented the wage with other work, how the woman found seasonal and part-time jobs and grew food in a kitchen garden and processed it and made over old clothes for the children, and how the children took baby-sitting jobs and ran errands for money and did unpaid work for their parents.[24]

Oral history reveals daily life at home and at work—the very stuff that rarely gets into any kind of public record. Thompson said that these are the areas where we can begin to see how social change is operating.[25] North Carolina millworkers, talking about courtship practices during and just after World War I, described not being allowed to be alone with a sweetheart. A chaperon was always in the parlor with them—one couple sat side-by-side and held hands under the sofa pillow. Then a few people were able to buy cars. At first, the chaperon went along, riding in the back seat. Then another couple went along—safety in numbers. Then two sweethearts started going on excursions alone.[26] Courting practices changed forever. Concrete details in these oral histories made understandable the textbook generalizations about the advent of the automobile changing social life.

The in-depth interview can reveal the informal, unwritten rules of relating to others that characterize any group. I reflect now on my interviewing project among artists in a women's cooperative gallery. The formal rule was that if an artist could not pay her dues after a stated length of time, she would be expelled from membership. In fact, the women were reluctant to expel anyone. They always found some strategy to keep the artist with them if she wanted to stay.[27] Another rule was that membership was open to both men and women and indeed men regularly exhibited at the gallery. But when asked if they would vote for a man to become a regular member, the women hedged and finally indicated that that would be a hard decision to make.[28]

The ramifications of personal relationships that do not get told in official documents are revealed. Again I am reminded of the art gallery and of a heated discussion that went on for months over the difference between art and craft. Hard positions were taken: Individuals seemed unmovable. As time went by, they softened their positions. Friendships mattered too much for anyone to maintain a rigid stance; in the end, personal relationships were more important even than the definitions of their work. And only in the in-depth interviews did the interweaving of personal relationships, work, and definitions of work become clear.[29]

It is through oral history that the dimensions of life within a community are illuminated. Studying the role of the two churches in the mill village showed me how this can come about. The programs in which members offered songs and poetry emphasized family and mutual help. Over and over, testimony was given about the family, such accounts as taking into the house two maiden aunts when they were old and could not work. In the mill, people also helped one another. If a spinner was trying to tie a broken thread and another thread broke, a fellow worker would leave her machines and come over to help.[30] The philosophy of what it meant to be "a good person" was linked to a commitment to help one another and was experienced in several ways and dimensions in this mill village. There was nothing about this in the mill records or in superintendents' observations of workers. Lummis summed up this important use of recorded testimony:

> There is no doubt that the strength of having the account of the various dimensions of life together in one lived experience gives all the data a particular strength lacking in virtually any other source of evidence; and certainly lacking in any other widespread documentary form.[31]

Personal testimony enables the researcher to understand the meaning of artifacts in the lives of people. British historian Raphael Samuel, discussing artifacts such as a measuring book and a price list, explained: "Sources like this may only come to life when there are people to explain, to comment and to elaborate on them, when there are other kinds of information to set against them, and a context of custom and practice in which they can be set."[32] In the mill village just before World War I, a family saved enough money to buy an organ for the two daughters. If I had seen "organ" in a list of household goods, I would have regarded this artifact as a tangible symbol of "the arts" among working-class people. For the narrator it was the symbol of the intimate bond between her sister and herself as they shared the organ in their adult lives after each married and lived in separate houses.[33] The organ had a significance for them in a way I did not at first imagine.

The in-depth interview also reveals the images and the symbols people use to order their experiences and give them meaning. In his book *Listening to Old Voices*, Patrick Mullen described a man (born in 1900) who had come from a background of poverty to land-ownership and from a wayward life to that of a lay preacher. This narrator took Mullen to the top of the highest mountain on his land, the landscape symbolizing his rise from poverty to prosperity, from sin to spiritual elevation.[34]

The in-depth interview can reveal a psychological reality that is the basis for ideals the individual holds and for the things he or she does. How the subject sees and interprets her experience, given her view of herself and of the world, can be gleaned in no better way than to ask in the context of the life review. For past times, historians searched for a diary or personal journal only to be disappointed by finding a daily account of weather and a brief synopsis of events. The ones that offered the writer's interpretations of the events on a psychological level were rare.

Such a situation arose during research John Bodnar conducted among Polish immigrants to the United States. He said that as a social scientist he might have seen immigration only in the context of economic and social forces. Using one of the oral histories to illustrate his point, Bodnar showed how the narrator expressed his experience in terms of the struggle to move from dependency on others to independence. In his personal psychology, independence was necessary to his sense of being a worthwhile person: This achievement, not amount of money, was the most important thing to him.[35]

Closely related to psychological disclosures is the way individuals see their own histories, both personal histories and the history of the group with which they identify. Indeed, this becomes important in understanding a culture. Ronald Grele, in analyzing two oral history interviews from working-class neighborhoods of New York, commented that "relatively obscure people do create their own history, and they do so within their own conceptions of its value and use in the culture." He concluded that these two narrators, like many others, did so in spite of the fact that before the interview no one had asked them.[36] They had felt a need to make clear the place that their group and they as individuals occupied in history.

Limitations of the Recorded Life Review

Consider now the limitations of the life review and how to use these limitations. Trevor Lummis, in *Listening to History,* rightly said that oral history testimony can give us a detailed account of wages paid in a factory to a specific level of worker but may be "silent on the question of profits." We can learn in the interview what families spent their money on, but not how profits were invested internationally. Lummis expressed this limitation concisely: "Given that so many dimensions of economic life occur at the level of institutional, national and international finance and of technology it is not surprising that those aspects are not recorded in most oral accounts."[37]

The use of life reviews may result in a picture that is narrow, idiosyncratic, or ethnocentric. Studs Terkel's book *Hard Times: An Oral History of the Great Depression* presented more than 150 testimonies of what it was like to live during the Depression years of 1929 and the 1930s.[38] The informants talked about how *they* made it during the Depression, rather than about the failure of capitalism to provide even the necessities of life for the people. As historian Michael Frisch pointed out, the narrators saw this as a personal experience.[39]

And yet there is the other side to this coin of limitations. In discussing the personal views presented in *Hard Times*, Frisch reminded the reader that taken together, the life histories reveal an important assumption in American culture: An individual can survive through hard work and ingenuity, no matter how bad the situation. He pointed out the advantage of using individuals' reflections on their personal experience of history:

> Anyone who has wondered why the depression crises did not produce more focused critiques of American capitalism and culture, more sustained efforts to see fundamental structural change, will find more evidence in the interior of these testimonies than in any other source I know.[40]

The in-depth interview is not necessarily idiosyncratic. In his article "What Is Social in Oral History?" Samuel Schrager pointed out that often there are references to the larger community and to national and international events, that the testimony is given in relationship to others. He gave this excerpt from an interview with immigrant Anna Marie Oslund: "I was born in eighteen ninety-one. And in eighteen ninety-two, the end of that summer—it was a late summer—my father went to America to find a better life for all of us. It was *hard* all over and he thought he'd try, he'd come."[41]

The narrator indicates she will offer two points of view, her own and her father's. She also refers to conditions being "hard all over" and articulates the reality of the wider society. She relates the story as she has been told it. And this is a family story, one that embodies a view of the past that sustains and guides the family in the present. It is assumed that it is in general terms like that of other families immigrating from the same place at roughly the same time. Schrager summed up the use to which this personal narrative can be put: "A migration story can be a very personal account and at the same time an incarnation of the peopling of an era, the exigencies of pioneering, and the aspirations of all who risk relocating to find a better life."[42] So the individual testimony may indeed contain references to the larger group and articulate a shared reality.

And it is possible by using the approach of grounded theory—the examination of a large sample of recorded life histories, the multiplicity of incidents of thick description—to make generalizations about a society. Paul Thompson and Thea Vigne did exactly this in their study of British society at the turn of the century: Their project resulted in the recorded life histories of more than 900 narrators who represented contemporary occupational categories.[43] They used these interviews inductively to arrive at an understanding of several important aspects of Edwardian society.

A second limitation—one related to the ability to generalize from the testimonies—lies in the selectivity of narrators: It is the articulate who come forward to be participants. In interviewing clerical workers for a project in Rhode Island, my fellow researchers and I found that our narrators were feisty, articulate, witty, sociable women. They had volunteered to talk.[44] Would we have gotten a different picture if those who were not enthusiastic had been represented in the collection of taped life reviews? We went on the assumption that the articulate spoke for the others, but I wish I had been more assiduous in seeking out the nonvolunteers and more persuasive when I found them. Probably, most interviewing projects are selective in that the shy or inarticulate individual—or the person valuing privacy—does not come forward.

Furthermore, as a historian interviewing the generation of millworkers who began work as children in the new cotton mill at the beginning of the century, I only heard *about* those who had died. My sample was biased in the direction of the healthiest simply because they were the ones who survived. If this had been a study of safety conditions (they were nonexistent) in the mill, this selectivity of narrators would have seriously limited interviewing evidence and biased the conclusion.

Consequently, these are limitations in oral history research that the researcher must take into account. He or she must ask about the evidence: How have passage of time and self-selectivity affected the sample of narrators available?

A third limitation is the fact that the in-depth life review presents retrospective evidence. But before I discuss this problem, consider the questions always asked of a written document no matter how much time has elapsed: What motive does the witness have for writing this? For whom is this document intended? How close was this witness to the event itself? How informed is this witness about the event observed? What prior assumptions did the witness bring to the observation? What kinds of details have been omitted?

These are questions to be asked of any primary source, including the recorded life narrative. Traditionally trained historians see the oral history document as especially faulty because, in addition to the above questions, there is the question of how much the narrator slanted the story to make it interesting or at least acceptable to the interviewer. This is a valid question to ask. But slanting the story to make it acceptable to the receiver occurs even with the diary writer: Even here the individual who writes only for him- or herself tries to protect the ego. And letter writers always have in mind their correspondents' interests. Motivation for describing oneself in the best light is always there, no matter what the form of expression. People who write their accounts without an interviewer often make themselves heroes of the stories, justifying their actions to themselves, as they reflect on their experiences.

On the other hand, like other interviewers, I have found that people tend with the passage of time to be more rather than less candid. When a career is in progress, there is much to lose by an untoward admission. Near the end of a life, there is a need to look at things as honestly as possible to make sense of experiences over a lifetime: This need strongly competes with the need to make oneself look good.

As for deliberate omissions, this is as likely to happen with official documents such as government press releases or personal documents such as letters as with oral histories. Perhaps the omissions are less likely with oral histories if the interviewer keeps probing.

And now to the issue of retrospective evidence. This is especially problematic for historians who are the most concerned about the past and who evaluate the reliability of evidence according to the amount of time that elapses between the event and its written description. A journal entry on the day the event occurred is considered more reliable than the event remembered 20 years later and recounted in a memoir. Actually, research indicates that people forget more about a specific event in the first hour after it happens than during any other time and that much forgetting continues to go on nine hours afterward; in other words, more is forgotten the first day than in the succeeding weeks, months, and years.[45] Nevertheless, although much has been forgotten a couple of hours later when the diarist writes, some more has been forgotten after 20 years. All of us who have used the in-depth interview in research realize that ability to recall depends on the individual's health, on the topic under consideration, on the way the question is asked, on the degree of pain (or pleasure) required to dredge the topic up, and on the willingness of the narrator to participate in the interview in a helpful way. And even when the narrator thinks she or he can recall the event vividly, the account may not be accurate. That old cliche about memory playing tricks has some truth to it.

Beyond the impressions gained from experience in interviewing, we can look at the research on memory carried out by psychologists. Early research was done in a laboratory in which subjects heard and then attempted to recall syllables or numbers or even whole words— none of them intended to be meaningful. In the last 20 years, however, there have been several psychologists who have researched autobiographical memory to understand how "people use memories of personal experiences to plan, solve problems, instruct and guide others, and justify and explain their actions to themselves and others."[46] Many of their findings have direct application in evaluating retrospective evidence in the life review.

Psychologist David C. Rubin found that people begin reminiscing in their 40s, but that from age 50 on this is an important and continuing endeavor. His research indicated that from middle age on, most people have more memories from childhood, adolescence, and young adulthood than for the most recent years of their lives. Rubin theorized that some periods of life are prominent in memory because they are periods that define the individual—first date, first job, marriage, birth of children.[47]

Psychologist William Brewer, in reviewing the research literature on remembering and forgetting, concluded that characteristics of events that lead to well-recalled personal memories are (1) uniqueness, (2) consequentiality, (3) unexpectedness, and (4) emotion provocation. Poor recall occurs when events were repeated or were trivial.[48] Possibly, the events of everyday life, because they were so ordinary and routine, were not thought about as much and were not as well remembered in Brewer's research project.

In my own experience of interviewing, however, I have found that certain kinds of daily events are remembered. Women could recall the kinds of dishes they prepared for a Sunday dinner as well as the things the family ate during the week. Men could recall not only the year they got a tractor but also how the tractor was used and how they fixed it when it broke down. They could remember daily work in a certain season.[49] These were details of daily life—humdrum, yes—but important to survival. Perhaps, a behavior's survival value may be an exception to Brewer's conclusion about forgetting daily events.

Single incidents that affected a life have a high rate of recall. Australian researcher R. Finlay-Jones found that there was consistency across reinterviews with adults in the general population with respect to separation from parents in childhood. The subjects were interviewed once, then again after eight months and by different interviewers. Ninety-one percent were consistent in their accounts; only 9% (23 out of 244) were inconsistent in their answers.[50]

Events of public significance also may be easily recalled if they affected the individual and if there was an association with personal action. For example, most studies use a question such as "What were you doing when you heard of John Kennedy's death?" Nearly every subject, alive and at the age of reason at the time, has been able to remember, and people remember the event in terms of what they were doing at the time.[51]

Lee Robins, sociologist in the department of psychiatry at Washington University in St. Louis, did a follow-up study of 542 child guidance clinic patients then in their 40s. He found that siblings, asked to remember events in the home life they shared, agreed most of the time about parents' one-time or habitual behaviors. For example, they could agree on whether the parent disciplined them. When they were asked to *judge* these events, however, agreement was reached only 29% of the time. They simply could not agree on whether the parent was hard on the children in terms of discipline.[52]

Each child, now grown, made sense of the past experience in his or her way. Such judgment, or interpretation of actions, is very much an individual process and is influenced by subsequent experience and present situation.

However, there is usually consistency within an individual's testimony about memories of strong feelings. In in-depth interviewing it is the very interpretation of the event and the remembered feelings about it that are sought. These are usually consistent within an individual's testimony, as Robins' research indicates. Oral historian Paul Thompson found the same in his oral history research. For example, he showed how a narrator in his study for *The Edwardians* might confuse details about where her father came from, but her memory about her feelings for her father were consistent over three different interviews.[53]

What then can we conclude about memory in in-depth interviews, given the above research findings? Beginning in their 40s and continuing through the rest of their lives, people reminisce. Memories of childhood, adolescence, and early adulthood may be more easily recalled than those from middle and late years. If the event or situation was significant to the individual, it will likely be remembered in some detail, especially its associated feelings. However, the interpretation may reflect current circumstances and needs.

Given the situation that human memory is selective and sometimes faulty in what is remembered, two aspects of the critical approach to the oral history are involved here: consistency in the testimony (reliability) and accuracy (or validity) in relating factual information. Consistency within testimony is easily checked, and questions about inconsistency pursued. Accuracy (the degree of conformity with other accounts) can be checked by consulting other sources and comparing accounts.[54]

After subjecting the oral history to such scrutiny, we may see that it does indeed offer information about an event that is consistent within the document and with other accounts. In other words, social scientists recognize that some "facts" have a shared reality with multiple means of verifying their facticity, no matter their interpretative frame.[55] And everyone views some facts as more reliable than others, and so a degree of acceptance is occurring, dependent on the means of verifying.

By accumulating sources of information and comparing them, we can arrive at an approximate understanding of what happened or is happening and hold this information with some certainty. But there is never absolute certainty about any event, about any fact, no matter what sources are used. No single source or combination of them can ever give a picture of the total complexity of the reality. We cannot reconstruct a past or present event in its entirety because the evidence is always fragmentary.

Another consideration is that the interpretation of the evidence depends on the interpreter. Placing kinds of evidence on a continuum, starting with the least mediation and ending with the most, such artifacts as vases, ditches in the land, tombs, and so on have had the least "mediation." A personal account has the most. A vase is what *you* make of it: A human being's past experience is what he or she makes of it before the historian begins to interpret it.

We can base a tentative conclusion on what the critical review of the evidence indicates. R. G. Collingwood described this process: "For historical thinking means nothing else than interpreting all the available evidence with the maximum degree of critical skill."[56] This means there is always the possibility that new evidence may appear. Although Collingwood was referring to historical research, interpreting the available evidence with critical skill is applicable to any research that social scientists carry out, and all of us hold our conclusions tentatively.

And yet, is it not the meaning attributed to the facts that makes them significant or not? After all, history does not exist outside human consciousness. History is what the people who lived it make of it and what the others who observe the participants or listen to them or study their records make of it. Likewise, contemporary society does not exist outside human consciousness: Our definition of it is what it is.

Special Strengths of Oral History

So, what if the narrator is dead wrong about a number, a date, or an event? The factual information may be incorrect, but look more closely at the document to discover what significance the discrepancy may reveal. Oral historian Alessandro Portelli reminded us that "untrue" statements are psychologically "true" and that errors in fact may be more revealing than factually accurate accounts. He insisted that the "importance of oral testimony may often lie not in its adherence to facts but rather in its divergence from them, where imagination, symbolism, desire break in."[57]

To illustrate this, Portelli showed how narrators might get dates incorrect but hold steadfastly to an account of a historical event that fits their view of history:

> For example: over half of the workers interviewed in the industrial town of Terni tell the story of their postwar strikes placing the killing of a worker by the police in 1953 rather than, as it really happened, in 1949; they also shift it from one context to another (from a peace demonstration to the urban guerrilla struggle which followed mass layoffs at the local steelworks). This obviously does not cast doubt on the actual chronology; but it does force us to rearrange our interpretation of events in order to recognize the collective processes of symbolization and myth-making in the Terni working class—which sees those years as one uninterrupted struggle expressed by a unifying symbol (the dead comrade), rather than as a succession of separate events.[58]

Portelli asked the question, Why is there this discrepancy between dates recorded elsewhere and dates given in the oral histories? This led him to an understanding of the way the narrators had used the death of a comrade to construct a history of their own, one that expressed their worldview. A similar concept was expressed by sociologist W. I. Thomas when he discussed "definition of the situation." He argued, "If men define situations as real, they are real in their consequences."[59]

The researcher can use this limitation to learn something important by asking of the narrator's self-serving account, *How* does he construct this view? *Where* do his concepts come from? *Why* does he build this persona and not another? *What* are the consequences for this individual?

Closely related to this is the use of oral history to discover habitual thinking (often below the level of conscious thinking), which comes from the evolving culture in which individuals live. Although the term *culture* has differing shades of meaning according to its interpreter, most students of human society would accept the definition given by ethnographer Clifford Geertz: "Believing, with Max Weber, that man is an animal suspended in webs of significance he himself has spun, I take culture to be those webs."[60]

French historian Jacques LeGoff explained the concept this way: "Automatic gestures, spontaneous words, which seem to lack any origins and to be the fruits of improvisation and reflex, in fact possess deep roots in the long reverberation of systems of thought."[61] The example he gave is from medieval history but is definitely applicable to the work of the scholar engaged in the search for an understanding of contemporary society. Pope Gregory the Great, in his *Dialogues* (written between 590 and 600) recounted the story of a monk who, on his deathbed, confessed to have kept for himself three gold coins. Keeping material possessions to oneself was against the rules of the order. Gregory refused to let the man have the last rites, insisted on neglect of the dying man, and after the culprit's death, punished him still again by having the body thrown into the garbage. His stated reason was that he wanted to show other monks they must adhere to the order's rules, but this was definitely a negation of the Christian ideology, which would have been to forgive. Le Goff concluded, "The barbarian custom of physical punishment (brought by the Goths or a throwback to some psychic depths?) proves stronger than the monastic rule."[62]

In the recounting of events, the deeper layers of our thinking may be revealed, indicating the centuries' long development of the culture in which we have our being. For this, oral history testimony is a research method par excellence because the researcher can question the narrator. We cannot drag Pope Gregory from his tomb, prop him up, and ask, "What were you saying to yourself at the time you threw that monk in the garbage?" "How did you feel?" "Ever seen this done before?" "Where do you think the idea came from?" But we surely can ask a *living* witness.

Summary

The interaction of interviewer and narrator is a special characteristic of this research method. This is shared work. This is a collaboration. The possibility of discovering something not previously known to the researcher is pursued. The understanding of the multiplicity of experiences in a total life context is the objective.

Retrospective evidence, like any evidence, is never accepted unquestioningly. Some things may have been forgotten; other things may be recalled. And the remembered version may have discrepancies within itself or when compared with other sources. Memory will be fairly accurate, however, if the event or an attendant emotion was significant to the individual. Nevertheless, the individual's interpretation of the event may have shifted because succeeding events cast a different light on the evidence. Discrepancies within testimony and differences in comparison to other sources point to truths not factually accurate but psychologically true. Levels of thinking deeper than the conscious, stated ones may be revealed.

Oral history is therefore inevitably subjective: Its subjectivity is at once inescapable and crucial to an understanding of the meanings we give our past and present. This is the great task of qualitative research and specifically oral history interviews: to reveal the meanings of lived experience. The in-depth interview offers the benefit of seeing in its full complexity the world of another. And in collating in-depth interviews and using the insights to be gained from them as well as different kinds of information from other kinds of records, we can come to some understanding of the process by which we got to be the way we are.

Notes

1. Judith Stacey, "Can There Be a Feminist Ethnography?" in *Women's Words: The Feminist Practice of Oral History,* eds. Sherna Berger Gluck and Daphne Patai (New York: Routledge, 1991), 111-119; see p. 115.

2. I am indebted to Jane Adams for dialogue with me on this subject; Jane Adams, communication to author, June 22, 1993. And I draw from Renato Rosaldo, *Culture and Truth: The Remaking of Social Analysis* (Boston: Beacon Press, 1989), 19-21, 50.

3. Louis Starr, "Oral History," in *Oral History: An Interdisciplinary Anthology,* eds. David Dunaway and Willa K. Baum (Nashville, Tenn.: American Association for State and Local History, 1984), 3-26; see pp. 10-12.

4. Ibid.

5. Charles Morrissey, "Why Call It Oral History? Searching for Early Usage of a Generic Term," *Oral History Review* (1980): 20-48; see p. 35.

6. Ibid.

7. James Bennett, "Human Values in Oral History," *History Review* 11 (1983): 1-15; see p. 14.

8. Sharan Merriam, *Case Study Research in Education: A Qualitative Approach* (San Francisco: Jossey-Bass, 1988), 6-7.

9. Ibid., 16.

10. Paul Thompson, *The Edwardians: The Remaking of British Society* (Bloomington: Indiana University Press, 1975), 6.

11. Trevor Lummis, *Listening to History: The Authenticity of Oral Evidence* (London: Hutchinson, 1987), 75.

12. Arlene Daniels, "Self-Deception and Self-Discovery in Field Work," *Qualitative Sociology* 6, no. 3 (1983): 195-214; see p. 197.

13. Jack D. Douglas, *Investigative Social Research* (Beverly Hills, Calif.: Sage Publications, 1976), 25.

14. Barney Glaser and Anselm Strauss, "The Discovery of Substantive Theory: A Basic Strategy Underlying Qualitative Research," *American Behavioral Scientist* 8, no. 6 (February 1965): 5-12.

15. Clifford Geertz, "Thick Description: Toward an Interpretative Theory of Culture," in *The Interpretation of Culture* (New York: Basic Books, 1973), 3-30; see pp. 3-5.

16. Fern Ingersoll and Jasper Ingersoll, "Both a Borrower and a Lender Be: Ethnography, Oral History, and Grounded Theory," *Oral History Review* 15 (Spring 1987): 81-102; see p. 83.

17. Leonard Schatzman and Anselm L. Strauss, *Field Research: Strategies for a Natural Sociology* (Englewood Cliffs, N.J.: Prentice-Hall, 1973), 19.

18. Rosaldo, *Culture and Truth*, 7.

19. R. G. Collingwood, "The Philosophy of History," in *Essays in the Philosophy of History* (Austin: University of Texas Press, 1985), 121-139; see p. 137.

20. Lummis, *Listening to History*, 43.

21. Valerie Raleigh Yow, *Patient Care: A History of Butler Hospital* (Providence, R.I.: Butler Hospital, 1994); see Chapter 2, "A New Kind of Hospital."

22. Bill Williams, "The Jewish Immigrant in Manchester: The Contribution of Oral History," *Oral History* (Spring 1979): 43.

23. Paul Thompson, *The Voice of the Past: Oral History* (Oxford: Oxford University Press, 1988), 3.

24. Paraphrase of Lummis, *Listening to History*, 150.

25. Paul Thompson, "Introduction," in *Our Common History: The Transformation of Europe*, eds. Paul Thompson and Natasha Burchardt (Atlantic Highlands, N.J.: Humanities Press, 1982), 11.

26. Valerie Raleigh Yow (listed as Valerie Quinney), "Childhood in a Southern Mill Village," *International Journal of Oral History* 3, no. 3 (November 1982): 167-192; see p. 171.

27. Valerie Raleigh Yow, *The History of Hera: A Woman's Art Cooperative, 1974-1989* (Wakefield, R.I.: Hera Educational Foundation, 1989), 8-9.

28. Ibid., 19.

29. Ibid.

30. Yow, "Childhood in a Southern Mill Village," 184.

31. Lummis, *Listening to History*, 110.

32. Raphael Samuel, "Local History and Oral History," *History Workshop Journal* 1 (1976): 191-208; see p. 200.

33. Mrs. V. P., tape-recorded interview with author (listed as Valerie Quinney), Carrboro, North Carolina, May 29, 1974, side one, tape counter number 300. Families of Carrboro, Chapel Hill Historical Society Records 4205, Southern Historical Collection, University of North Carolina Libraries, Chapel Hill, North Carolina.

34. Patrick B. Mullen, *Listening to Old Voices: Folklore, Life Stories, and the Elderly* (Chicago: University of Illinois Press, 1992), 189-190.

35. John Bodnar, "Reworking Reality: Oral Histories and the Meaning of the Polish Immigrant Experience," in *Workers' World: Kinship, Community and Protest in an Industrial Society, 1900-1940* (Baltimore, Md.: Johns Hopkins University Press, 1982), 59-68.

36. Ronald Grele, "Listen to Their Voices: Two Case Histories in the Interpretation of Oral History Interviews," *Oral History* (Spring 1979): 33-42; see p. 41.

37. Lummis, *Listening to History*, 42.

38. Studs Terkel, *Hard Times: An Oral History of the Great Depression* (New York: Avon, 1970).

39. Michael Frisch, "Oral History and *Hard Times*: A Review Essay," in *A Shared Authority: Essays on the Craft and Meaning of Oral and Public History* (New York: State University of New York Press, 1990), 11.

40. Ibid., 12.

41. Samuel Schrager, "What Is Social in Oral History?" *International Journal of Oral History* 4, no. 2 (June 1983): 76-98; see p. 80.

42. Ibid.

43. Thompson, *Voice of the Past*, 125-126.

44. Valerie Raleigh Yow (listed as Valerie Quinney), "Office Workers and Machines: Oral Histories of Rhode Island Working Women," in *Life and Labor: Dimensions of American Working-Class History*, eds. Charles Stephenson and Robert Asher (Albany: State University of New York Press, 1986), 260-281.

45. H. Ebbinghaus, *Memory: A Contribution to Experimental Psychology*, trans. H. A. Roger and C. E. Bussenius (New York: Columbia University Press, 1885). The findings of this early study have not been disproved by subsequent research.

46. John A. Robinson, "Autobiographical Memory: A Historical Prologue," in *Autobiographical Memory*, ed. David C. Rubin (Cambridge, U.K.: Cambridge University Press, 1986), 19-23; see p. 23. See also in the same volume, William F. Brewer, "What Is Autobiographical Memory?" 25-49; see p. 25.

47. David C. Rubin, Scott E. Wetzler, and Robert D. Nebes, "Autobiographical Memory Across the Lifespan," *Autobiographical Memory*, 202-221; see p. 212.

48. Brewer, "What Is Autobiographical Memory?" 44.

49. "Farm Families of DeKalb County," Northern Illinois Regional History Center, Archives, Northern Illinois University, DeKalb, Illinois.

50. R. Finlay-Jones, "The Reliability of Reports of Early Separation," *Journal of Psychiatry* (Australia) 15 (1981): 27-31. Cited in Lee N. Robins et al., "Early Home Environment and Retrospective Recall," *American Journal of Orthopsychiatry* 55 (January 1985): 28-29.

51. Norman R. Brown, Steven K. Shevell, and Lance R. Rips, "Public Memories and Their Personal Recall," *Autobiographical Memory*, 137-158; see p. 157.

52. Robins, "Early Home Environment and Retrospective Recall," 19-31, 37.

53. Paul Thompson, "Problems of Method in Oral History," *Oral History* 4 (1972): 14-17.

54. Alice Hoffman, "Reliability and Validity in Oral History," in *Oral History: An Interdisciplinary Anthology*, 67-73.

55. Jane Adams, communication to author, June 22, 1993.

56. R. G. Collingwood, "Limits of Historical Knowledge," in *Essays in the Philosophy of History*, ed. William Debbins (Austin: University of Texas Press, 1965), 90-103; see p. 99.

57. Alessandro Portelli, "Peculiarities of Oral History," *History Workshop Journal* 96, no. 12 (Autumn 1981): 96-107; see p. 100.

58. Ibid.

59. Quoted in "W. I. Thomas: On the Definition of the Situation," in *Sociology: The Classic Statements,* ed. Marcello Truzzi (New York: Random House, 1971), 274. Original discussion and quotation appeared in William Isaac Thomas, *The Child in America* (New York: Alfred A. Knopf, 1928), 572. See a treatment of this concept in Peter McHugh, "Defining the Situation: The Organization of Meaning" in *Social Interaction* (Indianapolis: Bobbs-Merrill, 1968), and Robert B. Stebbins, "Studying the Definition of the Situation: Theory and Field Research Strategies," *Canadian Review of Sociology and Anthropology* 6 (1969): 193-211.

60. Geertz, "Thick Description," 5.

61. Jacques Le Goff, "Mentalities: A History of Ambiguities," in *Constructing the Past: Essays in Historical Methodology,* eds. Jacques Le Goff and Pierre Nora (Cambridge, U.K.: Cambridge University Press, 1985), 166-180; see p. 170.

62. Ibid.

Recommended Reading

Discussions on Research Methods

Denzin, Norman K. *The Research Act: A Theoretical Introduction to Sociological Methods.* Chicago: Aldine Publishing, 1970. This book presents a discussion of qualitative methods that is focused on participant observation; nevertheless, there is information useful to the interviewer.

Douglas, Jack D. *Investigative Social Research.* Beverly Hills, Calif.: Sage Publications, 1976. This is a general guide to fieldwork research; it presents a comparison of quantitative and qualitative methods in the introduction. Although it is not focused exclusively on the in-depth interview, it offers discussion on such concerns as self-deception and biases.

Ellen, R. F., ed. *Ethnographic Research: A Guide to General Conduct.* New York: Academic Press, 1984. Although primarily on fieldwork methods other than the in-depth interview, there are general discussions of use to the interviewer, such as ethics in relation to informants.

Glaser, Barney, and Anselm Strauss. *The Discovery of Grounded Theory: Strategies for Qualitative Research.* Chicago: Aldine Publishing, 1967. This is the original source for discussions about grounded theory. An early statement can be found in their article "The Discovery of Substantive Theory: A Basic Strategy Underlying Qualitative Research," *The American Behavioral Scientist* 8, no. 6 (February 1965): 5-12.

Jensen, Richard. "Oral History, Quantification and the New Social History," *Oral History Review* 9 (1981): 13-25. The author states that the use of a questionnaire offers the advantage of providing systematic answers to identical questions, but it gives up the richness of narrative detail offered by the in-depth interview.

Merriam, Sharan B. *Case Study Research in Education: A Qualitative Approach.* San Francisco: Jossey-Bass, 1988. A lucid treatise, slanted toward scholars in education but containing information on using the in-depth interview applicable to other disciplines.

Price, Richard. *Ethnographic History, Caribbean Pasts*. Working Papers No. 9, Department of Spanish and Portuguese, University of Maryland, College Park, 1990. Insightful brief essay—and witty. The author refers to ethnohistory as "the history of the bare-assed."

Sharpless, Rebecca. "The Numbers Game: Oral History Compared with Quantitative Methodology," *International Journal of Oral History* 7, no. 2 (June 1986): 93-108. The author suggests ways in which oral history and a testing instrument for quantification can be used together, and she compares intrusion of the interviewer in both methods.

Spradley, James P. *The Ethnographic Interview*. New York: Holt, Rinehart & Winston, 1979. Clearly ahistorical and centered on ethnographic research, this is nevertheless a book with insights for the interviewer in other disciplines as well.

General Works on Oral History

Allen, Barbara, and W. Lynwood Montell. *From Memory to History: Using Oral Sources in Local Historical Research*. Nashville, Tenn.: American Association for State and Local History, 1981. See this for discussions of the combined use of history and folklore and for the evaluation of an oral history.

Dunaway, David K., and Willa K. Baum, eds. *Oral History: An Interdisciplinary Anthology*. Nashville, Tenn.: American Association for State and Local History, 1984. This collection of articles from journals covers many aspects of oral history research.

Friedlander, Peter. "Introduction, " *The Emergence of a UAW Local, 1936-1939: A Study in Class and Culture*. Pittsburgh: University of Pittsburgh Press, 1973. The author discusses the ways that narrators construct the narrative and, therefore, a view of history. The essay offers a convincing example of the benefits of repeated in-depth interviews with the same narrator.

Grele, Ronald, ed. *Envelopes of Sound: Six Practitioners Discuss the Method, Theory and Practice of Oral History and Oral Testimony*. Chicago: Precedent Publishing, 1992. These articles contain numerous insights, such as why created stories are revealing, how attitude affects memory, and how oral history affects the interviewer.

Henige, David. *Oral Historiography*. London: Longman, 1982. This is an especially helpful guide for researchers going into field research in non-Western cultures.

Lummis, Trevor. *Listening to History: The Authenticity of Oral Evidence*. London: Hutchinson, 1987. See especially the chapters on assessing interviews and on memory and theory.

Portelli, Alessandro. *The Death of Luigi Trastulli and Other Stories: Form and Meaning in Oral History*. Albany: State University of New York Press, 1991. This is a collection of journal articles (several of which I have mentioned singly) that have helped to define the purposes of oral history.

Thompson, Paul. *The Voice of the Past: Oral History* (2nd ed.). New York: Oxford University Press, 1988. This is an insightful account of the uses of oral history by a veteran interviewer.

Oral History and Folklore

Davis, Susan G. "Review Essay: Storytelling Rights," *Oral History Review* 16, no. 2 (Fall 1988): 109-115. This article briefly discusses how oral history and folklore are different but can be used together.

Dorson, Richard. "The Oral Historian and the Folklorist," *Selections of the Fifth and Sixth National Colloquia on Oral History.* New York: Oral History Association, 1972. This is a treatment of folklore's distinguishing characteristics and its differences from oral history. See also his book *American Folklore and the Historian* (Chicago: University of Chicago Press, 1971).

Montell, William Lynwood. *The Saga of Coe Ridge: A Study in Oral History.* Knoxville: University of Tennessee Press, 1970. See the preface for a discussion of the ways that historians can use folklore. Montell argues that folk tradition is itself a historical fact.

Research on Memory

Aube, Mary Elizabeth. "Oral History and the Remembered World: Cultural Determinants from French Canada," *International Journal of Oral History* 10, no. 1 (February 1989): 31-49. The author points out the ways in which memory is stored in narrative form and explores the relationship between culture and memory.

Neisser, Ulric, ed. *Memory Observed: Remembering in Natural Contexts.* San Francisco: Freeman, 1982. This collection of articles from the 1970s is based on naturalistic research on remembering.

Rubin, David. *Autobiographical Memory.* Cambridge, U.K.: Cambridge University Press, 1986. This series of articles reports on research done on memory in the late 1970s and 1980s.

Works on the Interviewer-Narrator Relationship and Subjectivity in Research

Anderson, Kathryn, Susan Armitage, Dana Jack, and Judith Wittner. "Beginning Where We Are: Feminist Methodology in Oral History," *Oral History Review* 15 (Spring 1987): 103-127. This is a discussion by a psychologist, sociologist, and historians about the influence of "particular and limited interests, perspectives, and experience of white males" on research. It explores the use of subjectivity in research.

Cottle, Thomas. "The Life Study: On Mutual Recognition and the Subjective Inquiry," *Urban Life and Culture* 2, no. 3 (October 1973): 344-360. This reflects on the "new selves" emerging because of the research.

Daniels, Arlene. "Self-Deception and Self-Discovery in Field Work," *Qualitative Sociology* 6, no. 3 (1983): 195-214. This is a candid, searching account of the author's behavior as an interviewer.

Gluck, Sherna Berger, and Daphne Patai. *Women's Words: The Feminist Practice of Oral History.* New York: Routledge, 1991. This collection of articles examines listening, using words, relating to narrators, looking critically at one's work, and interviewing Third World women.

Kleinman, Sherryl. "Field-Workers' Feelings: What We Feel, Who We Are, How We Analyze." *Experiencing Fieldwork: An Inside View of Qualitative Research.* Eds. William B. Shaffir and Robert A. Stebbins. Newbury Park, Calif.: Sage Publications, 1991. This is a sociologist's presentation of how the field researcher's feelings affect a study and how failure to recognize feelings affects a study.

Lebeaux, Richard. "Thoreau's Lives, Lebeaux's Lives." *Introspection in Biography: The Biographer's Quest for Self-Awareness.* Eds. Samuel H. Baron and Carl Pletsch. Hillsdale, N.J.: Analytic Press, 1985. The entire collection is interesting in the questions it raises about the effects of studying an individual life on the researcher.

Patai, Daphne. *Brazilian Women Speak.* Rutgers, N.J.: State University Press, 1988. In her discussion of methodology, the author explores her feelings about research among women in Brazil, pointing out how her intervention affected both researcher and the researched.

Studies on the Philosophy of History and on Ethnography

Clifford, James. "Introduction: Partial Truths." In *Writing Culture: The Poetics and Politics of Ethnography,* eds. James Clifford and George Marcus, 1-26. Berkeley: University of California Press, 1986. This is a perceptive and influential essay on the "webs" of culture.

Collingwood, R. [Robin] G. [George]. *Autobiography.* London: Oxford University Press, 1939. This uncommon autobiography presents the intellectual journey taken by an important theorist of historical research.

Collingwood, R. G. *Essays in the Philosophy of History.* Ed. William Debbins. Austin: University of Texas Press, 1965. See especially "The Limits of Historical Knowledge" and "The Philosophy of History."

Geertz, Clifford. "Thick Description: Toward an Interpretive Theory of Culture" in *The Interpretation of Culture,* 3-30. New York: Basic Books, 1973. This is an early, provocative discussion of the use of "thick description" in researching a culture.

Le Goff, Jacques, and Pierre Nora. *Constructing the Past: Essays in Historical Methodology.* Cambridge, U.K.: Cambridge University Press, 1985. See especially the chapter "Mentalities: A History of Ambiguities" by Le Goff.

Rosaldo, Renato. *Culture and Truth: The Remaking of Social Analysis.* Boston: Beacon Press, 1989. In this provocative study of ethnographic research, the author discusses his own fieldwork to illustrate the importance of acknowledging and using one's own feelings and assumptions in the process of researching and analyzing.

2

Preparation for
the Interviewing Project

Choose a subject for research that is of great interest to you. In the old view of research, the researcher was objective, noninvolved. However, even before the 1960s when that model began to be questioned, the best research was done by people much involved because they were highly motivated to do a good job, were intensely committed to the project, and could thus endure the setbacks. They had an intrinsic interest in the topics under discussion, and the narrators sensed this. The narrators were in turn motivated to respond. (This does not mean that interest prevents us from stepping back and taking a critical look at the project when that is needed.)

Imagining what topics the project will focus on and how you will do this is, of course, the first step in the research. Becoming conscious of assumptions, formulating questions, even defining tentative hypotheses, and critically examining all of these are necessary activities even at the beginning. (And here I depart from the usual approach of grounded theory.) These are the things that influence us in choosing topics and specific questions.

This chapter contains the information that helps move the researcher from this beginning to the interviewing phase. We cannot skip careful preparation and achieve anything but random conversations, so this is a crucial phase in the project. Doing careful background research, deciding what we want to find out, drawing up the interview guide, selecting narrators carefully, and getting tape-recording equipment ready are discussed in this chapter.

Conceptualization of the Research Project

Ask the question, "What do I want to find out?" Write out the list of questions, then express them as topics. Locate everything published on these topics and skim them until you decide which written sources will be helpful and begin a close study of them.

Some researchers using the approach of grounded theory object to the literature-review-first rule because this prevents the researcher from keeping an open mind and viewing evidence in new ways. I urge you to take advantage of the work that has been done before and its critiques. Knowing the pitfalls and possibilities that other researchers have encountered can be helpful if you also maintain awareness of how preconceived notions may be influencing the course of your research.

Whether this is an event, movement, community, set of social problems, or individual biography you are researching, look for names of people involved. Start asking librarians, agency directors, ministers, teachers—whoever might know something about the history of the community or whoever is involved in the aspects of community you want to study—"Who was involved in this? Who would know something about this?" Write notes to the individuals named as having knowledge of the subject and ask if they would talk to you. Then follow up with a telephone call to say you would like to meet them briefly to talk about the event, movement, or individual. These are informal conversations: do not record, just take notes.

Because you are dealing with living persons, you have the opportunity to find out what is important to them in their history and in their present lives. As you carry out these informational interviews, ask, "If you were writing this study, what would you include?" and "Who would you recommend I interview?" In a community history, I carry out informational interviews with various individuals in that community, asking the questions above and, "If you were writing this history, what would you consider important?" I also ask, "Who was present at that event? Who was instrumental in making this happen? Who was affected by this?" In a family history ask, "What were the events in the family that you would expect to be in the history? What were the hopes and joys and sorrows I should talk about?" In a biographical study, ask the person what he or she considered to be the most important events, which persons were significant in the life. Or if the individual is deceased, ask those who knew him or her well what they think were the pivotal events, the most significant relationships, the most important joys and sorrows, the aspirations, the defeats. Ask for names of people with whom you should talk. Find out if they have letters, photographs, or newspaper clippings.

How you go about conceptualizing the interviewing project depends on the kind of project you are doing. The chapters on community studies, family research, and individual biography later in this book present more detail on procedures relevant to the particular kind of project; but this chapter offers a general strategy.

As you reflect on the information in these oral and written sources, your knowledge and understanding grow. You begin to have questions in addition to the ones you started with. Think about how the community, family, or individual is typical for the time and place and how it may be different. For example, a small group of people in an oral history methodology class I taught were interested in how DeKalb, the small Illinois town in which they lived, experienced World War II. They narrowed the project to an exploration of the ways that management and workers converted a Wurlitzer factory from the manufacture of organs to gliders and guided bombs. We invited men and women who had been workers there during the war to tour the now-defunct empty factory with us and then return to the classroom to talk. We listened to what they had to say about their experiences and found out what they considered important. We compared these local experiences with our readings in the social history of the United States during World War II. We began to think about the ways that the DeKalb workers' experiences might turn out to be similar to those of workers in other places and other kinds of war work and how they might be different.[1]

We composed a list of topics based on these issues as well as the events and situations that the workers noted as important to them. We also included questions of importance to us as historians, anthropologists, or psychologists, such as:

How did the skilled men who had made beautiful organs adapt their skills to the manufacture of gliders?

How did they view the influx of unskilled women workers?

How were women workers treated in this plant?

How did the acquisition of manufacturing skills and increase in job responsibility affect the self-concept of these women who had formerly done farm work or retail sales?

To what extent and in what ways did co-workers help one another?

How were these workers affected by the national movement to unionize labor?

How did people react to wartime propaganda in the plant? To surveillance in the plant?

How did they respond to the news of the death of former co-workers overseas?

Because we had thought through the information we needed to place the experiences of these workers in a historical context, we were able to write the interview guide so that both the unique aspects and the shared aspects were discussed. Planning the interview guide carefully means that you will obtain testimony on a range of topics. After the project is over, you might wish you had asked questions about an overlooked topic, but you cannot go back to all of the narrators. If you have done the preliminary work with written and oral sources described above, you can compose an interview guide that is inclusive. This stage of conceptualizing the project is of utmost importance.

Composing the Interview Guide

An interview guide is not a questionnaire. A questionnaire is a series of questions that limit the range of answers the respondent can give, such as "agree, agree slightly, disagree slightly, or disagree." The questionnaire has a fixed set of questions, each with a stated limit on the kinds of answers acceptable. The interviewer may not depart from the questionnaire to follow different topics: If the answer does not fit one of the stated categories, he or she has to make it fit. An *interview guide* (sometimes referred to as the interview *format*) is a plan for an interview. The guide contains the topics the interviewer will pursue but does not limit the interview to those topics because the narrator will have the freedom to suggest others. The guide will have specific questions phrased in an open-ended way as much as possible—that is, there will often be no stated limit to the number of ways the narrator may answer. An order strictly following the guide will not be imposed on the narrator who may wish to follow a different order that makes more sense to him or her. However, the guide provides a strategy for following a line of questioning. You may change this plan—that is, what you think is significant enough to ask about—but you do not flounder because you do not know what to ask next.

The interview guide is not just a plan the interviewer can throw away once the interview begins. The topics and their specific questions cover the information that the interviewer needs, but leeway is built into the situation to allow the emergence of the unanticipated. This flexibility allows the narrator to teach the interviewer things he or she did not already know, while ensuring that the information the interviewer sought also is obtained.

A much higher level of skill is required in using the guide as compared to the questionnaire. The interviewer must understand the specific objectives of the interviewing project so well that even if the narrator suggests following other lines of investigation or chooses a different order of topics, the interviewer can still return to the unanswered questions he or she has come with if they still seem significant.

This is why it is imperative that the interviewer carefully think through and write out the interview guide. While some experienced interviewers may skip writing the specific questions, I believe that giving thought to the wording of the question is useful. I am more likely in the actual interview to phrase my questions in the clearest and strategically best way because I have thought about them ahead of time. (Spontaneous questions that arise in the interview situation—such as probes, follow-ups, challenges—are discussed in the next chapter on interviewing techniques.)

After I have become thoroughly familiar with the interview guide, I jot down headings of topics on index cards. I take the cards with me to the interview and glance down at them only at the end of a line of questioning and before I am ready to begin another. But having thought through the questions very carefully, I have them in my mind when I need them—before me, I have only the reminder in a simple phrase on an index card. This way, I can watch the narrator, respond to what he or she is saying, think about what is happening in the interpersonal relationship, and listen carefully so that I know when to probe, follow up, ask for clarification, or challenge. After you have used the interview guide several times in this condensed card form, you may not even need the cards because you will know the topics and questioning strategy so well. This confidence and ease will come as a result of careful preparation of the guide and your thorough knowledge of it.

In arranging topics for the interview guide, place the nonthreatening questions first. People generally like to talk about their birthplace, early childhood memories, and significant people and events in the years they grew up.

Although this information may seem off the subject, a full life history is very useful. As I will stress several times in this book, the taped life history should not remain in your study closet: This is a social enterprise, and the collection of tapes from your project should be deposited in archives, available to other researchers. Whoever listens to the tape will want to know the background of the speaker, will want to place him or her in a specific time and place to understand how the narrator came to do what he or she did.

The necessity of a full life history was an early learning experience for me. In 1974 and 1975, during an interviewing project among three generations of mill village families in Carrboro, North Carolina, my co-researchers, Brent Glass and Hugh Brinton, and I recorded full life histories although we sought information chiefly on the transition from farming to millwork. Later I published an article on childhood from the data, as well as several other articles comparing the lives of three generations of women. My co-researchers also used the data in ways they had not envisioned, and our entire collection was used with many others' interviews in the book *Like a Family: The Making of a Cotton Mill World.*[2] Biographers feel very lucky when they find that someone interviewed the subject of the biography while he or she was still living and deposited the tape. Thus it is important that you record a life history rather than concentrate only on your specific objectives. You do not know how useful the information will be in the future to someone else, but you do know that you have the opportunity to record a range of information and that someone else may not get the chance to tape this narrator's experiences again.

A chronological order is one way to proceed: childhood, adolescence, work and relationships in youth, work and family in middle age, tasks of old age, reflections. This requires integrating paid work with other activities and with human relationships at each stage. Another way is organize the interview topically, such as early family memories, marriage, parenting experiences, preparation for a profession, active years in the profession, reflections on the profession, community involvement, hobbies, and so on. Appendix A offers a sample interview guide, but you must decide what is the most logical progression given the research project you are beginning.

Compose the core interview guide. Perhaps you plan to code parts of the narrators' responses and use the data for a quantitative analysis. In any case, the core will be the topics every informant will be expected to deal with. But you also tailor the guide to the individual narrator. The guide for the Wurlitzer plant study contained a core that we asked every narrator, but managers were asked some questions specific to their experience, and workers were asked questions specific to their experience. Women workers were asked several questions about the ways they were treated in the plant; men were asked different questions about the ways they perceived women being treated.

The guide is not, however, an inflexible instrument. It is the nature of qualitative research that the researcher gains information not imagined at the beginning. As you learn new things from each narrator, insert new questions or even whole topics into the guide that you pursue in subsequent interviews.

Strategies for Questioning

When you have the topical outline for the interview format, you are ready to plan the questioning strategy. Do you start with a broad question and proceed to the narrowly focused question? When do you use questions that elicit a simple yes or no? And when do you use questions that allow the narrator to handle the topic any way he or she wishes? Do you tip off the narrator to the answer you are looking for by using a "leading question" or just specify the subject you expect the narrator to deal with in the answer?

Consider first the use of the leading question—the kind of question that indicates what the interviewer wants in the answer. In the past, this has been a technique interviewers were taught never to use because the narrator will be likely to give the indicated answer. He or she wants to be cooperative, polite, or just finish the ordeal. The interviewer learns nothing new, only what he or she has asked for. I blush over a memory at the beginning of my interviewing career when I asked people who had worked as children in a cotton mill before World War I (project mentioned above): "Gosh, you didn't *like* mill work?" Fortunately, they risked disappointing me by not giving me the expected answer. One narrator explained, "Honey, if you had ever chopped cotton in the hot sun, you would see why I liked mill work."

Another way to tip off the narrator about what you want and expect in an answer is to set the stage. For example, the interviewer says, "Serbs are not for free trade. Are you?" If you know the narrator is from an ethnic background with a history of strife with Serbs, this is a sure way to bias the answer.[3]

Raymond Gorden argued that a leading question can be used to ensure the narrator that he or she can go against the requirements of etiquette. You are fairly certain that the narrator has the information and can give it accurately so that he will not be influenced by your wording. The narrator already knows you well enough to realize his answer will not harm the relationship he has with you.[4] Look at this example from Gorden.

INTERVIEWER: What time did the meeting start, 8 or 8:30?
NARRATOR: We always start at 7 as we did last night.
INTERVIEWER: Did you just have an informal discussion?
NARRATOR: No, we also had a speaker from Columbus.
INTERVIEWER: Was his talk about the usual sort of things which education people have to say about child psychology?
NARRATOR: The topic was "What can the taxpayer buy for his school tax dollar?"
INTERVIEWER: Oh, I see. Did you feel that the speaker had little of value to say as is so often true of people speaking on this topic?
NARRATOR: No, he had quite a bit to say; we selected him because of his objectivity.[5]

In this excerpt it is obvious that the narrator knows exactly what he wants to say and will not be swayed by the way the interviewer asks the question. However, the interviewer could have gotten the same answers in this case by asking the question without prejudging and thus making it a leading question. And even Gorden advises, "It is a good plan to avoid the use of leading questions rather than hope they are of the harmless variety unless the situation calls for their intentional use."[6]

A closed-ended question calls for a short answer such as yes or no, a date, or a number. It can be used profitably at the beginning of a line of questioning. If the interviewer needs to know what it was like to be raising a family during the Depression, he or she must first find out if the narrator was married at the time. "No" means you have to follow a different topic. Or if the interviewer needs specific, factual information before progressing along a line of questioning, he or she can ask a closed-ended question, expecting a short answer: for example, "How many people were living in the house at that time?" Or the interviewer may need to clarify something, such as a date: "Let's see, what year would that have been?" The problem comes when you elicit a *string* of one-word answers. When that happens, start thinking about questions that open up the possibilities for the narrator to choose the direction and to elaborate. (Otherwise, you could have given a paper-and-pencil test, which calls for limited choices and short answers.)

An open-ended question gives the narrator scope to develop the answer as he or she chooses. Whereas the closed-ended questions above gave the narrator only limited choice in the answer, the open-ended question allows the narrator to define the choices. If the narrator had answered "yes" to being married during the Depression, the interviewer would have asked one more closed-ended question, "Did you and your husband have children at that time?" If the answer was "yes," the interviewer would have followed with an open-ended question: "We want to know how mothers and fathers managed to raise families during the Depression. Could you tell me how you got by during the hard time when your husband was out of work?"

There are degrees of open-endedness. Consider these questions Payne offers from a wartime survey among farmers:

What would you say have been your main difficulties in farming during
   the past year?

How did those difficulties affect your farm production?

What are some of the shortages that have bothered you the most?

As you look forward to your farming this next year, what in the line of
   supplies or equipment is causing you the most concern?[7]

Each question becomes more restricted in the range of choice in
the answer. In the first example, the narrator is restricted to talking
about the past year, but he can define difficulty in any way he wishes
and talk about it in his terms. In the second, the narrator must focus
on farm production. By the third, he must discuss not only production problems but also shortages connected with production. By the
fourth, he must answer in terms of supplies and equipment. Each
level of specificity in the expected answer has its use for the interviewer, but the questions remain open-ended because the narrator
is still free to talk about his experience as he sees it and to elaborate
as much as he chooses.

Think about the best strategy for you to choose, given your topic:
Do you start with a broad question and gradually limit the scope of
the answer? Or do you start with more focused questions and come
to a broad question at the end of that progression?

Usually a broad question is the most open-ended you can ask,
such as, "Please tell me about your life during the Depression."
Much depends on the narrator's interest in and acquaintance with
the topic and readiness to deal with broad questions. A workable
strategy is to use a broad question at the beginning of a line of
questioning and then pick up on what the narrator says by asking
more specific questions. The advantage of the broad question coming at the beginning of a line of questioning is that the narrator
follows his or her own thought processes or paths of association.
You can learn much that you did not even guess about before the
interview, including a new framework in which to view this topic.
Rob Rosenthal, who interviewed people in Seattle to find out how
their experiences in a general strike had changed their lives, explained
the advantages of a broad question: "Letting people talk about their
worlds with as little structure as possible is a good way to see things
through their eyes, and ensure against interviewer bias."[8]

Figure out if the narrator is at ease with this approach (the broad question, then the specific questions): Some are not and prefer that you ask specific questions; others relax and enjoy "picking up the ball and running with it." A broad question I have used successfully at the beginning of a line of questioning is, "I'm very much interested in knowing the details of daily life. What was a typical workday during the week like for you in those years?" Or "When you were a young girl living on the farm with your mother and father, what was a typical Sunday like?"

One kind of broad question to be concerned about is the comparative question. In interviewing academics in a liberal arts college in New England, I began with a broad question: "How do you compare your experience as a woman teaching at this college in the 1930s with your experience here in the 1970s?" The narrators enthusiastically launched into descriptions, anecdotes, and reflections that usually lasted at least half an hour. It was obvious that the narrators had talked about this among themselves and not only were used to this kind of comparative question but also had considered this particular one already. I concluded that a comparative question at the beginning of a discussion is useful when you know that the narrator is invested in the success of the interview, tends to like this kind of question, will probably be interested in the particular question, and has much information in detail about the topic.

On the other hand, the comparative question at the beginning of the line of questioning may not be profitable if the narrator has not thought about this question before and is not used to this kind of analytical approach. At the beginning of the mill village project, I asked the women of the first generation, "How has your life been different from your daughter's?" They seemed dumbfounded. I thought about their reaction: If someone had asked me that question out of the clear blue sky, I also would have been stymied. I changed strategy and asked a series of focused questions about their lives, often asking how their daughters did the same things now. The very broad question I saved for the end; in that way, I was able to get full answers.

Providing a context for the question is very helpful. The narrator is trying to follow your train of thought just as you are trying to follow hers. The narrator wants to know why you are interested in this topic. Oral historian Charles Morrissey called this the *two-sentence format* and advised the interviewer to use similar wording in the question that was used in the introduction to the question. Morrissey gave the following example:

INTERVIEWER: In oral history interviews, after asking a person why a decision was made, we often ask why a different result didn't occur. During the merger discussions, did you at any time expect a different result to occur?[9]

Consider another example in which providing a context accomplishes two tasks. This kind of exchange occurred in an interviewing project with farm families in Northern Illinois in the mid-1980s:[10]

INTERVIEWER: It's puzzling to social scientists that Americans in rural areas started limiting their families in the last century and then drastically in this century. No one knows who made that decision—father or mother—and why. We can't call them back and ask these questions but we can ask the generation who married in the 1920s and 1930s. So, I would like to ask *you*. I notice that your parents had 6 children, while you and your wife had 2. Did you make a conscious decision? [Narrator nods yes.] Who made the decision?
NARRATOR: Well, we pretty much decided together. Well, my wife would have liked more children, but I didn't. With her bad hip and all, we knew it wasn't a good idea to have another baby.

Because of the explanation, the narrator understood why the question was important to the interviewer. Also, this is a situation that could come close to being too personal for this narrator's sense of propriety but by putting it into the context of scholarly investigation, the interviewer was able to avoid offense.

In the same interviewing project among farm families in Illinois, my co-researcher Terry Shea and I decided our interview guide was too focused on material things. We began to add questions on perception of quality of life. One question we asked, in the context of religious life, was whether the narrator had had a spiritual experience. None had. Undoubtedly they thought I referred to a religious experience within the context of a church service—because we had been just been asking about church-related topics—and the intense, emotional feeling of "being saved" was not part of their religion. Only later did I realize that I should have explained what I meant by a "spiritual experience" and left my definition open enough to allow them leeway in answering. I should have placed my question in a different context because the sequence of questions implied a context I did not intend.

Kinds of Words and Phrasing to Avoid

Just as gaining skill as an interviewer means planning a strategy for asking questions, it also means becoming sharply aware of your own use of words. In *The Art of Asking Questions,* Stanley Payne has a witty discussion about this. Clarity is the rule of thumb here. All of us know not to ask the "can't win" variety such as "Still beat your wife?" or to use a confusing question such as "What is Mickey Mouse, a cat or a dog?" What is more difficult to discern are things such as "unintended specificity." When an interviewer asks, "How many books do you have on your bookshelf?" the narrator does not know whether he should run over and count them or not. And academicians use specialized words so often they do not stop to think that these are not in everybody's vocabulary. "Do you eat the flesh of sensate mammals?" is an exaggeration of pompous speech, of course, but it is useful to remember as you write out questions. Or the interviewer may blurt out a question before thinking about the possible double meaning: "Do you ever get down on the farm?" The narrator may think, "Does he mean depressed?"[11]

Worse still, the interviewer uses words that indicate he or she thinks the narrator is not very intelligent: "How do you feel about your income tax—that is, the amount you have to pay the government on the money you take in during the year?" A better way to phrase a question when you are not sure the narrator will be familiar with a term you are using is to describe, then add the term: "How do you feel about the amount you have to pay the government on the money you take in during the year—I'm referring to the federal income tax here." Or the interviewer asks, "What year did you get the electric?" The narrator knows that the interviewer is not "just folks."[12] The interviewer strikes a false note by using slang words or colloquialisms and also insults the narrator.

Using a conversational style is fine. End the sentence with a preposition if you feel like that is informal and clear. And if in the interview, you fumble, that is all right, because people fumble in conversation and this implies that you are thinking things through, too, as you speak. You look a little more human, a little less in control of all the words flying about. It is confusion and talking down to the narrator that is the concern here.

Avoid the use of emotion-laden terms as you phrase the questions in the guide. If the narrator chooses to use such words, he or she reveals something important about attitude. But the interviewer should not suggest it. In *Interviewing*, Gorden gives these two sentences in which changing just two words makes a critical difference:

How do you feel about Negroes moving into this area?
How do you feel about Negroes invading your neighborhood?[13]

Scrutinize the questions you are planning to use for terms that have an effect that you do not intend.

Selecting Narrators

During the informational interviews in the first phase of the research, you have gleaned names of individuals to interview formally. You may need other ways to find narrators. For the mill village project, my co-researchers and I visited the ministers of the two churches and asked who the oldest members were. We wrote to these members. In addition, we put an advertisement in the local newspaper but got a poor response; nevertheless, other researchers have had better luck with this method. For the college history, I scanned the list of faculty for each year, then checked with the alumni office to find out which individuals were still living after the 30- or 40-year interim. In researching the history of the Wurlitzer plant in DeKalb, Illinois, during World War II, we read the company newsletter, looking for names of employees. Then we checked the current city directory to see which of these names appeared. The best method in my experience, however, has been personal recommendation. Once we identified a few of the superintendents and workers at the plant, we asked them who among the employees still lived in the vicinity and were well enough to participate. We then asked the employees they named to whom they thought we should talk. This process of asking narrators to refer others who might be interested in the project is called *snowball sampling* by ethnographers.

The next step is to draw up a tentative list of narrators: I use the word *tentative* because you will probably add to the list as the interviewing project goes on and narrators think of others you should interview. In selecting narrators for recording, you will want to choose narrators who were involved in pivotal events. In a community history, you also choose narrators who have lived in the community the longest; for a family history, you might want to record the life story of every family member; for a biography, you will want to talk to the individual's associates, relatives, friends, and critics.

In the chapters on community studies, family research, and biography, there is information relevant to the appropriate kind of selection process. Here I will assume that the researcher is engaged in searching for information about an event or movement. Some individuals' recorded memories are essential: If one woman or man made a decision that changed the direction of the community, then that woman or man should be sought. When you seek to understand the effects of decisions on the community, a wider net is cast. But for recent periods, there may be so many narrators that you have to consider sampling techniques. Sampling design is simply the plan whereby the researcher selects cases for study; in oral history it is the choice of persons to be interviewed.

In quantitative research, such as a survey, 10% of the population might be designated by selecting every 10th name on an alphabetical list. These individuals would be called and interviewed. The researchers consider this a random sample. Such a random sample is often not helpful to a historian dealing with specific events: The 10% who are interviewed, for example, may tell you how the general public viewed the decision to drop the atomic bomb at the close of World War II, but they cannot say what was in the minds of the few people who made the decision.

In a qualitative research project, a different approach often will be necessary. If the project is concerned with decisions that changed the community, then the key decision makers must be interviewed. But these few at the top of the hierarchy do not make up the community. Certainly a study of a community or a movement requires interviewing in all strata because people at all levels not only felt the effects of decisions, but also implemented them, sometimes changed them, and often made their own decisions, regardless of the ones handed down.

In the history of a psychiatric hospital—which I viewed as a work community—I insisted on interviewing narrators at every level in the work force: grounds workers, housekeepers, maintenance people, psychiatrists, mental health workers, social workers, nurses, occupational therapists, cooks, carpenters, the administrative director, and members of the board of trustees. (Patients were not included in this list because state law forbids access to patient records unless the researcher is directly involved in the individual's clinical care.) The assumption was that the psychiatrist is the authority on diagnosis and prescription, but the mental health worker is the authority on the work that he or she does on the ward. By using this stratified sample, I was able to obtain information on a variety of experiences as well as many different perspectives on developments at the hospital. If I had interviewed only the directors and members of the board of trustees, I would have gotten a far different picture.[14]

I also sought out people who no longer worked in the hospital, people who were for and against the union, people known to be favored by the administration, and those reported to be dissatisfied with the way things were going. In other words, I sought a variety of opinions on controversial topics and a variety of levels of allegiance to the formal organization as well as witnesses in each occupational category. I added to my stratified sampling technique *purposive sampling*.

In the research project for *The Edwardians* (see Chapter 1 of this volume), British oral historians Paul Thompson and Thea Vigne selected a group representative of the population in Britain early in this century. They designed a *quota sample*—one based on the 1911 census—that numbered 444 persons. Thompson described the way the sample was drawn up:

> The proportion of men and women was as in 1911; so were the proportions who had then been living in the countryside, the towns, and the conurbations; and so too the balance between the main regions of England, Wales, and Scotland. We tried to ensure a proper class distribution by dividing the sample into six major occupational groups, taken from the adjusted census categories of Guy Routh's *Occupation and Pay, 1906-65*.[15]

In addition to stratified, quota, and purposive samples, there are other ways to select narrators. In the history of child workers in a mill village before World War I, I sought out every person mentioned to me as a worker in the mill early in the century. This method is referred to as a *universal sample* or *nonprobability sample*. At that point, the narrators were in their 70s and 80s, and I contacted all living persons who had been part of that history and still resided in that town. The number was so small that it was feasible to contact all survivors. In fact, the narrators finally numbered 30 men and women who were able and willing to talk to us.[16] In a universal sample, the number of potential narrators is less than 100, and you contact each one, hoping a fair number will be in good health, have good memories, and be willing to participate.

Often the interviewer wants to know how many interviews are enough. When you find that narrators are repeating for the 20th or 30th time, from about the same perspective, the same information, you know you have enough in that category. Glaser and Strauss refer to this as *saturation*.

A problem remains to be considered, however: Some narrators may choose not to talk to the researcher at all. Others will come forth because they are interested in the history and want to talk. As Thompson notes, the sample is to some degree self-selective because it is the confident, articulate people who agree to be interviewed. Laconic, isolated, or withdrawn individuals do not often appear in the sample of an oral history project.[17]

Bear with the inarticulate: Try to get them to talk when you know that they have been directly involved in the event you are studying. In your own sample, you will know the individuals you must seek out, no matter how laconic they may be. But if they refuse to talk except in monosyllables and your good interviewing techniques are of no avail, do not be discouraged. Knowing that you have done your best to interview this key witness, turn to the next narrator and try to get the information from other witnesses and written records.

Finally, look at the list of narrators and prioritize. Individuals who were most involved in pivotal decisions, were most active in important events, or were most directly affected should be at the top. Also, those who are very elderly or those with health problems should be sought in the first phase of interviewing.

Contacting Narrators

Write a letter to prospective narrators. If anyone the narrator might know is supportive of your project, ask if you may use his or her name in the letter. Describe your project and your training and interest in the project. Explain why it is important to learn from people who have firsthand knowledge of the subject. Tell them why you are contacting them, and ask for their help. Include your telephone number so they can call you if there are questions. End the letter with a statement that you will call.

If the narrator calls you to ask what this is all about, send a brief list of general topics to be covered in the interviewing session. Avoid sending the specific questions because you are likely to receive rehearsed answers.

This initial contact is almost always done best by letter rather than by telephone call. After the narrator has had time to receive the letter, then telephone; the narrator will know who you are. The exception to this procedure is a situation in which the individual has reason to distrust anything in print or to feel apprehension about such an invitation. Some elderly people have good reason to be skeptical about strangers, and the politically vulnerable will certainly want to know something about you. In either situation, having someone they trust explain the project to them will be the best method of contact.

Keep a file of index cards. On each narrator's card, record the name, address, telephone number, the name of the person who referred the narrator to you, and any pertinent information such as state of health. You need to know this information at the time you call. Keep a file folder on each narrator in which you can insert newspaper clippings or comments made by others about the narrator or any notes you take as you read through the written records. And, finally, make a huge chart, providing space for date of the preliminary interview (see the next chapter), for the recording interviews, whether the release form has been returned, when the thank you letter was written, whether there were photographs or any documents to be returned, and the date of return. If a transcript is to be made, then allow space for the date transcribing began, who is transcribing, when the transcript was finished, when this was sent to the narrator, and when returned. (A model for this form is given in Appendix E.)

Scheduling the Interview

When you call, schedule the interview at the narrator's convenience as much as possible. With elderly narrators or narrators who have had health problems, ask what time during the day they like having a visitor. Scheduling is not easy with very busy people: The time they suggest may sound strange to you—6:45 in the morning, for example, while the person crunches breakfast cereal. Because the narrator's good will is necessary for the interview to take place at all, be accommodating as much as you can.

Preparing the Equipment

As you prepare for the interview, you will be getting your recording equipment ready. Although I was at first cavalier about technical aspects of oral history, I soon found to my dismay that the sound quality of a recording was so poor that my work was of little use to anyone. And even as an experienced interviewer, I have had mishaps with equipment. I agree with Dale Treleven's statement about this: "Sloppily done interviews are a menace to the historical record, a pain to archivists, a disservice to researchers, and, above all, an insult to respondents who so willingly share their memories for posterity."[18] If you are concerned about what is happening technically or if you have had problems with sound, then here are suggestions about equipment. (If you are an experienced interviewer who is comfortable with your equipment and sure of sound quality, then skip to the next chapter.)

Use two remote microphones (attached to the lapels of narrator and interviewer) or one remote placed between interviewer and narrator. The voices are clearer and there is not as much extraneous noise (such as the whir of turning tape) as with recorders having only built-in microphones. When you are using only one remote microphone, place it between yourself and the narrator near enough so that the voices of both will be loud and clear. Microphones are sensitive and pick up vibrations, so nestle it on a scarf or some soft padding.

Place the recorder so that you can see how much tape you have left as the interview goes on. (A recorder that gives you a signal that the tape side is about full is a great help.) Glance down to make sure the record button is pressed in. And then check again. After the interview has gone on a few minutes, stop and play back. Explain to the narrator what you are doing, "I need to check the machine to make sure the sound is okay and that we are recording." Get in the habit of checking to make sure the record button is pressed in. Use

60- or 90-minute tapes because 120-minute tapes have a greater chance of breaking when rewound and played back during transcribing. Always carry extra tapes: You never know if the interview you thought would last an hour goes into three hours.

The use of batteries eliminates the problem of interference from other things in the house on the same circuit. Once when I was using a plug-in, someone started a vacuum cleaner in the next room and blitzed the sound on the tape recorder. I had just checked the sound and did not check again for 15 minutes—none of that part of the interview was audible. I discovered the problem, the maid changed rooms and vacuumed upstairs in the room above us, and another portion of the sound was obliterated. If you are using the house's current, check every 20 or 30 minutes or when there is a pause in the conversation.

It is best to buy a recorder that has a battery strength indicator. If not, one strategy with a tape recorder without such an indicator is to jot down the hours used in recording and change the battery before you use up the time. Then you do not have to use the house current, and you can feel confident that when you check the sound, the battery will be strong. You can expect that it will not weaken before the 90-minute interview is up. (But always take along extra batteries, just in case the sound starts to get weak, and an extension cord for the worst of times.)

When you use up one side of the tape, mark it quickly before you turn it over. This is a bother, of course, but you do not want to make a mistake and record over a side that is full. It is too easy to make a mistake: You record on both sides of a tape, put it aside, record on both sides of the second tape. By this time, you are tired, but the interview has not yet ended—the narrator is still going strong. Without noticing, you pick up the first tape and put it in the recorder, thinking you have a blank tape. The first side recorded gets erased.

When the interview session is finished, as soon as you can, fix the tape by removing the recording tab so no one can record over it. Label each side with project title in brief, narrator's name, interviewer's name, date, and place. Immediately make a notation in your records so that you can, just at a glance at your chart, see what interviews are completed, which are yet to be done. Of course, if you are carrying out only four or five interviews, this is not necessary, but if the project requires more than that, good record keeping saves much time. You do not have to rummage through tapes and correspondence, wracking your brain trying to remember. You avoid making unnecessary telephone calls or writing duplicate letters.

Summary

Choose a subject for research that engages both your mind and your heart. This is a head start on a successful project.

Carry out informational interviews to find out what the people who lived the history judge important. In drawing up the interview guide, you have the opportunity to ask the questions that will enable you to situate your findings in a historical context. You can get information unique to individuals and place them and the events of their lives in a wider framework that makes these events significant beyond them. Here you can draw on your background reading to suggest questions that will reveal how the people you talk to were like the rest of the state or the nation, how they were different. Be aware, though, of how background reading may influence you to stay with original hypotheses rather than frame new ones as you hear the testimony.

In the wording of your questions, strive for clarity. Avoid talking down to the narrator. Choose a strategy that will work best, given the topic and the particular kind of narrator: Ask focused questions first in a line of questioning and end with the broad questions when the narrator needs time to think the matter through in some detail before considering the broader picture. Choose a broad question when you know the narrator can easily handle it and when you need the narrator to be completely free in the response. Then you can follow up with questions on details the narrator has offered. Start with nonthreatening topics first. Closed-ended questions are often necessary at the beginning of a line of questioning to establish suitability of the narrator to deal with the topic or to clarify. Open-ended questions give the narrator scope to define the direction the answer will go in and to elaborate as much as he or she wishes.

Careful attention to the mechanics of recording pays off in clear, strong sound. Use a remote microphone, placed between narrator and interviewer, or two microphones, one attached to the lapel of the interviewer, one to the narrator. Use batteries and test frequently to make sure they are strong enough. Equipment in good working order and conscientious record keeping enable you to stay in control of the project.

Notes

1. *Life at the DeKalb Wurlitzer Plant During World War II*, eds. Char Henn, Estella Metcalf, and Valerie Yow. Northern Illinois Regional History Center, Northern Illinois University, DeKalb, Illinois.

2. Jacquelyn Dowd Hall et al., *Like a Family: The Making of a Cotton Mill World* (Chapel Hill: University of North Carolina Press, 1987).

3. Raymond L. Gorden, *Interviewing: Strategy, Techniques and Tactics* (4th ed.) (Chicago: Dorsey Press, 1987), 332.

4. Ibid., 219.

5. Ibid., 217.

6. Ibid.

7. Stanley Payne, *The Art of Asking Questions* (Princeton, N.J.: Princeton University Press, 1957), 35.

8. Rob Rosenthal, "The Interview and Beyond: Some Methodological Questions for Oral Historians, *Public Historian* 1, no. 3 (Spring 1979): 58-67; see p. 66.

9. Charles Morrissey, "The Two-Sentence Format as an Interviewing Technique in Oral History Fieldwork," *Oral History Review* 15 (Spring 1987): 43-53; see p. 46.

10. "Farm Families of DeKalb County." Northern Illinois Regional History Center, Northern Illinois University, DeKalb, Illinois.

11. Payne, *Art of Asking Questions*, 120-123.

12. Ibid., 116.

13. Gorden, *Interviewing*, 332.

14. Valerie Yow, "Effects of Change in Treatment Philosophy on Clinical Practice in a Psychiatric Hospital." Paper delivered at annual meeting of the Association for the History of Medicine, Cleveland, Ohio, May 1991.

15. Paul Thompson, *Voice of the Past: Oral History* (New York: Oxford University Press, 1988), 125-126.

16. Valerie Yow (listed as Valerie Quinney), "Childhood in a Southern Mill Village," *International Journal of Oral History* 3, no. 3 (November 1982): 167-192; see 167-168.

17. Thompson, *Voice of the Past*, 130.

18. Dale Treleven, "Oral History and the Archival Community: Common Concerns About Documenting Twentieth Century Life," *International Journal of Oral History* 10 (February 1989): 50-58; see p. 53.

Recommended Reading

On Phrasing Questions for the Interview Guide

Gorden, Raymond. *Interviewing: Strategy, Techniques and Tactics.* 4th ed. Chicago: Dorsey Press, 1987. This has useful information on the phrasing of questions.

Morrissey, Charles. "The Two-Sentence Format as an Interviewing Technique in Oral History Fieldwork," *Oral History Review* 15 (Spring 1987): 43-53. The author offers an important discussion on placing the question in context.

Payne, Stanley. *The Art of Asking Questions*. Princeton, N.J.: Princeton University Press, 1951. This remains the best single source on how to ask productive questions.

On Using the Interview Guide

Lummis, Trevor. *Listening to History: The Authenticity of Oral Evidence*. London: Hutchinson, 1987. The author discusses differences between the questionnaire and the interview schedule (or interview guide) and the usefulness of the guide.

3

Interviewing Techniques

" Interviewing is rather like marriage: everybody knows what it is, an awful lot of people do it, and yet behind each closed front door there is a world of secrets."[1] In this chapter, I will tell you some secrets. I also present interviewers' wisdom based on hours of interviewing experience. I have gleaned what can be useful to the interviewer from various disciplines, from the work of oral historians, sociologists, journalists, anthropologists, folklorists, psychologists, and communication specialists.

I point out steps to begin the interview and ways to build rapport. The chapter also presents a discussion on productive kinds of spontaneous questions to use as well as ways to handle delicate matters and ask hard questions. Meanings of nonverbal signals are pointed out, especially how to read the signs of impending difficulties, and there is advice on what to do when there is trouble. Finally, there is a checklist you can use to critique your own interviewing style.

The Preliminary Meeting

Everything you do before the interview will contribute to the establishment of the character of the interviewer and narrator relationship. It helps to make a brief visit to the narrator before the day of the interview (unless you already know the narrator well). Even though you have written and called, you are still a stranger. A meeting in person, however brief, means that you are not a stranger when you appear with your recorder.

Drop by at a time convenient for the narrator. Explain the project briefly and show enthusiasm about interviewing this person. Say something positive about the place and the person. Use some humor. This sets up the expectation that you are not a threatening person, that this could be a pleasant experience. In his book *Creative Interviewing*, Jack Douglas asserts that "small talk and chitchat are vital first steps on the way to intimate communion."[2]

I have arrived at a time when the narrator was washing the dishes. I dried them while we talked. Another asked if I had any canning jars, and I said I had a few empty ones I could bring, which I did. However, in scheduling an interview with a bank president, I was warned I would have only 30 minutes. Any preliminary meeting with him was not possible. In another project, I realized that a physician who was on the board of the college I was researching was too busy at the hospital for me to talk with her there. I asked her to stop by the archives and meet me when she came to the college for a board meeting. She did, which gave me a chance to show her how the project was organized, how many tapes we had done to that point, and so on. She started saying more positive things about the project. This preliminary meeting is not always possible, but make it happen if you can.

At this preliminary meeting, you can talk about what work will be done during the recording session. Explain that the recorder will pick up sounds in the house. Insist on a noise-free environment. If the narrator wants to sit in her rocker on the back porch and the sound of car horns and heavy trucks is in the neighborhood, explain that the noise will be on the tape and will obscure words from time to time. Ask her to find a different place. If the narrator wants you to come to his office but the telephone keeps ringing and the secretary keeps popping in, then point out that constant interruptions will be on tape and that they also obstruct the flow of the conversation. You might explain, "We'll spend a lot of time after each interruption, trying to reconstruct the conversation to that point so we can go on." Ask, "How can we keep the telephone from ringing and stop the interruptions?" If you are sitting in a living room and the television in the next room can be heard, then request in a firm, serious tone that the television sound be turned down when you come to record. And ask the narrator to move a barking dog somewhere else. I have even suggested muffling a grandfather clock that chimed loudly every 15 minutes.

The place where you meet the narrator to record makes a difference. An individual who meets you in his office will present himself differently in the conversation and will emphasize different things from the way he would if you record in his living room at home. Once a student of mine recording in ethnic communities in Providence, Rhode Island, interviewed the proprietor in an Irish bar he owned. The narrator declared several times that it is a myth that Irish men drink a lot, but in the background were the tinkle of glasses and the gurgle of liquids. His testimony would have been more convincing if the recording had been done in a different setting. And if he had recorded at home, he might not have chosen that topic to discuss at all: His life at home and in his neighborhood would have been more prominent in his thinking.

About 8 times out of 10, it is best to record, just the two of you, without a third voice. The presence in the room of another person changes the interview. On rare occasions, however, a third person can be helpful. I have interviewed a mother in her 90s whose daughter insisted on being there. The daughter was very quiet unless there was some information for which the mother wanted confirmation, such as, "I think that was 1934—do you remember your Dad talking about this?" The presence of the daughter seemed reassuring to the mother, and she might not have talked to me otherwise. And sometimes an interpreter is required or the culture prevents an outsider from interviewing a woman alone; a female relative will sit by the narrator's side.

On the other hand, I have had the experience of a husband insisting on staying in the room. He dominated the interview. My categorical advice is never permit a husband and wife to be interviewed together unless the project specifically calls for joint interviews. As much as married couples like the illusion that they are of one mind, they are not. The presence of one often inhibits the performance of another or at least slants it.

However, in some kinds of interviewing, especially projects in the sociology of the family, the research strategy requires conjoint interviews. Anthropologist Linda Bennett and social worker Katharine McAvity discussed their research methods for a psychosocial research project on alcoholism and family heritage. They argued that there are advantages to interviewing couples together when "marital negotiation of family identity" is the general aim of research. This is the easiest way to detect lack of consensus on an issue. The spouses provoke each other to expand on information and to clarify differences.[3] Other researchers, however, have found that information comes out that creates or exacerbates problems. (This situation is discussed further in the chapter on ethics.)

A different situation occurred when two women who had worked together in a munitions plant during World War II wanted to be interviewed together. They had been best friends for 40 years. As long as the conversation was focused on their war work, they sparked each other's memory. Answers to questions about their personal lives were truncated, however. Possibly, they considered the narrator a member of the out-group and used this to solidify their feeling of being in their own in-group.

For an in-depth interview, insist on being alone with the narrator. The exceptions to this are:

- when you know the two people well,
- when the situation requires them to be together,
- when the research strategy requires couple interaction,
- when the presence of an interpreter is necessary, and
- when the culture prevents an outsider from having exclusive conversation with the narrator.

Beginning the Interview

On the day of the interview, before you take out the recorder, your comments can reduce tension. Douglas explained, "When you talk about the weather, the view from her mountain top chalet, or the lack of view from her cellar den, a certain offhandedness indicates that nothing earth shattering (like headlines) is going to happen here."[4]

Explain the purpose of the project again, tell the narrator how it is coming along. Assure the narrator that he or she is not obliged to answer all of the questions. Because people do not wish to be impolite, let them know that you will not be offended if they decline to answer a question.

After the recording begins, give the narrator the chance to talk; except for introducing and asking the questions and answering the narrator's questions, be silent about your experiences. Otherwise, your story gets recorded 30 times (or as many tapes as you make in a project). Some interviewers see the interview as a "dialectic with speech and counterspeech," as Martha Ross observed. She objects to this model on the basis that the "authentic interpretation by the narrator of his own experience may be difficult to separate from that inspired by the interviewer."[5] This is the narrator's story: Give him or her the chance to tell it.

If the narrator does not like the idea of you using a tape recorder, then explain that you cannot take notes fast enough and that you lose ends of sentences or beginnings of the next. If you are doing historical research, remind the narrator that the taped memoir is a historical document that others will listen to and benefit from. (Or, in case studies requiring confidentiality, remind the narrators that you will not use their names on tape or reveal their identities to anyone.) You might say something reassuring such as, "In these interviews, we just ignore the recorder. Usually we forget it's on." If there is some hesitation because the narrator does not know how the conversation will sound, play the tape back after a few moments to let her or him hear the voices. Of course, if the narrator absolutely insists that you put away the recorder, then you will have to take notes. Type them up as quickly as possible before you forget specific sentences. If you are a historian, deposit them in the archives with your tapes: At least others can check your evidence, but notes are not a substitute for the taped interview.

Begin the taped interview by stating the name of the interviewer, the name of the narrator, the location of the interview, and the date. To any listener years from then, explain the purpose of the interview very briefly. If you have a special relationship to the narrator, inform the listener, because this will make a difference: "The narrator and interviewer have been friends for 20 years." Then ask for the narrator's oral consent (a nod will not suffice) to the taping of your conversation that day. If this is a research project where confidentiality is required, of course you do not give the real name. But if you are using a pseudonym, explain that; you still need acknowledgment on tape that the narrator knows the conversation is being recorded.

Begin with routine questions such as, "Where were you born?" Follow with uncomplicated questions about the place or family. These nonthreatening questions help both of you ease into the interview.

Building Rapport

In *The Ethnographic Interview,* James Spradley observed four stages in the interview situation: (1) apprehension, (2) exploration, (3) cooperation, and (4) participation.[6] Every first interview begins with uncertainty on the part of the interviewer and the narrator. The interviewer does not know how the interview will go. The narrator does not know what is expected of him or her. Often the narrator says something like, "I don't think I know enough to be of any help to you."[7]

The interview begins, and soon the interviewer and narrator are exploring the situation; this is a period of listening and observing. Spradley suggested that running through the minds of these two are questions such as, "What does he want me to say? Can she be trusted? Is she going to be able to answer my questions? What does she really want from these interviews? Am I answering questions as I should? Does he really want to know what I know?"[8]

The narrator will decide whether or not to trust the interviewer. It is thus crucial for the interviewer to be honest and straightforward about the project and to answer the narrator's questions honestly and respectfully. This may require repeated explanations of what the project is about and why he or she is there interviewing this particular individual. Douglas recalled a moment in an interviewing session that had been preceded by several sessions. He thought everything was understood. Suddenly, the narrator asked, "What is the point now? Why are we doing this?" Douglas realized that he would have to explain in far more detail than he had exactly what he was doing and why.[9]

Taking the time to make sure the narrator understands also builds trust. It is not productive to echo repeatedly the narrator's statements, but sometimes if you are not sure of the meaning, ask: "Do

I understand you right? You had mixed feelings about the decision to take the plane that morning?" The narrator appreciates your effort to understand and to represent the meaning correctly.

Reassurance that the narrator is responding in a helpful way should be given. Spradley suggests communicating to the narrator, "I understand what you're saying; I am learning; it is valuable to me."[10] The interviewer should express appreciation that the narrator is offering his or her time to answer questions. And especially the interviewer should make it clear that the narrator's expertise or special effort is appreciated: "I know I am asking you some questions that are not easy to answer, and I really appreciate your helping me with these." "You know the details of that situation better than anybody else. Talking to you really helps me understand." "You've explained this so clearly that I feel like I understand it." Positive appraisal of the narrator's work in the interview contributes to the narrator's motivation to continue and to cooperate in the endeavor.

Although this may seem too obvious to mention, listen carefully. Listening with only part of your mind will be detected, and who wants to talk to someone who is only halfway listening? This means not following an interview format slavishly but instead following the narrator's thought processes. In the old style of questioning by social scientists, the interviewer's attitude might have been like this description given by Douglas:

> How much more proud and worthy—serenely confident and powerful—we feel when we can *impose* the structure of discourse and of reality itself upon our little "subjects": "Sit there, 'subject.' Now here is a questionnaire with five hundred questions on it. They are written in stone and encompass the entire realm of possible questions concerning these realities. There are only five possible responses to each one."[11]

In in-depth interviewing, because you seek the unexpected, the information you do not already know, you must listen carefully and give the narrator scope to develop his or her train of thought. The narrator may tentatively offer another line of investigation. Careful listening enables you to pick up on this. Consider this interchange after the interviewer asks the narrator if his father had been involved in the Irish Republican Army.

NARRATOR: My mother was active. She received several medals for
    bravery from the Irish government.
INTERVIEWER: Very good! And how about your father?[12]

The interviewer missed a very promising line of questioning. However, this does not mean that you can allow the narrator to digress
to the extent that he or she uses the interview for a catharsis for some
current problem not connected to the subject of the interview. (Of
course, if you are writing a biography, every concern of the narrator
will be of interest.) Gorden points out that afterward, in listening to
the tape, the narrator may feel embarrassed or resentful that the
interviewer let him talk on and on about irrelevant or trivial matters.[13]
I realize that I have stressed equal sharing in the direction of the
interview and it seems like a contradiction for me now to advise you
to return to the intended topic. You must depend on your judgment
here: If you judge that this is totally irrelevant, listen, but when
there is a pause, tactfully draw the narrator back to the subject
under discussion.

When you change topics in the interview, explain what connection there is to the previous topic or how it fits into the overall plan
of the interview. The narrator appreciates your letting him know
what you are doing. After all, he or she is trying to follow *your* train
of thought.

Indicate that you are interested in the unique point of view the
narrator can give you by personalizing the request. You can say
outright, "I want to be sure I understand *your* point of view on this
issue."[14] Or "I'd like to know what *you* did that day."

Needless to say, you do not interrupt or finish a sentence for the
narrator. The matter of silence is not so easy to state categorically,
however. You have to sense the narrator's pacing and keep your
own compatible. If the narrator is a reflective person, pausing to
think something through, wait for her to take the time she needs.
On the other hand, if the narrator answers with a clipped efficiency
and seems to expect a rather brisk pace, you can proceed a little faster
than you might ordinarily. Gorden suggests that before you ask the
next statement, you should give the narrator at least a 10-second
pause to see if he or she wants to add anything.[15]

Sherry Thomas, who had just completed an interviewing project
with farm women, talked to her audience at a National Women's

Studies Association Conference about learning to keep silent, to give the narrator time to think. She said, "Sometimes the answer to a question from fifteen minutes before comes the next hour if you'll let the silence drag on."[16] Too long a pause, however, is a silent way of putting pressure on the narrator to add, and I suspect that this produces resentment after a while. Sensitivity to the narrator's pace is the key here.

Your nonverbal responses are important. Avoid responding with "Uh huh," because it is recorded and transcribed. Nod, smile, shake your head to show that you are following. It is important to maintain eye contact. Looking down to take notes and not looking into the person's eyes makes you seem to be thinking about something else (and it prevents you from observing the narrator's nonverbal behavior). Often it is necessary to keep a small pad of paper and a pencil handy to jot down names or terms for which you need to ask correct spelling after the interview or to jot down a word to remind yourself of a line of questioning to pick up on later; but make this note taking quick.

Both people, however, look away from time to time because that is what we do in any conversation. Communication researchers Byron Lewis and Frank Pucelik found that people often look up and to the right when they are constructing images, up and to the left when they are remembering images, level and to the right in constructing speech, level and to the left remembering sounds, down and to the right in concentrating on feelings, down and to the left in holding an internal dialogue.[17] (The researchers warn that this represents a generalization about human behavior, one that may be reversed for some left-handed people.) You might keep these possibilities in mind as you observe the narrator's behavior.

Sometimes the interviewer can anticipate how difficult it will be for a narrator to answer a question and that the narrator may be strongly tempted to lie. Gorden advises letting the narrator know immediately that you have some information on this topic already and that you are making no judgment about it.[18] Another way is to depersonalize the question. For example, "I know that some women in the neighborhood donated their gold wedding rings to Mussolini's cause; of course, they did not know what was to come later in Italy. Did you know people who were asked to donate their rings?"

The usual advice is to communicate positive regard. It is difficult, however, to do this when you are interviewing people whose values you abhor. Consider, for example, the interviewing project with former Nazis that William Sheridan Allen undertook for his book *The Nazi Seizure of Power*.[19] Allen interviewed a range of adherents and opponents to the Nazi regime, and these first-person accounts do indeed enlighten the reader about the reasons that the movement gained supporters. Allen had to show that he wanted to understand and that he appreciated the fact that their dilemmas were not the same that he had faced in his life. This does not mean that he had to show approval or agreement. However, he did get across an earnest desire to understand the variety of experience in which we humans have been involved.

Take the time to review background material thoroughly on the subject of the interview. You should not show off your knowledge, but the narrator will sense that you are informed and that you take the interview seriously. Do not try to convey the impression that you are in the in-group by using jargon. This is false, and the narrator knows it. But learn as much as you can about terms specific to the topics to be discussed before the interview begins; ask the narrator for meanings if you do not know them. Sometimes, even if you know a dictionary meaning, you may want to ask for the narrator's definition. (See the discussion on asking for meanings later in the chapter.)

These techniques will help you win the narrator's cooperation, but the most important basis for a good interview is sensitivity to the narrator's feelings. Show the narrator that you have empathy, that "I can imagine how you felt." The narrator is grateful for this understanding. Gorden shows how the interviewer can respond with empathy to a narrator.

NARRATOR: At that time I had three babies still in diapers, and that made it a bit difficult to adjust to the divorce.
INTERVIEWER: Three babies all in diapers! How did you manage?[20]

Diminishing Rapport

Up to this point, the discussion has been focused on ways to build rapport. Consider also the ways that rapport can be damaged. Contrast the interviewer's reply in the next example with the previous one.

NARRATOR: At that time I had three babies still in diapers, and that
    made it a bit difficult to adjust to the divorce.
INTERVIEWER: What were some of the problems?[21]

The second example creates the message, "I am detached from
this. I just need some information." Here is a similar interchange.

NARRATOR: Jim and I were going down highway 67; we didn't see the
    tornado, but just as we came to one of those banked turns we
    couldn't make it because the car was off the ground. We were jerked
    up in the air and I remember seeing a flash as our car hit the high-
    tension lines. Then we landed bottom side up in a swamp about
    four feet deep. One more gust of wind came and just flipped the
    car right side up again.
INTERVIEWER: Were you going north or south on highway 67?[22]

Ask yourself if you would wish to continue to talk to someone
you have just met who responded to you in the way the interviewer
did in the last example. From Gorden's examples, you can see that
this interviewer showed no sensitivity to the feelings of the respondent, no appreciation of what this experience was like for the person
going through it.

The subtle communication of a negative attitude also can damage
rapport. The narrator can sense disapproval. Gorden cites an interview with an individual in a metropolitan slum. The interviewer
was taken aback by the casual attitude displayed toward middle-
class ideals of parenthood and of legalities such as adoption procedures. His disapproving attitude was somehow communicated.
Gorden observed, "From this point on, the respondent ceased to
express herself so candidly, and any constructive working relationship was made more difficult."[23]

In interviewing farm women, Sherry Thomas found issues that
the ideal picture of our society does not permit us to acknowledge.
She said that she had expected her narrators to talk about pregnancy, child rearing, and even sexuality, but she also got surprises:
"What I didn't expect was, I got a lot of wife battering, incest,
lesbianism, from women aged fifty to 100 in midstream America."
She advised, "You have to be real comfortable about dealing with
[such issues] and real able to keep that conversation going, and not
by your face or your body manner or anything else put a stop to it,
because it's some of the most powerful material that's going to

surface, and to me, it's the material that blows the statistics wide open."[24]

I have talked about being animated—nodding, smiling, for example—during the interview; now I am advising that you control your face and body language. It is one thing to show interest, another to show judgment.

In his discussion of inhibitors of conversation, Gorden explained that negative attitudes toward the narrator also show up as errors of omission (such as forgetting what the narrator has said and just passing over topics important to the narrator) and the use of a condescending tone of voice or "cautious rigidity" (a reluctance to depart from the interview guide).[25]

When the interviewer shows interest and respect, a desire to understand, and a sensitivity to the feelings of the narrator in a life situation, a real partnership in the interview may begin. Spradley defined *participation* as a situation in which the narrator accepts the role of teaching the interviewer.[26] I see this as occurring when the narrator takes on some of the responsibility for making the interview productive. There is an earnest and intense involvement in the process on the part of both interviewer and narrator.

Using Skill in Questioning

Gorden listed as interviewing skills (1) wording the question so that it is clear and appropriate for the topic, (2) listening to the narrator, (3) observing the narrator's nonverbal behavior, (4) remembering what the narrator has said, and (5) judging the relevance, validity, and completeness of the answer so that you know when to follow up, probe, and so on.[27]

Probing is used when you sense that something has been left out, that the narrator could give a more complete answer. In an example in the preceding chapter, the interviewer rightly gave a context for asking the question about family limitation. The narrator answered with the explanation that he and his wife limited their family because the wife had a bad hip. The interviewer thought there might be additional reasons.

INTERVIEWER: Were there any other considerations that dissuaded you from having a larger family?

NARRATOR: Hell, it was expensive. I knew I wanted both of mine to
    go to college. And farming's an "iffy" thing. If it's not too wet, if
    it's not too dry, if the price of machinery doesn't go up (laughs).
    You can't count on being able to take care of the ones you've got.

Because of the interviewer's probe, another level of motivation was
articulated: higher expectations for the next generation that would
require so much of the resources of this family that having more
than two children would be defeating.

Another kind of probe asks for the meaning of a word when you
suspect it has a special meaning in a subculture or for that narrator.
In defining meaning, the narrator will tell you a lot about her values.
Look at the following interchange.

INTERVIEWER: Everybody thinks about the meaning of this word dif-
    ferently. I suspect it means something different to everybody. What
    does "sisterhood" mean to you?
NARRATOR: Well, I guess it means we all go out of our way to help
    another woman, that we look on her like we do a sister, help her
    when we can.

Often, asking the meaning of a technical word you do not understand will give you an insight that the narrator takes it for granted
that you have. At the beginning of this century, Beatrice Webb, social
investigator par excellence, learned that she had to become familiar
with the technical terms appropriate to a line of investigation. She
said, "Technical terms and technical details . . . are so many levers
to lift into consciousness and expression the more abstruse and
out-of-the-way facts or series of facts; and it is exactly these more
hidden events that are needed to complete descriptive analysis and
to verify hypotheses."[28]
    Sociologist Arlene Daniels describes such an event in her research
on psychiatrists in the military:

Once, for example, a key informant said, with lowered, confidential
voice, "Since Colonel X has been to Vietnam, he's caught a bad case of
Oudai fever." I had no idea what that meant; but I said nothing. In the
course of another conversation, I said, "I understand he has a bad case of
Oudai fever," hoping that I would find out what that meant. But this
offended officer frowned and changed the conversation. Later, I learned
that Oudai fever refers to the relentless pursuit of Vietnamese women:
the Oudai is the name of the silken garment the women wear. And

this I learned only when I discovered that the officer whom I offended was giving me a bad reputation for spreading malicious gossip. So much for the use of a standard technique for trying to learn insiders' ways without asking directly for information.[29]

Sherry Thomas described her puzzlement over the meaning of the statements farm women made about themselves. They never called themselves farmers; rather, they said something like, "Well, *really* I only helped out on the farm." Thomas thought this over: "And by about the third interview I realized that I needed to find out what that phrase meant, because either I was wrong in what I was seeking to find out or something else was going on." She sensed that there was cognitive dissonance. She began asking questions such as, "Tell me what you did in 1926 on a typical day." These questions evoked responses that brought her nearer the truth:

> And "helping" turns out to mean that those women got up at five in the morning, milked as many as twenty-four cows by hand, did all of the cream separating and milk preservation, ran a poultry herd, sold eggs for money, which was a significant part of the cash income, produced all of the vegetables and fruit for the family, *and* did at least a third, and frequently a half, of all the field crop work for the family, as well as doing all the housework, all the cooking, all the food preservation, and all the child care.[30]

Her advice is not to stop with the socially accepted response but to keep probing until the narrator reveals the reality of the situation.[31]

The excellent interviewer knows the culture well and is conscious of gender roles. Men in our culture will have a hard time articulating some feelings, and women also will be most hesitant to admit certain ones. Interviewer Dana Jack explained:

> Oral interviews allow us to hear, if we will, the particular meanings of a language that both men and women use but which each translates differently. For women, the ability to value their own thought and experience is hindered by self-doubt and hesitation when private experience seems at odds with cultural myths and values concerning how a woman is "supposed" to think and feel.[32]

Sherry Thomas was able to probe by asking a different kind of question, trying a different tactic. This is a delicate matter because you neither want to "lead the witness" by eliciting the answer you desire nor make the witness feel that he or she has violated cultural expectations.

A general probe may also follow a line of questioning. The interviewer senses that the narrator is still thinking about the topic or seems to be expecting further questions or might talk more if encouraged. Then ask, "You have done an excellent job in giving me insight into this problem. Is there anything else you would like to add before we go on to the last topic?"[33]

The follow-up kind of question is closely related to the probing question. The interviewer picks up a clue in the narrator's statement and pursues it. The narrator may just slide past the topic, indicating in an offhand manner that he could tell you more, as he does in the following example.

NARRATOR: Well, the Thirties were lean around here. People weren't actually starving, but they weren't eating very much. By the way, I know how that DeKalb winged ear of corn sign got started. But as I said, people tried to live off hope and you get mighty thin on that.

INTERVIEWER: I'd be interested in knowing how the winged ear of corn began. Please tell me.

An interviewer can also use a follow-up question when a narrator has given a factual account but no indication of feelings. The interviewer senses that something important is being left out here.

NARRATOR: So, we sold the farm and moved to town. I got a job at the dairy.

INTERVIEWER: I am imagining how I would have felt in that situation. Would you tell me how you felt about this change in your life?

Sometimes, a gentle suggestion can evoke information. This is helpful especially when you have come to the end of the line of questioning and you believe the answers have been honest but that the narrator could be encouraged to reflect and go beyond a factual account. It's tricky, though, because you run the risk of "leading" the witness.

NARRATOR: They had a ballfield for the workers. Christmas, gave out a turkey for each family. Picnic in the summer.

INTERVIEWER: Did you feel at the time that was enough or did you wish the mill had done more for the workers?

The "reason why" question is useful when you need to know motivation. The narrator has told you that a decision was made but has not told you the reason for it.

NARRATOR: We decided to go along with the administration, whole committee did.
INTERVIEWER: Why did the committee make that decision?

In some cases, the simple reason why question can open up a new line of inquiry. By asking, "Why did you prefer that uncle to the other one?" the interviewer got a detailed account of family interaction.

Still another kind of question is aimed at clarification. The simplest kind is to make sure you and the narrator are talking about the same thing.

INTERVIEWER: Was that the situation in World War I or World War II?

The interviewer also may be confused because something has been left out: "I'm a bit confused here. Would you explain the relationship between these two people that existed prior to this particular meeting?"

Another kind of clarification question is the request for the source of the information. You need to know whether the event described is a firsthand account or a handed down story. The credibility of the account must be established. Ask something like "Did you see it happen?" Establish the location of the narrator relative to the event described: "How close were you to the man who was making that speech?" "Were they using a microphone?" If the narrator was there, but yards away and no microphone was in use, then he may not have heard correctly.

The narrator may be used to taking shortcuts in conversation, such as saying, "You know what I mean." Usually the person listening politely nods or says, "Uh huh." During a recording session, you will have to be less polite and say, "I'm not sure of your meaning here. Could you tell me more about it?"[34]

If the narrator gestures to show you how large the fish was or says the stream was only as wide as the living room and dining room together, the next person listening to the tape will have no understanding of this. As interviewer, you must indicate on tape what the nonverbal communication means: "Would you say the fish was three feet long?" Or "I think these two rooms together measure about 24 feet, so the stream was about 24 feet wide?"

The hypothetical question is interesting for finding out the narrator's wishes or aspirations or the things she thought would have made her happy. "If you could have gone to work wherever you wished, where would you have worked?"

The comparison-type question gives the narrator a chance to explore a topic further. Some narrators are not analytical, and this type may not appeal to them, which you will be able to judge after some period of interview time. The question "How do you compare working in the telephone office and working in the munitions plant?" brought out some interesting observations on social life in a small office composed of women as compared to social life in a large plant where both men and women were working. (See the discussion of broad questions, including comparisons, in Chapter 2.)

The challenge question is risky. You must use your judgment as to whether the narrator can tolerate a challenge, and you must be very careful in wording it. Take care that your tone of voice and nonverbal gestures soften the challenge. For example, imagine that you are interviewing the mill superintendent about a strike in 1936 at his mill. He has just told you that the strikers were armed and that one accidentally shot the strike leader. You know from reading the newspapers that the eyewitnesses said the strikers were not armed. You suspect that the mill owner had hired armed men, and you would like to know how, in retrospect, the mill superintendent feels about what happened even though he has given you the official line. Indeed, to ask him is to challenge the official line, and you are putting him on the defensive.

INTERVIEWER: We do know that the mill had hired armed guards. Just about everybody questioned saw their guns. I'm wondering how you felt about having these men with guns there?

NARRATOR: Needed to protect the building. Didn't want any burning, wrecking.

INTERVIEWER: Was the decision to bring in armed guards your decision?

NARRATOR: No.
INTERVIEWER: Were you against it or for it?
NARRATOR: (Brief silence.) I never had any trouble talking, I'd rather we kept talking. Don't like to see anybody get killed. I was afraid that would happen. (Narrator shifts feet, looks at watch, looks directly at interviewer, not smiling now.)

Here the interviewer took a chance and kept pushing beyond the official line. But reading the nonverbal signals told her to stop there, at least for the time being.

Below is a narrator who also could be challenged, even though this is going to puncture her long-held myth. She is describing the neighborhood in the early part of the century and her Italian-American heritage.

NARRATOR: The Irish people and Italian people lived in the building with my mother and they lived next door, all along the lane. They got along so wonderfully you would think that they were all one family.
INTERVIEWER: Your family moved when you were two years old, did you say?
NARRATOR: Yes, only about five or six houses down. And they were all Irish people down there, too. Then as the Italian people started to move in, the Irish started to move out.[35]

The discrepancy in the narrator's two statements tip the interviewer off that a challenge is needed here: "Why did the Irish move out?" As in the preceding example, the interviewer must observe the nonverbal communication and listen to the tone of voice. If the narrator is annoyed, stop this line of questioning and return to it later, phrasing it differently.

Coping With Troublesome Situations

In any interview situation, the narrator keeps having to decide what to disclose, how much to tell, what to keep silent about. There is always a kind of tug going on within the narrator and between narrator and interviewer. You must sense from the nonverbal response as well as from the spoken words how uncomfortable you are making your narrator and stop challenging before you get ordered out.

One strategy in asking troubling questions is to stop that line of questioning at the moment you can tell from tone of voice or look that the narrator is getting upset. Wait, then return to it later in the interview, phrasing it differently, more gently, maybe more obliquely. Once, in interviewing an Italian-American woman on Federal Hill in Providence, Rhode Island, I asked where she had gotten the money to start her flower business. This was a project where I was recording the life histories of ethnic women, and I was especially interested in ethnic women who had "made it in America" as businesswomen. She ignored my question but continued talking. From her tone I knew she was offended. I did not pursue that but instead asked the next line of questioning about how she built up her business. At the end of the hour, my student who had accompanied me said innocently, "You sure made the business a success but you never did tell us how you got your start." I felt my heart drop to my knees. The narrator, who had meanwhile warmed up to us, said, "Oh, I stole it from my husband's funeral parlor business—I kept the books for both."

Jack Douglas described a similar situation when he was trying to ask a personal, troubling question during an interviewing project with beautiful women. He refers to the narrator here as the Goddess:

> I try to put these [delicate questions] off until optimum trust and inti-macy are established by going around them, if necessary. But always the point is to return to them by an indirect route. The hope is always that the Goddess will herself find her own way to talk about it, at her own time, and in her own words and tones. Allow her the lead once she has learned what you want to know. Then, if she does not find her own way back to what you need to know, gently nudge her with the reins toward the potentially sore spot. Do not lunge for it. Weave a cir-cle of relevance around it, homing in on it in a downward spiral. If the dis-ease [sic] becomes great, pull back and circle further away, or take up another point, keeping it in mind to come back and try an-other day when intimacy and trust are greater.[36]

Asking a string of questions at once or even two questions at the same time can confuse the narrator. You usually get an answer to only one—the last one asked. The exception to this rule against asking two questions occurs when you are approaching an emotion-laden topic. You let the respondent "off the hook." In interviewing in the

Italian-American neighborhood in Providence mentioned above, I learned to say, "Were some people in the community for Mussolini and some against him?"[37]

Another troubling situation occurs when the interviewer assumes a meaning the narrator has not given to something. Beware of expressing the narrator's feelings or drawing a conclusion that he or she has not stated. Instead of saying, "I conclude that . . . ," just ask, "What do you conclude from that experience?"

Sometimes the narrator wants to be helpful, but the questions come so long after the event that his or her memory is not clear. Artifacts are very useful in this situation. Sven Lindquist, in his article about in-depth interviewing aptly termed "Dig Where You Stand," described this technique:

> If you come with a document, like the household book, or a report from the Factory Inspectorate, or a plan of the workplace from the archives of the insurance company, or a collection of photographs, or something else that captures the interest of the old person, this will awaken their memories and make the interview more worthwhile for both of you.[38]

If you have none of the above, ask the narrator if she or he has photographs or souvenirs that you could look at together. You then might ask, "Did this have a special meaning for you?" "What was that event like?"

At one point during an interviewing project on farm families, I asked a farmer to draw a diagram of the family's house. Questions around this drawing (suggested to me by anthropologist Jane Adams), such as "When the new bride came, did you build on?" revealed a lot about family change.[39] During the same project, a narrator mentioned that his mother kept a diary and asked me if I would like to see it. Reading some lines out loud stimulated his memories of her as he explained to me what she was referring to. In a class project on the history of a local, defunct Wurlitzer organ plant, the students visited the plant with former employees. The employees explained the part of the manufacturing process that was done in each room. These narrators turned out to be highly motivated, and their recall was very good when they were interviewed: possibly seeing the setting again stimulated memory.

Sometimes the narrator is just wrong about some detail. You do not wish to point that out in such a way that it hurts feelings. Unless the error is seriously confusing the narrator and preventing the conversation from going forward, keep silent. You can put a note correcting the error in the transcript or the interviewer's comments to the tape. If it is causing serious trouble, say, "Just a second. Let's check this date. Let's see, if the war ended in 1945, do you think this might have been. . . ."

Chronology is indeed one of those areas where narrators are apt to depart from the expected answer because people often remember things according to significant life events rather than dates. Alessandro Portelli explained this process in his article "The Time of My Life":

> Historians may be interested in reconstructing the past; narrators are interested in projecting an image. Thus, historians often strive for a linear, chronological sequence; speakers may be more interested in pursuing and gathering together bundles of meaning, relationships and themes, across the linear span of their lifetimes.[40]

Portelli quotes from an oral history transcript to show how this may be done.

AMERIGO MATTEUCCI: One more thing I remember, about Bianchini's farm. It was a farm with thirty-four hands. On Sunday mornings, the overseer would come in and say, "Say, you guys, no going to town today. We have work to do . . ." Can you believe that? It was slavery. That's what it was, slavery.

Portelli commented, "He wishes us to perceive the slowness of change in the lives of farm workers."[41] Interviewers must ask when this occurred, must establish some kind of time frame; but the narrator has another objective—to indicate what was significant from his or her point of view.

Very often, it is neither time nor chronology but the association of events that are important, as Barbara Allen pointed out. In reflecting on her experience interviewing in middle Tennessee and south central Kentucky, she wrote:

> The stories the narrators related that afternoon were not told in chronological order, nor were they linked together topically, for they dealt with more than just the episodes of violence that were the ostensible subject of the interview. Rather, they seemed to be grouped according to the association the narrators made among the events they were recounting,

the individuals involved in those events, and the relations that bound those individuals to each other and to others in the community.[42]

Follow the thought process of the narrator, allow him or her to develop the story as needed. The narrator may well answer all the questions you have; if not, you can return to them later in the interview. If a date is not correct, ask yourself if the narrator has unconsciously changed it and why. What significance might this switch have for the narrator?

This chapter earlier stressed the importance of listening. I bring this up again, now with a different meaning. We may listen but not *hear.* Sometimes our own anxieties or assumptions prevent us from understanding the significance of what the narrator is saying. You may feel vaguely troubled at some point in the interview but do not realize what happened until the interview is over. An excellent interviewer told me about a project she had undertaken with a Russian Jewish immigrant. She asked him if he had experienced anti-Semitism in pre-World War I Russia. He talked about quotas for attending high school and added "I was never pressed," intimating that the worst had not happened. Because the worst had not happened, she went on with the interview but felt bothered. In the second interview, she returned to the subject, this time probing. He talked about restrictions on movement, pogroms, derogatory names for Jews. She asked what being "pressed" meant. He explained that he had never been forced to consider discontinuing his practice of Orthodox Judaism. Her vague discomfort with his answer during the first interview tipped her off: She sensed that somehow she had not understood his meaning, the significance of this for him. She explained that the subject of anti-Semitism is an emotionally charged one for her and that she might not have wanted to hear.

For all of us who do in-depth interviewing, being aware of our own fears, aversions, and assumptions and checking to see where we might have failed to hear and understand fully is a beneficial strategy. In the above example, the interviewer listened to an internal voice to detect a troublesome interchange.

To figure out what is going on inside the narrator, pay attention to nonverbal signs. Squirming, glancing at a wristwatch, and making a comment about what he still has to do that day signifies that the narrator is losing interest and that the interview can be stopped for that day or, at least, the topic switched to something he really wants to talk about. Drooping eyes, yawning, and stretching might prompt you to ask if the person is tired and would like to continue at another time. The narrator who crosses her arms over her chest and stares at the interviewer is working up some hostility. Soften your challenges, give the narrator an expression of appreciation for what she has offered, and forego for the time being asking questions that you know will cause discomfort.

The narrator who resents your questions at some level will attempt to gain control of the interview. Turning your questions into his questions is one way to do this. Being vague in her answers, mumbling "I don't know" is another way. Sometimes the narrator will keep the interviewer on the defensive by continually asking him or her to clarify the question. Sometimes the narrator will talk in such a low tone of voice that the interviewer can barely hear.[43] Or he will encourage constant interruptions that will sabotage the interview. Usually, the anxious or disgruntled narrator just talks about a remotely related subject and does not answer directly. Or else he takes the conversation on an irrelevant tangent. Or she gives short answers and refuses to elaborate.

These are tough situations. If you continue to get "I don't know," try some open-ended questions about a nonthreatening topic. You might say something like, "Tell me about your childhood. I'd like to hear more about those trips to the Farmers' Market with your grandmother." (Of course, you should not jump around in the conversation: Your question has got to be on the topic discussed or you must give a reason for changing suddenly.) If you are getting answers in a scarcely audible voice, try saying cheerfully, "Let's just listen and see if we are getting a good sound quality." Listening to the tape may reveal to the narrator how strange this mumbling person sounds and she may speak a little louder. Ask only nonthreatening, routine questions until you sense that she is relaxing. If she keeps obstructing the interview by going off on a tangent, explain again in different terms this time why these questions are important to you and how she will have the right to restrict use of the tape. Or, you might confront her by saying something like "I notice that you change the subject when I mention your father. Would you prefer not to discuss this?"

On one occasion, I persisted in the interview even though the narrator's questions to me indicated she trusted no one, including me. At the end, she demanded the tape and threw it into the fire in her fireplace. On another occasion, I wound down the interview because the narrator kept asking me questions and was consistently evasive. I realized the interview was useless.

Sometimes, when you have done everything you know to do and the narrator is still distrustful, resentful, and hostile, give up. Thank the narrator politely and leave. Further struggle with so little promise of constructive work is a waste of your time.

Consider one last situation: The narrator breaks down and weeps. You could not have known that you would touch on a topic that would evoke such sad memories for the narrator. At one point in our mill village project, I blithely asked the standard question about courtship practices in the early part of the century. The narrator started to cry as she remembered a sweetheart she had loved 50 years ago. When this happens, be silent for a few minutes. Every person is entitled to express his or her private grief. Then apologize for stumbling onto a topic that was painful. Ask the narrator if he or she would like to go on with the interview. If the narrator gives assent, change the topic and go on.

Ending the Interview

As the interview winds down, thank the narrator on tape. As you reach for your belongings and chat with the narrator, leave the tape running. Inevitably, the narrator thinks of something else to add. Don't turn off the recorder until the last minute. And if he or she starts talking again, unpack the recorder and turn it on again. Always ask, in addition, for names of other people and written documents that will lead you further in your research.

If there is any indication at all that the narrator has more to tell you, ask for a second interview. On the second and third interviews, rapport is better. Your questions have stimulated memory, and the narrator will continue to think about them during the intervening time. You also will think of questions you would like to ask. Interviewer and narrator now have a history together on which they can build.[44]

Hand the release form to the narrator and explain it. Give him or her time to read it and ask questions. If the signing takes place then, you can take the release form with you. If the narrator insists that you leave it so a son or daughter or husband or wife can look it over,

---

Box 3.1. Checklist for Critiquing Interviewing Skills

A. Positives (Add 10 points for each item checked.)
1. Indicated empathy when appropriate.
2. Showed appreciation for narrator's help.
3. Listened carefully.
4. Followed narrator's pacing.
5. Explained reason for change in topic.
6. Used a two-sentence format when introducing line of questions.
7. Probed when appropriate.
8. Used a follow-up question when more information was needed.
9. Asked a challenge question in a sensitive manner.
10. Requested clarification when needed.

B. Negatives (Subtract 10 points from the score above for each item checked.)
1. Interrupted the narrator.
2. Kept repeating what the narrator had just said.
3. Inferred something the narrator had not said.
4. Failed to pick up on a topic the narrator indicated was important.
5. Made irrelevant, distracting comments.
6. Ignored narrator's feelings and failed to give empathic response.
7. Failed to check the sound on the recorder.
8. Let the narrator sidetrack the conversation with a long monologue on an irrelevant topic.
9. Asked a leading question.
10. Asked several questions at the same time.

---

try to get a date specified when you can return to pick it up. Otherwise, give the narrator an addressed, stamped envelope and request that you get it in the mail by a specified date.

As soon as you get home, write a thank you letter and notes about the interview. Write the notes immediately while the information is fresh in your mind. If you are a historian, you will need these for the interviewer's comments that are deposited in the archives with the tape. Putting off writing the field notes and procrastinating about the thank you letter will result in a backlog of work. And the longer you wait, the harder it gets because you will forget observations. The Checklist for Critiquing Interviewing Skills (see Box 3.1) can help you assess and improve your interviewing techniques.

In this chapter, I have stressed attention to details and discussed techniques that are essential to expert interviewing. It is worthwhile to learn them. Beyond techniques, however, you bring to the interview your own unique approach to others and to life. Beatrice Webb said it best:

> Hence a spirit of adventure, a delight in watching human beings as human beings quite apart from what you can get out of their minds, an enjoyment of the play of your own personality with that of another, are gifts of rare value in the art of interviewing.[45]

Summary

A meeting before the day of the interview means that you do not appear at the interview as a stranger. It permits you to survey the interviewing environment and establish some expectations about a good environment for recording. Explain the purpose of the project and give some indication of what will be discussed.

Begin the recording session by giving pertinent information on tape and get the narrator's verbal consent to the taping. Start with nonthreatening topics and questions that are easy to answer.

The first interview with a narrator usually begins with apprehension on both sides. After a period of exploration, if the interviewer can build rapport, the narrator may feel like fully cooperating and may end up taking responsibility for the success of the interview. Rapport is built by being sensitive to the narrator's feelings, showing appreciation, listening carefully, explaining why you change topics and why you ask a line of questions, following the narrator's pacing, and communicating interest and respect.

Know when to probe, when to use a follow-up, when to ask for clarification, to try a suggestion, to ask for a reason why, and to pose a hypothetical question. Challenging questions are appropriate but must be pursued with caution.

In troublesome situations, watch nonverbal communication and listen to the tone of voice. If the narrator is getting angry or uncomfortable, stop that line of questioning. Return to the topic later, using a different approach if possible. Try to get dates correct but understand that narrators have their own organization of thoughts. Be aware of your own assumptions that might prevent you from probing as needed.

Resentful narrators try to sabotage an interview by giving only short answers, getting the conversation offtrack, encouraging interruptions, and mumbling. Steer the conversation to a nonthreatening topic. If the obstruction persists, ask outright in as friendly a manner as possible what is bothersome in the interview.

At the end of the interview, get a signature on the release form if you can. Ask for names of other possible narrators. If you think the narrator has more to tell and is willing, schedule a second interview. As soon as possible, write the interview notes and thank you letter.

Notes

1. Ann Oakley, "Interviewing Women: A Contradiction in Terms," in *Doing Feminist Research,* ed. Helen Roberts (London: Routledge & Kegan Paul, 1981), 31.

2. Jack Douglas, *Creative Interviewing* (Beverly Hills, Calif.: Sage Publications, 1985), 79.

3. Linda A. Bennett and Katharine McAvity, "Family Research: A Case for Interviewing Couples," in *The Psychosocial Interior of the Family* (3rd ed.), ed. Gerald Handel (New York: Aldine, 1985), 75-94; see pp. 76-84. See also Ralph LaRossa, "Conjoint Marital Interviewing as a Research Strategy," *Case Analysis* 1, no. 2 (1978): 141-149. For a discussion of the opposite point of view, see Marie Corbin, "Problems and Procedures of Interviewing," Appendix 3 in *Managers and Their Wives: A Study in Career and Family Relationships in the Middle Class,* eds. J. M. and R. E. Pahl (London: Penguin, 1971), 286-306; see pp. 294-295.

4. Douglas, *Creative Interviewing,* 82.

5. Martha Ross, "Interviewer or Intervener," *Maryland Historian* 13 (Fall/Winter 1982): 3, 4, 5.

6. James Spradley, *The Ethnographic Interview* (New York: Holt, Rinehart & Winston, 1979), 79.

7. Ibid.

8. Ibid., 80.

9. Douglas, *Creative Interviewing,* 100.

10. Spradley, *Ethnographic Interview,* 81.

11. Douglas, *Creative Interviewing,* 55.

12. Valerie Yow (listed as Valerie Quinney) and Linda Wood, *How to Find Out by Asking: A Guide to Oral History in Rhode Island* (Providence, R.I.: National Endowment for the Humanities Youth Planning Grant and the Rhode Island Board of Education, 1979), 20.

13. Raymond L. Gorden, *Interviewing: Strategy, Techniques and Tactics* (4th ed.) (Chicago: Dorsey Press, 1987), 251.

14. Ibid., 232.

15. Ibid., 188.

16. Sherry Thomas, "Digging Beneath the Surface," *Frontiers* 7, no. 1 (1983): 54.

17. Byron Lewis and Frank Pucelik, *Magic Demystified: A Pragmatic Guide to Communication and Change* (2nd ed.) (Lake Oswego, Ore.: Metamorphous Press, 1984), 121.

18. Gorden, *Interviewing*, 303.

19. William Sheridan Allen, *The Nazi Seizure of Power: The Experience of a Single German Town, 1922-1945* (New York: F. Watts, 1984).

20. Gorden, *Interviewing*, 226.

21. Ibid.

22. Ibid., 227.

23. Ibid., 225.

24. Thomas, "Digging Beneath the Surface," 51.

25. Gorden, *Interviewing*, 249.

26. Spradley, *Ethnographic Interview*, 81.

27. Gorden, *Interviewing*, 43.

28. Beatrice Webb, *My Apprenticeship* (New York: Longman, Green, 1926), 409.

29. Arlene Daniels, "Self-Deception and Self-Discovery in Field Work," *Qualitative Sociology* 6, no. 3 (1983): 195-214; see p. 198.

30. Thomas, "Digging Beneath the Surface," 51.

31. Ibid. In a similar way, James Spradley advised interviewers to ask for the use of the word rather than for meaning, but this strategy may depend on the situation. James Spradley, *The Ethnographic Interview* (New York: Holt, Rinehart & Winston, 1979), 156-157.

32. Kathryn Anderson, Susan Armitage, Dana Jack, and Judith Wittner, "Beginning Where We Are: Feminist Methodology in Oral History," *Oral History Review* 15 (Spring 1987): 103-127; see p. 114.

33. Gorden, *Interviewing*, 234.

34. Ibid.

35. Yow and Wood, *How to Find Out by Asking*, 20.

36. Douglas, *Creative Interviewing*, 138.

37. Yow and Wood, *How to Find Out by Asking*, 9.

38. Sven Lindquist, "Dig Where You Stand," in *Our Common History: The Transformation of Europe*, ed. Paul Thompson with Natasha Burchardt (Atlantic Highlands, N.J.: Humanities Press, 1982), 326.

39. Jane Adams, "Resistance to 'Modernity': Southern Illinois Farm Women and the Cult of Domesticity," *American Ethnologist* 20, no. 1 (February 1993): 89-113.

40. Alessandro Portelli, "The Time of My Life," in *Death of Luigi Trastulli and Other Stories: Form and Meaning in Oral History* (Albany: State University of New York Press, 1991), 63.

41. Ibid., 67.

42. Barbara Allen, "Recreating the Past: The Narrator's Perspective in Oral History," *Oral History Review* 12 (1984): 1-12; see p. 11.

43. William Banaka, *Training in Depth Interviewing* (New York: Harper & Row, 1971), 17.

44. Eva M. McMahan, *Elite Oral History Discourse: A Study of Cooperation and Coherence* (Tuscaloosa: University of Alabama Press, 1989), 6.

45. Webb, *My Apprenticeship*, 411.

Recommended Reading

Banaka, William. *Training in Depth Interviewing*. New York: Harper & Row, 1971. This manual is slanted toward the interviewer in an employment counselor situation or a psychological intake interview; nevertheless, Banaka has things to say that are appropriate to interviews in general.

Douglas, Jack D. *Creative Interviewing*. Beverly Hills, Calif.: Sage Publications, 1985. Douglas has in mind the sociological or anthropological investigation, but interviewers in other disciplines also will find helpful information.

Dunaway, David. "Field Recording Oral History," *Oral History Review* 15 (Spring 1987).

Gorden, Raymond L. *Interviewing: Strategy, Techniques and Tactics*. Chicago: Dorsey Press, 1987. First published in 1969, this book is slanted toward the needs of sociologists doing survey research, but there is excellent advice on interviewing strategies, techniques, and ethics that is applicable to the in-depth interview no matter what your discipline.

Lindquist, Sven. "Dig Where You Stand," *Oral History* 7 (Autumn 1979): 26-30. (Also in *Our Common History: The Transformation of Europe*, eds. Paul Thompson and Natasha Burchardt. Atlantic Highlands, N.J.: Humanities Press, 1982). The author provides admonitions and examples on probing.

Morrissey, Charles T. "The Two-Sentence Format as an Interviewing Technique in Oral History Fieldwork," *Oral History Review* 15 (Spring 1987): 43-53. This is a helpful article on phrasing a question so that you provide a context and obtain collaboration.

Payne, Stanley. *The Art of Asking Questions*. Princeton, N.J.: Princeton University Press, 1951. This is a readable guide for phrasing questions for both survey research and the in-depth interview.

Portelli, Alessandro. *Death of Luigi Trastulli and Other Stories: Form and Meaning in Oral History*. Albany: State University of New York Press, 1991. This collection of earlier essays forms a thoughtful and provocative treatise on in-depth interviewing in general.

Spradley, James P. *The Ethnographic Interview*. New York: Holt, Rinehart & Winston, 1979. This book presents useful information in general, but concerning the in-depth interview it is very good for discussion of cooperation and participation and for techniques of building rapport.

Thomas, Sherry. "Digging Beneath the Surface: Oral History Techniques," *Frontiers* 7 (1983): 50-55. Thomas speaks candidly about her experiences interviewing farm women across the United States; she stresses the need for probing and for keeping silent.

4

Legalities and Ethics

Like a cat about to go into a yard full of dogs, step with full attention into this matter of legalities and ethics. The amateur just turns on the tape recorder and lets the tape roll. The professional reads as much as possible about the law, uses a release form, and saves hours of worry—and maybe a lawsuit. The main areas of legal concern to researchers recording people's words are copyright, libel, and privacy. This chapter will consider these legal areas. But often a legal issue is also an ethical issue, as well. Such ethical issues as responsibilities of interviewer to narrator, considerations of harm to others, and truthful presentation of research will be discussed.

Legal Issues

Copyright

About the legalities, first consider ownership of copyright as defined by the most recent copyright law, the Copyright Act of 1976 (which went into effect January 1978). At the moment you shut off the machine, the tape belongs to both narrator and interviewer. The two have a joint copyright.[1] If the interviewer is acting on behalf of an institution or agent, the copyright belongs to that agent and the narrator—but not to the interviewer—according to the 1976 copyright law.[2]

If the taped life history is to be deposited in archives, the archivist will need permission to let the public listen. If you intend to keep the tapes for a length of time to study for your own research and writing, you need permission to use the information in the published writing or your teaching. You must therefore secure from the narrator the right to use the information.

Use a *release form*, a formal acknowledgment that the narrator transfers his or her ownership of copyright to you or to the institution on whose behalf you are acting. This is not a guarantee against all lawsuits, but it will surely help in court. Sample release forms are included in Appendix F, and you may be able to use these models to tailor a form for your project. The best protection is to have a lawyer scrutinize the form you draw up. John Neuenschwander, a history professor, lawyer, judge, and oral historian, reminded oral historians that "preventative law is always less expensive than litigation."[3]

If you intend eventually to deposit the tapes in archives, note this in the release form. When the tapes are deposited, you must give the archives a release form from each narrator. Have the narrator sign a release stating that he or she relinquishes copyright and grants the archives ownership. If you are acting on behalf of an institution, you as interviewer also may wish to acknowledge this formally by signing an agreement to that effect with the institution. If at some time after the project is completed you decide to deposit the tapes, send a release form to the narrators at that time.

Before you begin recording, inform the narrator that you will have a release form that you will ask him or her to sign at the end of the recording session. Do not ask the narrator to sign before the recording, which would be tantamount to asking someone to give up control of his or her words before the questions and the answers are known. It is like telling someone to sign and hand over a blank check.

When the recording has been completed, give the form to the narrator. Explain how the release form is to be used: "This will allow me to use the information in my book." "This will allow people interested in this community who come into the library to listen to your tape." Remind the narrator why he or she was chosen to record. Explain options: unrestricted use of the tape, sealing the tape for a specified number of years, or sealing portions of the tape for a specified number of years. Be sure to write the narrator's decision under the designation "Restrictions." A final possibility is anonymity, which must be stated on the form. (If anonymity is promised, you must lock up this release form and refrain from using the name on tape.) If there are no restrictions, ask the narrator to write "None" and initial it. If the narrator chooses not to sign the release form, you must not pressure him or her to do so. This would be a denial of the narrator's right to choose to do whatever he or she wishes with his or her property.

Without a release form, you are allowed by the 1976 copyright law to use the tape in your own classroom for educational purposes.[4] You may not lend the tape to anyone else. You may, however, deposit a copy of the tape in the archives if you seal it for a period of 50 years after the narrator's death. Whenever you deposit a tape, remember that some archives have loose security systems. Make sure that if you promise the narrator that a tape will be sealed for 10 years, it will indeed be locked up and the public denied access to it for 10 years. If portions are to be sealed, make a duplicate copy, erase the sealed words, and place the original under lock. In the silence created by the erasure, indicate to the listener what has happened: "Here, Mr. Smith requests that information of a confidential nature be sealed for 10 years."

Also be aware that courts can subpoena tapes and government agencies can demand tapes made during government-sponsored research. The best protection you can give the narrator is to stop recording for a second if the conversation veers toward a topic that could be self-incriminating or result in a libel suit. Warn the narrator. If he or she continues unrestrained, after the recording advise sealing portions of the tape that are libelous. And still another possibility is to delete the identity of the person discussed, but this may not be a solution when identity is indicated elsewhere in the discussion.

Libel

Libel is a published statement that is false and which is intended to harm a person's reputation. Neuenschwander defines *defamation* as "a false statement which injures the reputation of another." If the defamation is in written form, it is libel; if it is spoken, it is slander.[5]

You may think that what the narrator chooses to say about someone else is the narrator's problem. But it also is your problem because the court's assumption is that "anyone who repeats, republishes, or redistributes a defamatory statement made by another can be held liable as well."[6]

What would a court of law find defamatory? Neuenschwander summed up four categories of published statements:

1. imputing falsehood, dishonesty, or fraud;
2. imputing crime and immorality;
3. injuring someone's business or professional reputation;
4. implying a lack of fitness for or misconduct or criminal acts while in office or employment.[7]

And if, by misfortune, you find yourself in court, what must the prosecution prove? The words must be lies. The lies must have been communicated at least to a third party. The person offended must be identified. The person's reputation must have suffered harm. And finally, the person bringing suit must establish that the defendant has been to some degree at fault.[8]

"Degree of fault" sounds problematic, and it is. Neuenschwander explained: "The degree of fault that must be established depends on whether or not the plaintiff is determined by the court to be a public figure or a private individual."[9] If a person has become a public figure, the court considers that so many accusations have been bandied about that one case will not ruin a reputation about which there is already so much known.

Several other conditions are important criteria for establishing libel. Intent is a crucial test. If the defendant can prove that he or she was simply mistaken and that no malice was intended, then the court will not convict. (However, absence of malice may be very difficult to prove.) Or if the accusation was just an opinion and there was no attempt to recite false information to prove the opinion, the defendant is off the hook. And finally, a deceased person is not thought of legally as having an ongoing career or reputation. Therefore, libel does not apply to a dead person.

A case begun in 1983 and judged in 1993—although damages have not been decided and an appeal will probably be made—illustrates some of the difficulties a researcher or writer can face. In the early part of the 1980s, journalist Janet Malcolm interviewed psychotherapist Jeffrey Masson for approximately 40 hours. She published a two-part article in *The New Yorker* titled "Annals of Scholarship: Trouble in the Archives" on Masson's work at the archives for Freudian research.[10] Masson brought suit against Malcolm and the magazine, charging libel. He pointed out five quotations attributed to him falsely and argued that these had damaged his reputation and professional life. The jury read the transcripts of the 40 hours of taped interviews as well as Malcolm's notes. The decision was that all five quotations were fabricated and that two fit the definition of libel.[11] Juror Patricia C. Brooks said that author Janet Malcolm "often connected Mr. Masson's remarks about sex and his remarks about work, building rhetorical bridges between the two that he may not have intended."[12]

Perhaps as a writer, one could argue that quotations from different sections of the oral history were pieced together in such a way that the true essence of the man's character was revealed. Nevertheless, when you deal with a living person's words and reputation, such artistic liberties can get you in a lot of legal difficulty.

Privacy

Consider the matter of *privacy*. Herbert C. Kelman, a social scientist who studied legal and ethical issues in social science research, defined invasion of privacy as "exposure of damaging information, diminishing a person's control and liberty, and intrusion into a person's private space."[13]

Secret listening by means of electronic bugging is an invasion of privacy. And recording without the speaker's knowledge and consent is another form of invasion of privacy. In oral history interviews, begin the recording by asking on tape if you have permission to record. Make sure you have the spoken consent on tape.

Another kind of invasion of privacy is the public revelation of information about an individual's intimate, private life. This is information that may be true but is intensely personal. It is not important that the public know about it because this very personal, private situation did not affect the individual's conduct in office or job performance.[14] Or perhaps in such research as studies of family life, intimate details from life histories are not necessary to the narration of the research findings.

I confronted this issue when I was writing the history of a psychiatric hospital and had to make a decision about a personal rivalry between two staff people. One psychiatrist drove spikes in the ground around his parking place so that his rival would blow out his tires if he went so much as an inch over the line. I left that out of the published book because it was not part of the institution's history. I reasoned that their rivalry had not affected the course of the history and that by pointing out these eccentricities in private life, I would damage the individuals' reputations.

Ted Schwarz, who has published several biographies and *The Complete Guide to Writing Biographies,* cautioned that anyone can openly reveal their intimate secrets and agree to publication; but be careful when they tell you someone else's. Discussing someone else's secrets in public is an invasion of privacy and could cause you a libel suit.[15]

Ethical Issues

General Principles in Professional Guidelines

Ethical and legal issues are often intertwined, and it is appropriate to consider them in the same chapter. Ethical issues, however, are even more difficult to solve than legal issues. John A. Barnes defined ethical problems as those we try to solve not in terms of expediency or gain but in terms of morality, of standards of right or wrong.[16] The resolution of ethical problems requires a solid understanding of professional guidelines and an ability to reflect on and critique one's own behavior. The discussion here is focused on ethics applicable to the recorded in-depth interview.

Readers should consult the guidelines and codes of ethics of the Oral History Association, American Historical Association, American Sociological Association, American Anthropological Association, and American Psychological Association (see, for example, "Principles and Standards of the Oral History Association" in Appendix B). There are normative restraints characteristic of each discipline and each arena of research. However, across disciplines there is a concern about protection of the well-being of the persons studied and truth in publication.

The historical profession insists that the practitioner of oral history has an obligation to tell the narrator honestly what the goals of the project are, the stages of the research as the researcher expects them to unfold, and the uses to which the taped information will be put. The researcher must inform the narrator of her or his rights. The narrator must be especially assured that she or he may refuse to answer any question or discuss any topic. The researcher must say where the tape will eventually be placed and who will be able to listen to it.

In a similar way, guidelines for sociologists, anthropologists, and psychologists seek to protect the narrator by insisting that the researcher clearly explain the purpose of the research and what will be expected of participants. This permits the narrator to judge whether or not this may be harmful. The narrator must be told that he or she can withdraw from the project at any time. If the narrator decides to participate, this constitutes *informed consent*. Furthermore, the researcher must provide for anonymity and confidentiality of information if that is promised. If there is any possibility that the privacy of the narrator cannot be maintained, then the narrator must be so informed. Risks of harm to the participants must be small in comparison to the good resulting from the research.

Informed Consent

Consider application of these guidelines in specific situations where problems may rise in the in-depth interview. Some researchers have argued that the narrator cannot be told in any detail where the project is going. In qualitative research, conversations may take an unanticipated turn; information from several interviews may result in new hypotheses so that the research takes a different turn. Sociologist Norman Denzin said about long-term field studies not only that it is not possible for interviewers to reveal everything, but also that they should not, that the search for truth permits interviewers to keep the narrators in the dark about their intentions.[17] I reject this stance: If we want the narrator to be honest with us, we must tell the narrator as truthfully and fully as possible about the project's goals and methods. We must not abuse the trust the narrator places in us by hurting him or her.

Sometimes the researcher is reluctant to describe the chief aim of the research for fear of turning away informants. The real objective of the research is disguised. Kai Erikson argues that researchers should not misrepresent themselves or the research they are doing when they are seeking entrance into the narrator's private domain.[18]

Most sociologists make a distinction between observation of public behavior and intrusion into private space and apply the ethical guidelines more strictly in the latter situation.[19] In this debate, I argue that the extremely intense personal interaction between interviewer and narrator and the revelation of details about an individual's life in the recording of a life history require honesty on the part of the interviewer. The rule of thumb for ethical in-depth interviewing is, Don't carry out a project in which the narrators, if they knew the truth about your objectives, would not reveal themselves.

There is, however, an important exception to this that occurs when explaining fully slants the findings of the research. For example, you want to discover if there is a persistent bias against women in a company. When the interviewees know this, they try to eliminate their own bias as they recount their observations. In effect, you shape the data. In this case, if masking specific aims does not hurt the narrator, give a general explanation rather than a specific one. Barnes suggested that the researcher can explain to the narrator that as a scientist, he or she does not want to influence answers by explaining the purpose of specific research questions but will give a general explanation and as soon as possible a specific answer if the narrator is interested.[20] The question here is, "By not telling all, do I leave the narrator vulnerable to harm?"

Informed consent has to be voluntary. In some situations, the freedom of the narrator may be restrained. Barrie Thorne pointed out, for example, that prison administrators may have given consent for the prisoners to be interviewed, but the prisoners themselves have not consented.[21] The researcher must ascertain whether a refusal to be interviewed would have negative consequences for the individual and correct that situation or end the project.

Cost Versus Benefit

Often the consequences of the research process to the narrators are phrased in terms of the long-range good outweighing immediate harm to the narrators. This attitude is summed up in the term *cost-benefit analysis*. Joan Cassell asserted, "Risk and benefit in fieldwork occur at 2 different times, during interaction and when data becomes public."[22] This is highly problematic because you cannot always anticipate costs.

In an individual's interview, the historian can advise sealing the portion of the tape that could cause harm. The sociologist or anthropologist can decline to publish the information. But in conjoint interviewing, such as researchers studying the family carry out, information may be articulated by one partner that shocks the other and changes the marriage relationship.[23] If you can see that the conversation is edging toward a topic that could cause trouble, change topics and schedule individual interviews to deal with that one. If too late, then it is ethical to stay with the couple for a while after the interview to help deal with the feelings the untoward admission aroused.

And what about the good you expected to come from the publication of results of the interviewing project? Sometimes publication of a study causes distress instead. For example, individuals who had been promised anonymity are identified by themselves or by others according to the roles they played. This result was not anticipated. Howard S. Becker said that the interviewer can refuse to publish when individuals are bound to be harmed seriously or publish if the harm is judged minimal. For situations that fall in between, the researcher and those he studied must come to some decision.[24]

Anthropologist Jean Briggs did something similar to this. She had studied an Eskimo community and wanted to publish an account of her six years of research. She decided to identify the group and the geographical location: "I reasoned that the work would lose ethnographic value if the statements could not be put in historical and geographical perspective." She disguised the identity of individuals by using pseudonyms, but she realized that at least four people could be identified by their roles in the community. She omitted any information that could be used against individuals and any information told to her confidentially. She asked a missionary couple she had known well to write an explanation of her reasons for writing the book as she did. She also asked the people, through the missionaries, if she could put their pictures in the book. The missionary wrote back that the people did not object to the book and agreed to have their pictures in it. After the book was published, she returned to the community and was welcomed. But even her clearing some things with those studied may not have been sufficient: She had nagging feelings that some had been offended.[25]

In some cases, anonymity is maintained, but very personal information is published. The researcher must be aware of the shock a narrator feels on seeing in print intimate details about his or her life. Elizabeth Bott and her co-researchers studied intensely the social relations of two married couples. In the resulting publication, they disguised identities and used pseudonyms. They took the draft back to the narrators. The four people involved agreed to publication (even though they did not necessarily agree with the interpretations of the findings). The researchers could, in that way, go ahead with publication of very personal information; and even though they had disguised identities, they had informed the individuals, explained why the information was necessary, and gained consent so that publication would cause no surprise or harm.[26]

Anonymity and Confidentiality

Guaranteeing anonymity for the narrator and maintenance of confidentiality of information is highly problematic. M. G. Trend described what can happen when research is done under government contract. He had been involved in ethnographic research on low-income households, gathering data with a promise of confidentiality. The General Accounting Office (GAO), which audits expenditures of public funds for the U.S. Congress, requested the data. Trend found that the Privacy Act of 1974 (Public Law 93-577) provided that information collected by government agencies or their contractors should be released in certain cases. Among these was the enforcement of civil or criminal law and requests under the Freedom of Information Act, from congressional investigating committees, and from the GAO's comptroller.[27] If you do research under government contract, keep this in mind and do not promise confidentiality. But for any research project, the courts can subpoena your tapes.

Anonymity is also problematic in specific research situations. In longitudinal studies, David Jordan noted, the researcher has to identify the narrators so that the researchers who continue the project can locate them.[28] He asserted also that the anthropologist making the only record of a population needs to ask whether it is ethical to disguise the name of a village or a whole ethnic group—or withhold the study from the people when they need it. He pointed out that subsequent researchers should have access to names so that they can restudy the data and challenge data, methods, and conclusions.[29]

Also, there are degrees of anonymity: Although you do not publish individuals' names, you may have to inform a select few about them, trusting their adherence to professional ethics in not making the names public.[30]

Anonymity is just as problematic for the historian. Oral historian Linda Shopes remarked that the issue of anonymity was the most difficult the committee developing the Oral History Association's ethical guidelines had to deal with.[31] One of the necessities in reviewing a historian's conclusions is that others will have access to the same documents. If the source is anonymous and identified only by a pseudonym, how can the veracity of a statement be judged? The narrator is unknown and therefore does not take responsibility for his or her statements. The narrator's relationship to the events under discussion remains vague. In biographies and narratives of events and movements, you slide down a slippery slope away from credibility when narrators do not identify themselves and take responsibility for their words.

If you do promise anonymity, use a pseudonym on tape and omit identifying details. If the real name is left in, however, but the narrator requests that the name not be used in print, you have to rely on the archives to enforce the narrator's wishes. Once I came on staff when an oral history project was already finished; the project had concentrated on millwork and included questions about how families survived the Depression that began in 1929. A newspaper reporter was admitted to the archives and listened to the tapes. He published an account of how families survived, giving actual names. The members of one family had not wanted anybody to know how hard it was for them personally or to know the desperate strategies to which they had resorted. They had stated on the release form that they did not want to be identified publicly. The director apologized, but feelings were already hurt, the damage done. Protection of the individual's privacy depends on the security system in the archives. A surer way to protect is to seal the problematic segments; offer the public the edited tape (making it clear that it has been edited) and make sure the archivist has a locked case to keep the original.

It is important to caution all members of the project—other interviewers, transcribers, and office staff—to keep silent about information of a confidential nature and to resist using names of narrators who requested anonymity. In fact, no information can be transmitted even verbally until a release form is secured. Just as important is the feeling of respect for the narrator that you inculcate in those working with you on the project. Training of staff in an oral history project is crucial because they may be dealing with information whose spread will have regrettable consequences.

On the other hand, anthropologists, sociologists, and historians agree that is important to name individuals when they want to be identified. Historian Brent Glass was preparing informational plaques for the Carrboro, North Carolina, cotton mill (which was being preserved, although as a shopping mall) and wanted to use testimony from an oral history project with people who had worked there. In this project, he and I had carried out the in-depth interviews with sociologist Hugh Brinton, recording information not only about work, but also about family interaction, and promising anonymity. Glass went back to the narrators to ask if he could use their names and testimony about work, and they were pleased to have this chance to inform the public about their work and life in general in the village early in the century. He re-recorded conversations about work and mill village life for public information and identified the narrators. Now all of our narrators are deceased, but this public witness to their skill and labor remains.

Relationships and Reputations

Relationships among narrators are in your hands. Sometimes the interviewer can forestall harm by warning a narrator of consequences he or she may not know about. While I was taping the oral history of a physician in an oral history project on a college, she began a critique of the undergraduate education she had received there. Some of it contained negative critiques of individual professors. I stopped recording for a few seconds and suggested that she not name or identify individuals. I explained that those individuals came into the oral history office to listen to tapes of famous alumni, especially if they had taught them. The narrator did not realize this, and because it was not her intention to hurt anyone's feelings, just to influence change in the curriculum, she altered the approach. She made her points without hurting feelings in that rather small community of scholars and former students.

Take care not to exacerbate existing enmities by saying things like, "When I talked to Mr. Smith, he said that you wrecked his career." Figure out how you can get information on the topic without mentioning Mr. Smith's charges. Try something indirect, such as, "I'm wondering if you had any reservations about the action Mr. Smith took in this matter." And then, "Did you express your concern to anyone at the time?"

On rare occasions, although you have a release form and are legally correct in publishing something a narrator said or depositing the tape in public archives, the narrator was elderly and you suspect that he or she might not have understood the consequences of signing the release form. (Sometimes the narrator will want to please you and will be agreeable without thinking things through.) It would be ethical to go back to the individual and describe the segment you think might cause problems.[32] Once again, ask if it is acceptable to make this knowledge public. If not, seal that portion.

The Ethics of the Profession
Versus Humanitarian Concerns

Consider in some detail the problem of publishing material from taped life histories for which you have a release form but that nonetheless could cause harm. In a court of law, you could argue that you have ownership of copyright because you have a release form from the narrator, your account required that you use it, and that the statements are true. You prove that you correctly attributed the statements to the speaker by producing your transcripts or tapes. And you have fulfilled your obligation to your profession by presenting an honest account—no evidence was suppressed, the interpretation was fair to the best of your ability. But although ethically and legally correct, you have to live with the knowledge that you have caused much distress. You have satisfied your profession's requirements but violated your need to be a compassionate person.

Most discussions on ethics remind the reader of Immanuel Kant's guide to ethical behavior: People must be treated as ends in themselves, not as means to an end. The reality is that as interviewers we use people for our ends: Kant's meaning is that we cannot let our ends override our narrators' well-being. In "Ethical Issues in Different Social Science Methods," Herbert Kelman explained this rule of thumb: "We . . . have a moral obligation to avoid actions and policies that reduce others' well-being (broadly defined) or that inhibit their freedom to express and develop themselves."[33]

When I was researching the history of an institution, I found out that a director had a serious substance abuse problem at the time he was in office. What turn his life and career had since taken I did not know. I studied the historical situation carefully and decided that the institution was well managed then by the department heads and that the director's incapacity did not have an adverse effect. (A brilliant man, he had himself set up the administrative structure that had worked so well.) At the end of the chapter, in discussing his resignation—which did affect the course of the institution's history—I wrote about his troubles briefly. I used the description "emotional and physical problems becoming more and more serious over the last year which finally prevented him from continuing his work." I did describe the last board meeting when he passed out because this was dramatic proof to the trustees that he could not continue in the job. Without a description of the events at this meeting, their decision would have been incomprehensible to the reader.

In a similar situation in writing an institutional history, I soon became aware as I was taping that there was a bitter enmity at one time in the past between medical director and administrative director. Their private conversations were unknown to me, but the echoes of their confrontations rumbled through the hospital and in their own oral histories as well as in the taped recollections of their associates. Looking at the administrative structure objectively, I saw the conflict as situational: There were too many areas of decision making in the administrative structure of a dual headship that had been left undefined. It was inevitable that they would have confrontations. I decided not to blame this on personality but to show how the administrators and staff coped and how another structure evolved. An expose of personal faults would not have helped anybody, but information about flaws in administrative structure was educational in that it had relevance beyond the particular institution.

On the other hand, sometimes failure is due to personal actions, at least in part, and this is very difficult to deal with. Following the strategy of using oral history testimony for information about the individual's roles in the work community and concentrating on the individual's objectives—considering always the state of knowledge at the time—I tried to give a fair account without damaging anybody's reputation. But in one case, lacking warm, affectionate, or positive descriptions of a man from the oral histories, I used appraisals of his clinical work. I studied his published research, read reviews of it, and listened again to the taped recollections of his objectives. I felt uneasy about this approach (which had worked so well before) because I had practiced such selectivity in the history that I had skewed the account in his favor and glossed over real problems related both to personality and administrative style.

Saul Benison, an oral historian in the field of the history of medicine, said that when he was writing a history of a famous physician, he included a wild escapade the young intern had in approximately 1910. The doctor had approved of Benison's telling the story, but after his death his widow did not approve. Benison reasoned as follows:

> Should I retell the story when the book was printed? I felt that I didn't want to hurt this seventy-six-year-old lady. There was enough in the interviews to indicate that he was a hard drinker and I took out the story to save the sensibilities of this lady.[34]

Here are two dilemmas, both involving omission of personally damaging information. Raymond Gorden described the process of figuring out what to do: Ethics "does not merely involve some fixed hierarchy of abstract ideas isolated from knowledge of cause and effect in the empirical world; ethics involves decision making guided by both values and knowledge."[35] Looking at the two examples, Benison was right to omit the story of the intern's account. I was wrong not to indicate the individual's personality and administrative style because these characteristics had negative effects on the hospital work community. I bent over too far to protect the narrator.

Truth in Presentation of Findings: Commissioned Research

Researching and writing commissioned studies—where someone else pays the bill and demands the goods for the money paid—presents problems the academic scholar independently investigating does not encounter. Because interviewing projects are often funded by outside sources, consider here differences between independent research and commissioned research, or, in the context of the historical profession, the academic historian and the public historian.

Some scholars such as historian Ronald Tobey have considered these differences to be significant. Academics depend on peer review and individual integrity as checks, Tobey argued. He defined *peer review* as the referee process for funding grant proposals, reviewing manuscripts submitted for publication, book reviewing, and critiquing papers given at scholarly conferences.[36] The researcher writing commissioned studies may see the work published by the commissioner, but peer scrutiny is also operating in reviews of articles derived from the commissioned study, book reviews of the commissioned work, and critiques of papers on interpretation of the commissioned research given at scholarly conferences. The historian writing commissioned histories or social scientist preparing reports in sponsored research projects works on the basis of the same individual ethics as the academic scholar. But there is the additional check on sponsored research that Tobey calls *procedural* whereby information is reviewed in public hearings or the author is cross-examined in court.[37]

There is an even more stringent check when the public historian or commissioned researcher returns the manuscript to the principal oral sources for review—the community review process. Although the community members may not like the researcher's framework or conclusions, they will conscientiously point out inaccuracies. For example, Eliot Jacques and his co-researchers, who had interviewed in a factory, returned drafts of each section of their manuscript to groups of workers in the factory to get comments. The revised drafts were then sent to the factory's works council to be checked again.[38]

Looking at differences on another level, Tobey asserted that the academic historian is expected to research and analyze the data as objectively as possible, recognizing and correcting for his or her bias.[39] The public historian and any social science researcher also must do that.

The academic historian is not supposed to plead a cause; however, in the public sphere, Tobey argued, a hired professional is expected to plead a cause—but one cause only. The implication is that the public historian or any commissioned researcher as a hired professional does this. For example, a lawyer must defend the interests of one client only; objectivity and disinterestedness would be considered unethical.[40] I contend that the scholar and lawyer have different tasks to perform. The historian, sociologist, or anthropologist has the obligation to be truthful. A metaphor often used is that the scholar pleads before the "bar of history." That bar endures: When the present uproar over research some group does not like passes, the documentation will be as useful as the day it was published and to the extent that it was carefully gathered. Neither an academic nor a commissioned researcher can remain completely disinterested, but neither should he or she suppress evidence. In that sense, neither is an advocate.

Nevertheless, there is greater pressure on the public historian or sponsored social scientist: This is where the real difference exists, and it is one of degree. The problem is that no company or institution or governmental body wants to publish a study that shows the leaders in a bad light or increases respect for a competitor.[41] The commissioner may withhold written records or object to interviews with certain narrators or insist on omitting evidence from the published work. If the researcher presents evidence the commissioner does not like, there is the risk that the manuscript will not be published. And many of us who write public history have had the experience of completing a manuscript only to have a bureaucrat in the institution say that things in it would damage the public image. Many worthwhile scholarly histories probably have been quietly deposited in company files never to be seen again, and many research reports have been "lost" among some agency's papers.

Consider some specific situations in which pressure has been applied. Raymond Gorden discussed an incident from his own research in which pressure was put on the researchers to suppress information. In his book on interviewing in the social sciences, he described a study of social problem rates in a city, funded by a college, a private welfare council, and a city planning commission. Gorden reported that data indicated the Boy Scouts were not serving lower-class areas. Local scout officials, who needed support from the United Fund, wanted to suppress that information. And when data indicated that the boys who were Protestant were most likely to be delinquent, the Protestant Council of Churches wanted to suppress that information. The researchers refused. In the end, support came from the college, which insisted on publication of the entire report.[42]

One situation that involves ethics in researching commissioned histories is access to information. A company or college or institution may want to seal its private archives against public use. The very documents you need you may not be able to see, but this is a problem every scholar working in the period of the last 50 years may face. You can do some negotiating, however. In writing one institution's history, I wanted to see the union contract. That request was refused. I could have gone to union headquarters to read it, but I

felt like that would have been going behind my employers' back—
an unethical thing to do. I again requested access to the union contract,
stipulating the clauses I needed to see. Their compromise was that
these particular clauses would be read to me. Because I needed to
know what was in them in order to compare oral history testimony
with the wording in the clauses, I accepted this solution. This was
not an easy compromise to agree to: My ethical obligation to my
profession was to seek all extant documents on the topic; my ethical
obligation to the institution was to honor its rules. Because I did have
access to the clauses that were significant, I judged this compromise
acceptable.

Access to narrators is fully as important as access to written
sources. You may find that the company would prefer that you not
talk to union leaders or to individuals who are central figures in
incidents of dissatisfaction with the company. Sometimes, company
executives are afraid that workers "on the line" do not understand
the overall objectives of the company and will give you a jaundiced
view. You have some educating to do: Explain what the purpose of
the study is from your point of view and describe the research procedures you see as necessary. Insist on your need to record testimony
of witnesses at every level of the community.

On the other hand, the researcher may see trouble coming and
use professional judgment to decline a commission. When I was
interested in writing a history of the rural health centers in the state
I was living in, I encountered a pivotal individual in the health care
research bureaucracy who was concerned about his reputation in
the state. He demanded that he have a right to veto the publication
if I did not write the book he wanted. I declined the project on the
grounds that free inquiry and freedom from censorship in publication are necessities in a scholar's research. The project was important to me because of the developments in rural health care that
affected people I cared about. However, I realized certain things:
Without his cooperation, I would have had difficulty gaining access
to several important narrators and to necessary documents. With
his cooperation, I would have become a hired lackey, turning out
the usual laudatory account of "great men."

And in spite of all the effort to educate the community, inevitably
there will be members who object to including anything negative.
In the preface to the hospital history, I wrote that no effort had been
made to gloss over mistakes, that it was by trying to succeed and

failing that creative solutions were arrived at. One psychiatrist, important in the administration, wrote in the margin of the manuscript that he rejected that approach as destructive. He had some objections on specific points also. I looked at those places in the manuscript and agreed with him that improvements in wording could be made. I made changes in the wording without altering the meaning. I did not delete accounts of troubles, however, and continued to argue the value of a credible history based on the testimony of people who had lived it.

Finally, the company may cheerfully change your manuscript and go ahead and publish a version that the officers want the public to have. The public relations people may want a more positive public image or the institution's lawyers may scrutinize a manuscript for cause of a possible lawsuit. Truth in the published narrative is not their goal: They have been hired to protect the institution, and this is their priority.

I faced such a conflict when I was researching and writing the history of a college. The new campus had been built in the 1970s and consisted of a giant unistructure. In the middle of the building on the ground floor was a large swimming pool, and anyone walking the perimeter of the unistructure could look down and see the pool. At one time, the president was a single man in middle age who felt greatly attracted to young women. One fine summer day he took off his clothes and went swimming in the college pool with a woman companion. He was observed, of course.

This episode caused a shock wave that rushed through campus and public groups. Newspapers were full of descriptions of the incident. The president stayed on, but the incident damaged his credibility. In protest against his refusal to leave the college, all three vice-presidents resigned. This private deed could not be omitted from the written history because it affected the course of subsequent developments at the college. I did considerable oral history research and research in the written records, trying to write an honest account of the total administration, describing both positive and negative aspects. At the lawyers' request, I changed one phrase from "nude swimming" to "alleged nude swimming."

On reading the galleys, I saw that the account of nude swimming in the college pool had been deleted entirely. Only one phrase remained: "alleged incident."[43] These two words had been substituted by the college lawyers for my phrase, and several paragraphs had been omitted. I was powerless: As agent for this institution in the researching and writing of the history, I did not hold copyright. I insisted that the title page of the book bear the disclaimer, "Edited by So and So." Obviously, this was not a satisfactory solution.

It is also necessary to take a closer look before you begin a project to discover the source of funds and the use to which information from the research will be put. The infamous Project Camelot is an extreme example of research being used for a political purpose not beneficial to the people studied. Supposedly, this research was aimed at providing information for determining the nature and causes of revolution in underdeveloped areas and for eliminating causes of revolution. The funding agency was the U.S. Department of Defense.[44] The project was short-lived for reasons of political expediency but not before prominent social scientists had agreed to do the research. Consequences to the people studied—manipulation for another nation's political interests—should have been considered.

Unconscious Advocacy

Still another pitfall in any research is unconscious advocacy. For one thing, in commissioned research we are being paid and may feel reluctant to "bite the hand that feeds us." For another, we want to do a good job in the commissioner's eyes. Linda Shopes, oral historian and researcher in public history, compared the situation of the academic historian to the public historian: The academic historian is encouraged to develop controversial or bold conclusions. Often that enhances the career, and the sociology of the academy protects the academician by the rule of academic freedom. The public historian enjoys no such protection. The public historian is not expected to "shine" brilliantly, nor does the employer want a strikingly original interpretation.[45] And sometimes the thought that we have to continue to live or work in the community we write about may make us cautious enough to consider omitting some evidence.

Historian Carl Ryant called this reluctance to damage the reputation of a place or people we like *goodwill advocacy*. He did not have trouble gaining access to documents or narrators in researching the histories of three companies. He explained that in each case the company had reorganized or expected to do so, diversified, or even moved out of state. The companies' executives did not have any fear that information that could damage current reputations would emerge.[46] They were not looking for an advocate.

However, Ryant saw a drawback, especially when the institution is amenable to the writing of a truthful history: The pressure to present a favorable picture may come, not from the funding institution, but from inside the researcher. He explained: "Sympathy for a corporation (particularly when it is helping to fund a project) may cause an interviewer to leave certain questions unasked, in the belief—perhaps honest—that protecting the subject's image will do no real damage to the integrity of the research."[47] He cautioned the interviewer to be wary of the effects of warm feelings for the commissioner.

When you like and admire the people you are interviewing, you are also subtly influenced in the direction of goodwill advocacy. When I was doing the research for the hospital history, I had an office in the psychiatric hospital that happened to be across a courtyard from the emergency entrance. I would see people with serious illness enter the hospital and several weeks later would meet them walking around, looking calm and in control. The chief cook would come over in the middle of the night to prepare a meal for a patient just admitted if the nurses thought the patient should have something to eat. Or the director of nurses would come over on Sundays, her day off, to see if anybody needed help. Of course, I admired the work the hospital staff did. I cannot put a finger on any place in the history where I ignored evidence or consciously falsified an account, but respect for individuals working in that hospital must have influenced what I wrote. (In the account of the administrator given above, I was trying to protect his career; this would not have affected the hospital's reputation, but his.) And hospital personnel, too, many of them having worked there for years, must have toned down some negative aspects because they identified with the place.[48]

Ronald Tobey advised that in the preface to the collection of tapes or to the published history, the public historian must state clearly his or her bias, his or her interest in producing the history, and what qualifications he or she brings to it.[49] But this applies to all published social science research, commissioned or not. The limitations on the research must be clearly stated.[50] And the ways these limitations impinge on the work should be pointed out to the readers.[51]

Protection of Interviewer in Contracts

In the situation described above of the college deleting sections of the manuscript, I should have had a contract that would have prevented publication without the author's consent. When you begin to negotiate a contract with an institution or agency, make it clear that as a professional, you must write as truthful an account as you can. Explain that research results may not be altered. Get a commitment in writing that defines access to documents and narrators so that the employer will know what a professional requires and you will know if there are any limitations.

Find out where the money is ultimately coming from and anticipate where control on the research might be applied. Try to figure out what motives the commissioner has and how the information from your project will be used. If you can foresee that the information might be used in such a way that the narrators are harmed, refuse the commission.

If the commissioner offers a contract, look at the fine print to discover who has ultimate control over publication. Try to get a guarantee that if the commissioners choose not to publish, you may still use the information in a form that you deem feasible.[52]

Power in the Interview

The essence of in-depth interviewing is that there are subtle ethical issues in the interpersonal relationship not at all easy to define, and the researcher has trouble reaching conclusions even about what is happening, much less what to do.

Power in the relationship is not equal but tipped to favor the interviewer. Consider that the researcher takes and moves on, using the information to get a degree or a publication and a better job situation. The process of recording and using other people's words was described by a group of British oral historians in "Popular Memory: Theory, Politics, and Method":

> On the one hand there is "the historian," who specializes in the production of explanations and interpretations and who constitutes himself as the most active, thinking part of the process. On the other hand, there is his "source" who happens in this case to be a living human being who is positioned in the process in order to yield up information.[53]

The possibility of exploitation, Daphne Patai concluded, is built into every research project that uses human beings as sources of information. Interviewing women in Brazil in the early 1980s, she was led to reflect on the ethics of this kind of research. First, material inequalities heightened her sensitivity to the discrepancy between what she would gain from it and what her narrators would gain from it.[54] She decided to write a letter to several dozen people who in recent years had published books based on extensive oral history interviewing, asking them questions about the ethical implications of using recorded life histories.

One question concerned financial reward to respondents. In some disciplines respondents are often paid for their participation in a research project. However, most people who work with in-depth interviews do not have funds to pay their narrators. And many people chosen to be interviewed would not consider cash payments an appropriate exchange for their accounts. In Patai's survey, many interviewers answered that if they were visiting poor people, they took a gift of food to the narrator. There were diverse opinions on paying people for interviews.[55]

The question of further financial compensation was handled differently by authors who made money from the books. Joseph Cash, author of *To Be an Indian*, sent royalties from the book's sale to the University of South Dakota for a scholarship fund for Native American students.[56] Theodore Rosengarten used half of his royalties to set up a trust fund for Nate Shaw's children.[57] In other cases, where the book does not consist solely of one person's testimony, compensation has usually not been given. Mark Jonathan Harris observed:

> If I were one of Studs Terkel's subjects, I'd hate to think of him getting rich from my life history. Of course, my interview would be only one of hundreds, so when you divide the profits up, factor in Studs' time and effort, travel costs, etc., there obviously wouldn't be so much money to distribute.[58]

Journalist Vivian Gornick wrote that her obligations to narrators are to tell them the truth about the purpose of her research and to represent their meaning truthfully. Her obligation ends there, she believes.[59]

Many of the writers said that they had given their narrators something important other than material reward: attention and recognition and a chance to influence the public's understanding of history. And yet we must return to Patai's original question: Do both narrator and interviewer profit equally according to time spent? There is no easily arrived at answer, but certainly the researcher accomplishes his or her purpose, and so the reward is easier to see.

The reality is that rarely do oral historians or independent scholars have money to pay narrators for interviews. Rarely do academic books sell well enough to compensate narrators. But you can give something back: Give a copy of the narrator's taped history to him or her. Write a letter summarizing the research findings so the narrator can learn too. Publicly acknowledge the narrator's help unless he or she wishes to remain anonymous or there has been a promise of confidentiality.

Ethics in Relationships of Unequal Power

Possibly even more important than the issue of tangible reward is the dominant-subordinate relationship and the possibility of taking advantage of another person that arises from it. Patai described this situation inherent in interviewing:

> We ask of the people we interview the kind of revelation of their inner life that normally occurs in situations of great intimacy and within the private realm. Yet these revelations are to be made within the context of the public sphere—which is where, in an obvious sense, we situate ourselves when we appear with our tape recorders and note pads eager to work on our "projects." The asymmetries are marked, further, by the different disclosure that our interviewees make and that we are willing or expected to make—this goes back to the fundamental rules of the interviewing game. While shyly curious, interviewees never, to my knowledge, make a reciprocal exchange a condition of the interview. And researchers almost always are much less frank than they hope their subjects will be.[60]

The narrators usually trust us: They do not know how we will use the information. Will we describe the narrator in print as an ugly woman in late middle age, subsisting on irregular work as a cleaning woman? Will we use the details of narrators' intimate lives to sell books? Will we publish studies about their community that change the ways they think about themselves in a negative direction? As interviewers and authors, we know what we intend to do, but our narrators do not. We have the advantage of this knowledge.

We also control to some extent the interpersonal relationship, and we use rapport to get information. In her essay "Can There Be a Feminist Ethnography?" Judith Stacey cautions against seducing the narrator into "telling all" by being such a good confidante and defining the relationship as one between equals so that all defenses are removed.[61] A similar issue arises especially in in-depth interviews with couples for those researching topics in the sociology of the family. A couple in crisis or experiencing stress may divulge more than they might in ordinary circumstances. The researcher seems to know a lot about families; he or she has promised confidentiality, and this is taking place in the home, suggesting a friendship is developing. The couple may begin to think that by telling "all," advice or help of some kind may be forthcoming.[62] It is unethical to insinuate that you can help or to so disarm the narrator that he or she puts on tape information that will hurt.

Correct Representation of the Narrator's Meaning

Be careful not to misrepresent the narrator's meaning or change the sense of the words—this, too, is an ethical issue. In quantitative research, computations are made to check the statistics: It is assumed that anyone could duplicate the experiment and get the same statistical results. In qualitative research, errors are not so easily checked. Rereading the documents to see whether the transcription was accurate and whether interpretation was on the mark is one way.

For the historian, checking one primary source against another helps in writing traditional histories; for the oral historian, additional checking with oral sources is a necessity. And all social scientists who have used living witnesses as primary sources have the opportunity to take the transcript back to them so they can correct for errors. When you send the transcript back to the narrator, ask for corrections in spelling or punctuation or word order and for accuracy in transcription of words. When no transcripts have been made, send the chapter in which the oral testimony appears back to the principal narrators and ask, "Have I misinterpreted your words? Have I made factual errors in this chapter?" In the case of marginally literate narrators, you may want to call or visit and read the quotation or paragraph pertaining to their testimony.

When you return a transcript to educated narrators, there is often an occasion when narrators alter the text, especially to take out something they think might make them look bad or smooth out awkward sentences or correct their grammar. You have to leave the edited transcript as it is (although if the meaning has changed, say so in a footnote to the transcript).

In returning a manuscript chapter, I found that a few individuals objected to inclusion of a direct quotation when they thought the prose was less than elegant. But most sincerely looked for factual errors and pointed them out in a very helpful spirit. (See Chapter 9 for further discussion.)

And again, on important points, compare written and oral sources with one another. Sometimes a narrator is just wrong. If you quote in this case, present the facts that right this incorrect statement or contextualize it so that it is clear the statement represents one person's memory rather than an accurate account of the situation. Respect for the living witness is necessary, but this does not mean unquestioning acceptance of the veracity of the testimony.

Summary

Narrator and interviewer have joint copyright to the tape. A release form signed by the narrator is required before the interviewer can use the information in a publication. When the interviewer deposits the tape in the archives, a release form from both narrator and interviewer is necessary so that the public can have access to the tape. If a tape is to be sealed for a time or the narrator requests anonymity, make sure the archivist is willing and able to ensure that these provisions are carried out.

Do not promise anonymity unless you are certain you can enforce this provision. Be aware of publishing confidential information in a way specific enough for the information source to be identified. Discuss with the narrator the ways identity will be disguised and the information presented.

Warn the narrator about making assertions about others on tape that could result in a lawsuit. If the narrator persists, advise sealing that portion of the tape. And in publishing or repeating information from a taped interview, be aware of the possibility of the legal charge of defamation, a false statement that harms someone's reputation. Respect the right of privacy by not publishing personal, intimate details of an individual's life unless this is absolutely necessary to the meaning of the study.

Be sure to get on tape permission to record when you begin an interview. Tell the narrator what the project is about, how the taped information will be used, where the tape will be placed, and who will have access to it. Inform the narrator of rights—such as withdrawal from participation and refusal to answer every question or discuss a topic. Be sensitive to the possible harm that can come from encouraging a narrator to "tell all." In the unique situation of conjoint interviews in studies of the family, steer the discussion away from revelations that can cause serious discord and schedule an individual interview for these. Remember that relationships among narrators may be affected by taped memories and that the narrator's family may be affected. When it is possible to avoid harm, do so.

In researching and writing commissioned histories and institutional or community studies, the researcher must insist on a contract specifying access to information and narrators. Social scientists, in general, must examine the assumptions about the research that the funding agency has and scrutinize the origin of funds. Ownership of data and eventual access must be made clear. In situations where the commissioner wants to delete or change passages, the researcher must resist if such a change would seriously alter the truthful presentation of the research evidence. But in many cases educating the commissioner at the beginning of and all along the project can help avoid an impasse. The researcher must be aware, too, of the inclination to like the individuals involved, which may affect the kinds of information sought or color its presentation.

Power in the interviewing situation is most often on the side of the interviewer. Accept that there is inequality in the interviewing situation, but know also that the narrator's immediate and long-range good may not be sacrificed for the researcher's gain. Give the narrator a chance to review the transcript or relevant manuscript paragraphs so that the meaning is correctly conveyed.

Notes

1. This has not been tested in court yet, but joint copyright is the intention of the law, according to lawyers knowledgeable of oral history. John Neuenschwander, *Oral History and the Law* (Denton, Tex.: Oral History Association, 1985), 10. See also Andrea Hirsch, "Copyrighting Conversations: Applying the 1976 Copyright Act to Interviews," *American University Law Review* 31 (1982): 1071-1093; see pp. 1079-1083. Shirley E. Stephenson, "Protect Your Collection: Oral History and Copyright," *The Public Historian* 9 (Fall 1987): 21-33; see p. 30.

2. Neuenschwander, *Oral History and the Law*, 10.

3. Ibid., 18.

4. I based this on commonly accepted practice in the profession of oral history and on the doctrine of "fair use." See discussion in Hirsch, "Copyrighting Conversations," 1085-1092.

5. Neuenschwander, *Oral History and the Law*, 1.

6. Ibid., 2.

7. Ibid., 5

8. Ibid., 2.

9. Ibid.

10. Janet Malcolm, "Annals of Scholarship: Trouble in the Archives," *The New Yorker* Part I, December 5, 1983: 59-152; Part II, December 12, 1983: 60-119.

11. Jane Gross, "Reaching a Decision in *The New Yorker* Trial: A Juror's Account," *New York Times,* June 5, 1993: sec. 1, pp. 1, 6.

12. Ibid.

13. Herbert C. Kelman, "Privacy and Research with Human Beings," *Journal of Social Issues* 33 (1977): 169-195.

14. Neuenschwander, *Oral History and the Law,* 4.

15. Ted Schwarz, *The Complete Guide to Writing Biographies* (Cincinnati, Ohio: Writer's Digest Books, 1990), 111.

16. John Arundel Barnes, *Who Should Know What? Social Science, Privacy and Ethics* (Cambridge, U.K.: Cambridge University Press, 1979), 16.

17. Norman K. Denzin, "Ethics: The Value-Laden Context of Sociological Research," in *The Research Act: A Theoretical Introduction to Sociological Methods* (Englewood Cliffs, N.J.: Prentice Hall, 1989), 255-268, discusses the work of several theorists on this topic.

18. Kai T. Erikson, "A Comment on Disguised Observation in Sociology, *Social Problems* 14, no. 4 (Spring 1967): 366-373; see p. 373.

19. Barrie Thorne, " 'You Still Takin' Notes?' Fieldwork and Informed Consent," *Social Problems* 27, no. 3 (February 1980): 284-296.

20. Barnes, *Who Should Know What?* 110-111.

21. Thorne, " 'You Still Takin' Notes?' " 292.

22. Joan Cassell, "Risk and Benefit to Subjects of Fieldwork," *American Sociologist* 13 (August 1978): 134-143; see p. 137.

23. Ralph LaRossa, Linda A. Bennett, and Richard J. Gelles, "Ethical Dilemmas in Qualitative Family Research," in *The Psychosocial Interior of the Family* (3rd ed.), ed. Gerald Handel (New York: Aldine, 1985), 95-111; see p. 100.

24. Howard S. Becker, "Problems in the Publication of Field Studies," in *Reflections on Community Studies,* eds. Arthur J. Vidich, Joseph Bensman, and Maurice Stein (New York: John Wiley & Sons, 1964), 267-284; see p. 272.

25. Jean L. Briggs, "A Problem of Publishing on Identifiable Communities and Personalities," in *Ethical Dilemmas in Anthropological Inquiry: A Case Book,* ed. G. N. Appell (Waltham, Mass.: Crossroads Press, 1978), 202-204; see pp. 203-204.

26. Elizabeth Bott, *Family and Social Network* (2nd ed.) (London: Tavistock, 1971), 47; cited in Barnes, *Who Should Know What?,* 142.

27. M. G. Trend, "Applied Social Research and the Government: Notes on the Limits of Confidentiality," *Social Problems* 27, no. 3 (February 1980): 342-349; see p. 342.

28. David K. Jordan, "The Ethnographic Enterprise and the Bureaucratization of Ethics: The Problem of Human Subjects Legislation," *Journal of Anthropological Research* 37, no. 4 (1981): 415-419; see p. 416.

29. Ibid., 417.

30. Jane Adams, conversations with author, Chapel Hill, North Carolina, June 18, 1993.

31. Linda Shopes, letter to author, July 20, 1992.

32. Sally Smith Hughes, letter to author, December 4, 1992.

33. Herbert C. Kelman, "Ethical Issues in Different Social Science Methods," in *Ethical Issues in Social Science Research,* eds. Tom L. Beauchamp et al. (Baltimore, Md.: Johns Hopkins University Press, 1982), 41.

34. "It's Not the Song, It's the Singing," in *Envelopes of Sound: The Art of Oral History* (2nd ed. rev.), ed. Ronald Grele (Chicago: Precedent Publishers, 1985), 71.

35. Raymond L. Gorden, *Interviewing: Strategy, Techniques and Tactics* (4th ed.) (Chicago: Dorsey Press, 1987), 16.

36. Ronald C. Tobey, "The Public Historian as Advocate: Is Special Attention to Professional Ethics Necessary?" in *Public History Readings,* eds. Phyllis K. Leffler and Joseph Brent (Malabar, Fla.: Krieger Publishing, 1992), 127-134; see p. 132.

37. Ibid., 133.

38. Eliot Jacques, *The Changing Culture of a Factory* (London: Tavistock, 1951), 17; cited in Barnes, *Who Should Know What?* 142.

39. Tobey, "The Public Historian as Advocate," 128.

40. Ibid.

41. Donald Page, "Ethics and the Publication of Commissioned History," in *Ethics and Public History: An Anthology,* ed. Theodore Karamanski (Malabar, Fla.: Krieger Publishing, 1990), 65-71; see p. 66.

42. Gorden, *Interviewing,* 86.

43. Valerie Yow (listed as Valerie Quinney), *Bryant College: The First 125 Years,* eds. Peter Mandel and Elizabeth O'Neil (Smithfield, R.I.: Bryant College, 1988), 98.

44. Denzin, *The Research Act,* 329-331.

45. Shopes, letter, July 20, 1992.

46. Carl Ryant, "The Public Historian and Business History: A Question of Ethics," in *Ethics and Public History,* ed. Theodore J. Karamanski, 60-61.

47. Ibid., 61.

48. Valerie Yow, *Patient Care: A History of Butler Hospital* (Providence, R.I.: Butler Hospital, 1994); see author's preface.

49. Tobey, "The Public Historian as Advocate," 132.

50. Page, "Ethics and the Publication of Commissioned History," 66.

51. Ryant, "The Public Historian and Business History," 62.

52. Susan W. Almy, "Anthropologists and Development Agencies," *American Anthropologist* 79 (1977): 280-292.

53. Popular Memory Group, "Popular Memory: Theory, Politics, and Method," in *Making Histories: Studies in History Writing and Politics,* eds. Richard Johnson et al. (Birmingham, U.K.: University of Birmingham Center of Contemporary Cultural Studies and University of Minnesota Press, 1982), 219.

54. Daphne Patai, "Ethical Problems of Personal Narratives, or, Who Should Eat the Last Piece of Cake?" *International Journal of Oral History* 8 (February 1987): 5-27.

55. Ibid., 16.

56. Ibid. See Joseph Cash and Herbert T. Hoover, *To Be an Indian: An Oral History* (New York: Holt, Rinehart & Winston, 1971).

57. Theodore Rosengarten, lecture at the University of Rhode Island, Kingston, Rhode Island, 1978.

58. Mark Jonathan Harris, letter to Daphne Patai, January 5, 1986, quoted in Patai, "Ethical Problems of Personal Narratives," 23.

59. Patai, "Ethical Problems of Personal Narratives," 18.

60. Ibid., 21.

61. Judith Stacey, "Can There Be a Feminist Ethnography?" in *Women's Words: The Feminist Practice of Oral History,* eds. Sherna Gluck and Daphne Patai (New York and London: Routledge, 1991), 111-119; see p. 113.

62. LaRossa, Bennett, and Gelles, "Ethical Dilemmas in Qualitative Family Research," 101.

Recommended Reading

Appell, G. N. *Ethical Dilemmas In Anthropological Inquiry: A Case Book.* Waltham, Mass.: Crossroads Press, 1978. The author presents individual accounts of ethical problems in field research, some of which involve oral history interviewing.

Barnes, John Arundel. *Who Should Know What? Social Science, Privacy and Ethics.* Cambridge, U.K.: Cambridge University Press, 1979. This is an informative, thorough treatment of ethics in field research.

Beauchamp, Tom L., Ruth R. Faden, R. Jay Wallace, Jr., and LeRoy Walters. *Ethical Issues in Social Science Research.* Baltimore, Md.: Johns Hopkins University Press, 1982. See especially the articles by Terry Pinkard and Herbert Kelman concerning ethics in interviewing and Joan Cassell on risk-benefit analysis.

Denzin, Norman K. *The Research Act: A Theoretical Introduction to Sociological Methods.* Chicago: Aldine Publishing, 1970. See the chapter "On Ethics and the Politics of Doing Sociology."

Ellen, R. F., ed. *Ethnographic Research: A Guide to General Conduct.* London: Academic Press, 1984. See especially the section "Ethics in Relation to Informants, the Profession and Governments" by Anne V. Akeroyd, pp. 133-154.

Erikson, Kai T. "A Comment on Disguised Observation in Sociology," *Social Problems* 14, no. 4 (Spring 1967): 366-373.

Feldman, Kerry D. "Anthropology Under Contract: Two Examples From Alaska." In *Anthropologists at Home in North America: Methods and Issues in the Study of One's Own Society*, ed. G. N. Appell. Pp. 233-237. Cambridge, U.K.: Cambridge University Press, 1981.

Fluehr-Lobban, Carolyn, ed. *Ethics and the Profession of Anthropology: Dialogue for a New Era*. Philadelphia: University of Pennsylvania Press, 1991. See especially the article by Jay Szklut and Robert Roy Reed, "Community Anonymity in Anthropological Research: A Reassessment," pp. 97-114; and Barbara Frankel and M. G. Trend, "Principles, Pressures, and Paychecks: The Anthropologist as Employee," pp. 175-197.

Gorden, Raymond. *Interviewing: Strategy, Techniques and Tactics*. 4th ed. Chicago: Dorsey Press, 1987. See the chapter on ethics, which is slanted toward the sociologist rather than the historian. There is an excellent discussion showing how the researcher weighs benefits and costs in making a judgment.

Horowitz, Irving L. *The Rise and Fall of Project Camelot: Studies in the Relationship Between Social Science and Politics*. Cambridge: Massachusetts Institute of Technology Press, 1974. This offers a history and analysis of this example of government funding, control, and abuse of social science research.

Jordan, David K. "Ethnographic Enterprise and the Bureaucratization of Ethics: The Problem of Human Subjects Legislation," *Journal of Anthropological Research 37*, no. 4 (1981): 415-419.

Karamanski, Theodore. *Ethics and Public History: An Anthology*. Malabar, Fla.: Krieger Publishing, 1990. In this collection of informative articles on ethical issues, see especially Carl Ryant's "The Public Historian and Business History: A Question of Ethics."

Kelman, Herbert C. "Privacy and Research with Human Beings," *Journal of Social Issues 33* (1977): 169-195. This article defines invasion of privacy as "exposure of damaging information, diminishing a person's control and liberty, and intrusion into a person's private space."

Klockars, Carl B. "Field Ethics in Life History." In *Street Ethnography: Selected Studies of Crime and Drug Use in Natural Settings*, ed. Robert S. Weppner. Pp. 201-226. Beverly Hills, Calif.: Sage Publications, 1977. Klockars draws on his experiences in researching the life history of a dealer in stolen properties to examine the risk-benefit principle.

Langness, L. L., and Gelya Frank. *Lives: An Anthropological Approach to Biography*. Novato, Calif.: Chandler & Sharp, 1981. See the section "Ethical and Moral Concerns" for a discussion of the Principles of Professional Responsibility adopted by the American Anthropological Association.

Messerschmidt, Donald A., ed. *Anthropologists at Home in North America: Methods and Issues in the Study of One's Own Society*. Cambridge, U.K.: Cambridge University Press, 1981. See especially "Constraints in Government Research: The Anthropologist in a Rural School District," pp. 185-201.

Patai, Daphne. "Ethical Problems of Personal Narratives, or, Who Should Eat the Last Piece of Cake?" *International Journal of Oral History 8* (February 1987): 5-27. This is a focused and clear discussion of ethics, the in-depth interview, and field research methods, especially the interviewer's exploitation of the narrator.

Punch, Maurice. *The Politics and Ethics of Field Work.* Qualitative Research Methods, Vol. 3. London: Sage, 1986. This is an account of the problems Punch encountered as he attempted to write a history of a private school in Britain.

Thorne, Barrie. " 'You Still Takin' Notes?' Fieldwork and Problems of Informed Consent," *Social Problems* 27, no. 3 (February 1980): 284-296.

Trend, M. G. "Applied Social Research and the Government: Notes on the Limits of Confidentiality," *Social Problems* 27, no. 3 (February 1980): 342-349.

5

Interpersonal Relations
in the Interview

In this chapter, interpersonal relationships and the effects of the interviewing process on both interviewer and narrator are discussed. As an investigator, you may want "just the facts, Ma'am," but human conversations are much more than a recital of facts, and you, as an in-depth interviewer, can open a treasure chest that will enrich your own life—or maybe a Pandora's box of troubles.

Many or us, trained in traditional research methods using written sources, have little preparation in relating to the living witness. Because of the very nature of the main sources of information—living people—the oral historian or ethnographer has to delve into a study of interpersonal relationships in the research process.

First, the recording of an oral history is a collaborative venture. This does not necessarily make the two people, interviewer and narrator, feel equal, however. In any interviewing situation, a vague awareness of the power relationship impinges, and the power relationship is based on age, race, class, status, ethnicity, gender, and knowledge. The relationship between interviewer and narrator directly affects the quality of the recorded life history. Power in the interpersonal relationship is discussed in this chapter.

Second, present after the interview are the lingering reflections on what has happened. The interviewer has asked the narrator to tell things he or she would not normally tell a stranger. During this process, both interviewer and narrator are changed in some way. These changes are considered.

Effects of the Interview on the Narrator

The interviewer walks into a home. She or he asks questions the person living there has not thought to ask about a life. Suddenly, the process of analyzing, of answering someone else's questions about a life, of standing outside it and looking at its experiences in a different way makes the narrator feel strange. And you, as interviewer, also feel strange because you have asked questions that have taken you into another's world, and you are not sure of your place there.

Can the effect on the narrator be positive? Certainly the oral history interview gives the narrator an opportunity to make sense of scattered events. The narrator has a serious, eager listener. This is an opportunity to tell a life story to another person who accepts that this version is true for the teller and that it is important. There is validation for the narrator that he or she is worth listening to.

This validation is especially important to people our society often devalues—women, the elderly, political dissidents, and minorities. Interviewing working-class women for a study of millwork in Carrboro, North Carolina, I often heard the narrators say, "I don't know what I can tell you. There are people smarter than I am who will know more." During the course of the interview, they discovered that they knew a lot about the topics under discussion.

Certainly, in the process of telling our life stories, we describe things that happened and our reaction to them and learn something about ourselves by articulating things we were not consciously thinking about before. In his book on autobiography, James Olney explained that "the act of autobiography is at once a discovery, a creation, and an imitation of the self."[1]

In describing events and struggles, the narrator creates a story and gives her or his life a meaning. Judith Modell concluded that anthropologists realize that the individual is an "active creator of his surroundings each time he puts thoughts into words." Probably, she said, the narrator has already begun in mind to compose the story:

> As informant, the individual self-consciously unravels a plot and presents a character he has been constructing and coloring all along. Storytelling goes on with a relentlessness which illustrates, I would suggest, a special human strategy of survival.[2]

The process of reflecting during an oral history interview can be a way to understand anew some things that happened and a means of coming to accept the things that have hurt. Each person is creative in the way that she or he weaves from various life experiences—both the pleasant and the devastating—a whole cloth. Recording the life story gives the narrator not only formal encouragement, but also a way of doing this. Robert Butler, a psychiatrist and former director of the National Institute on Aging (National Institutes of Health), told members of the Gerontological Society at an annual meeting, "By reviewing the past events of their lives, old people put their lives in perspective, prove to themselves that their lives have been worthwhile and prepare themselves for death with a minimum of fear or anxiety."[3] He concluded: "Oral history can be a boon to both the patient and the practitioner—helping both to 'see and see again.' "[4]

Furthermore, the narrator learns something from the interviewer. He or she gets a perspective that was not there before. The very questions asked cause the narrator to look at the experience in a different way and to reflect on this long after the interview has been completed. (I assume here that the interviewer respects the narrator and that what the narrator learns is a different way to see things and not necessarily a negative way.) William Foote Whyte, in interviewing for *Street Corner Society*, found that his informants were becoming sophisticated in their observations about their own lives as they responded to his questions and thought about their experiences in new ways.[5] Years after publication of the book, one of the narrators, born in the Boston slum neighborhood Whyte was studying, said that Whyte showed him the community was well organized with a certain structure and social patterns (but others spoke of less beneficial effects).[6]

The presence of a listener who records words for a story of the past gives the process a sense of drama and importance the casual conversation cannot give. Through the use of the tape recorder, the narrator can speak to the community and to generations to come. Politicians make speeches that they assume will be recorded for posterity in history books, but most of us never make that assumption. It is tantalizing to think that we might have the chance to say to future generations: "This is the way it happened. This is the way we were." Theodore Rosengarten said of the narrator Ned Cobb, the principal witness to the history of the Southern tenant farmers' struggles for justice in *All God's Dangers*:

> He was racing against time to give his last confession. From me he wanted the affirmation he felt he had never gotten from his children—that he had always tried to do the right thing. Moreover, he was speaking to a higher judge. By offering his good works as proof of his intentions, he pinned his salvation on God's justice, not mercy. If he erred on the side of righteousness, he gambled that his last deed would win him forgiveness. The lies he exposed were monumental compared to the lies he concealed. He wanted his testimony to oppose the stories told about people like him in newspapers, court records, congressional reports, merchants' ledgers, and school books.[7]

Ann Oakley interviewed women in-depth in a research project on transition to motherhood. At the end, she questioned them about the effects of the project on them. She found that

> [nearly] three-fourths of the women said that being interviewed had affected them and the three most common forms this influence took were in leading them to reflect on their experiences more than they would have done; in reducing the level of their anxiety and/or reassuring them of their normality; and in giving a valuable outlet for the verbalization of feelings.

None judged that the interviewing had had a negative effect.[8]

In all of the situations discussed above, there is the assumption that the interviewer can communicate the following to the narrator:

1. You have something to say that I think is important.
2. I listen and accept that your version of the story is true for you.
3. I seek to understand rather than to judge.

This kind of encouraging, noncritical listening based on mutual respect between narrator and interviewer is crucial not only to a productive interview, but more important, to the narrator's self-esteem.

The interviewer who goes into an interview assuming that the narrator is nothing more than a bigot may get very little information. (He may indeed be a bigot, but even Shakespeare's villains were complex characters.) The interviewer who communicates to the narrator that she is just a lower-class, inarticulate woman who happened to witness a historical event will do much more harm to the narrator than he or she can imagine. And the interviewer's communication of disdain may make the narrator want to quit being helpful. In any case, this disdain can kill the chance for a frank, full discussion in an oral history interview.

Sometimes in the midst of answering questions, the narrator turns the tables and asks the interviewer a question. Often this is a request for information. This suddenly puts the interviewer in a different role—that of consultant or advisor. The old model in the social sciences was to keep silent. The reasoning was that the researcher should not say anything because it might bias the narrator's answer. However, oral historians Kristin Langellier and Deanna Hall believe that the interviewee's questions are "requests for reciprocity from the interviewer." They explain, "They [the interviewees] ask the interviewer to invest some of herself in the research relationship within and outside of the interview frame."[9]

Furthermore, the old model possibly biased information anyway because the narrator sensed that the interviewer was being less than candid. Ann Oakley, in her study of transition to motherhood (mentioned above), interviewed 55 women four times each—twice during pregnancy and twice after childbirth. She had found in previous research that refusing to answer questions honestly damaged rapport. In this project, she answered questions, and these were usually about pregnancy and childbirth, matters she had studied. She believed that the narrators, without the satisfaction of having their pressing questions answered, would not have been motivated to continue after the first interview.[10]

Sensitivity to questions asked by both parties is the key here. If you have information, give it. (Of course, I do not refer to information told to you in confidence.) If your own understanding of the topic is vague and you do not feel informed, tell the narrator. Be frank about the limitations of your own knowledge. If you can refer the narrator to other sources of information on the topic, such as books, agencies, and so on, do so.

On the other hand, consider also that this intervention may have unintended consequences. The researcher comes into a home, asks questions that compel people to think in new ways about their relationships to others. The researcher then leaves, but the narrators must come to terms with new perspectives about their significant others and must continue to live with them.

When I was beginning to interview, I suggested to a woman that she had worked hard for her political party and deserved some reward, that perhaps she herself should run for office. I must have started the ball rolling, but undoubtedly she consulted others, and she decided to run for mayor. She won, but it proved to be a difficult and most unrewarding experience. I learned there is a difference between giving information and giving advice.

The narrator may want to know if you agree with him. During an interview in the project on work in a North Carolina cotton mill in the early twentieth century, I was suddenly stymied. The narrator had just asked, "Do you feel like I do about black people?" I replied as gently as I could, "No, I don't, but I grew up in a different time." I tried to express disagreement without disapproval—a kind of "this is the way things are" attitude. I went on to the next topic. Traditionally, social scientists were told to avoid any expression of opinion: "I'm here to get *your* opinion—mine doesn't matter in this research project." However, I believe that when you expect your narrators to be open and honest with you, then you must be open and honest with them.

Effects of the Interview on the Interviewer

Up to this point, we have considered effects on the narrator of the process of being interviewed. Consider now the effects of interviewing on the interviewer. The interviewer may begin to feel a kind of strangeness, too, because he or she is welcomed into a home and treated like a friend. Information is confided that is often told only to a friend. And yet the interviewer is there to get information for her or his own use and in the traditional training of a social scientist should be an impartial observer. Still, the interviewer is affected by the situation and may feel a friendship developing. When the interviewing project is over and the interviewer leaves the area, there is guilt over terminating a friendship. So, what is the interviewer—friend or researcher? Is it possible to be both?

Arlene Daniels noted that she gravitated to particular narrators who caught her imagination and made close friends of them. Daniels described the way she became fascinated with an officer during her interviewing project with military psychiatrists. Later, during a research study on women in volunteer work, she accompanied a particular woman to various engagements, listening to her every word. Later Daniels reflected on the process of cementing friendships with these two narrators:

> It was difficult to see how the glitter of interesting personality that surrounded these figures was a product of how much I needed them. I did not realize how I had psyched myself up to admire extravagantly in order to enjoy the advantages they offered me.[11]

She realized that she had not confronted honestly the "self-serving nature" of these friendships, but she felt discomfort, an underlying sense of unease, and perhaps guilt about the unconscious manipulation involved. She tried to carry out "ritual expressions of friendship" to prove she was a good friend as well as a researcher.[12]

Lynwood Montell told a similar story in an article titled "Me 'n Ina." He described the early stage of the relationship with 75-year-old Ina Gilpin:

> Because of Ina's knowledge of the geographic area surrounding her home and its lifelong residents, I soon asked her to accompany me during an interview with an acquaintance of hers. She did, the idea caught on, and Ina traveled extensively with me from that point on. Our trips together served important functions for both of us. Her presence facilitated my work; thus I viewed our new relationship as totally professional. Having Ina along provided a natural entre to narrators who would have been difficult if not impossible for me as a stranger in the area to approach in successful terms. People recognized Ina immediately and invited us into their homes without a second thought. From

her point of view, these trips in the company of a college professor gave her a status in the community that she had not known previously.[13]

As the research progressed, he found that the "most distressing aspect of our affiliation is the manner in which she seemingly planned and maneuvered to have me in her company as much as possible."[14] He began to think that she had "strong emotional feelings" toward him. When the research came to an end, he tried to keep in touch by sending occasional letters, birthday cards, and Christmas cards. She complained of his neglect. He concluded, "It may be that my relationship with Ina represents the typical, yet largely unspoken, folklore fieldworker's dilemma of not knowing how to end a professional relationship without ending a priceless friendship in the process."[15]

I suspect the role of researcher obstructs the development of a disinterested friendship. It is possible that a true friendship may develop after the research comes to a close, but in the midst of a research project, the researcher has a purpose in talking with the narrator that is not friendship. The reality is that a professional relationship is not the same thing as a friendship.[16] And I do not think it honest or wise to indicate that there will be an ongoing friendship after the research ends unless you are sure that you want to continue the relationship and can do so.

Be aware, too, that the narrator may not understand the rules for a professional relationship. What you can do is indicate that this is a collaboration in a project that will have an end. Communicate your respect and liking and thank the narrator for this gift of memories. To the narrators I felt close to, I stated outright that they would always be significant to me not only in this research project but also in my life. I assured them that the time we had spent together was enjoyable and rewarding for me, that they had taught me a lot, that I would not forget them. In this way, I tried to bring about closure in the immediate situation but assure them of their ongoing importance in my thinking. And at the same time, I was aware that there is a tension inherent in this kind of ethnographic research and that the tension must be lived with.

In addition to this tension, there is guilt attached to learning about someone's misery and doing nothing to help. And merely revealing a group's plight by publishing the research study does nothing directly to improve the situation. The traditionally trained social scientist avoids this by assuming that his or her role is appropriately that of objective researcher. Those of us trained in qualitative research methods acknowledge that we are human beings as well as social scientists and that to be untouched by the sufferings of our fellow human beings is to be less than human ourselves. But the dilemma is there: One must be cognizant of the sufferings and feel empathy but also be aware that there are limitations on what an individual can do.

When I was interviewing farm women in DeKalb County, in northern Illinois, I was struck by how many elderly widows lived alone on isolated farms. They were glad to see me because they needed another person to talk to. If they were lucky, a daughter or daughter-in-law lived nearby and would drive them to the grocery store once a week or a church member would drive them to church on Sundays. But they longed for companionship. There was no way I could be a companion to the 20 or more women in the research design. I felt a failure in that respect. My only rationalization (a limp one) was that for that week, I was somebody to talk to. I found myself winding down the project and realized later that I had felt overwhelmed by their needs. As an isolated individual, there was not much that I could do.

Often the researcher does not live in the community, but if that is your own place and you can see possibilities for ameliorating a bad situation and this is a priority for you, organize. Collectively you can accomplish something and that is probably the most constructive way. But obviously you cannot organize for every cause: realize and accept limitations. Set priorities based on what you can actually do. At the least, you can become informed about the social services available in the area and tell the narrator about these.

There are possibilities for learning something about yourself in interviewing. As Thomas Cottle noted, in the interviewing process we watch ourselves as much as we watch the narrators.[17] During a project Arlene Daniels began to scrutinize her clothing: She had thought of herself as a "mud hen" (a rather drab bird) and dressed like one. But she wanted to impress the military psychiatrists she was interviewing that she was a sophisticated person. She began to dress in a chic way and began to think of herself as a peacock.[18] Sherry Thomas, who interviewed farm women, began to reflect on her own attitudes. She found that she was much more skittish about discussing sexual experience than she thought. She admitted, "I publish my sex life in feminist journals, and I'm a prude when I sit in front of an eighty-year-old woman and she starts to tell me about hers."[19]

The interviewer enters the narrator's world and learns another way of life and some things about her or his own assumptions. A professional woman herself, sociologist Arlene Daniels assumed when she studied society women who were volunteers in philanthropic causes that this was a form of amusement with which they filled their useless hours. She came to understand that these philanthropic endeavors were "hidden worlds of serious careers invisible to the sex-stratified and cash nexus economy." She began to see her narrators as women who performed invaluable services for the community and at the same time developed their own competencies. And in coming to this realization, she confronted her own "sexist views of nonworking (not gainfully employed) women."[20]

I learned some things about myself during an interviewing project for a college history. I taped several faculty women, many retired, some still teaching, all significant in the college's history. One day when I began an interview with a young woman, she said, "I've had a stroke and I may not remember everything—sometimes I lose a word, too." This was a statement, not an apology nor a plea for sympathy. Her frankness toward me and acceptance of herself was so reassuring to me that I immediately relaxed and said, "Okay." We both smiled. It turned out to be a productive interview. I started to work on admitting and accepting my own shortcomings and bad luck without feeling sorry for myself.

Interviewing can enlarge the sympathies of the interviewers as they hear the struggles of people in a world they have not known firsthand. Taping life histories of women clerical workers for the Rhode Island chapter of Nine to Five (a national organization of clerical workers), I talked to a lot of single mothers. As I listened to the details of how they juggle work and child care and budget to the penny, I gained an appreciation of their practical knowledge, financial acumen, and courage.

Blanca Erazo recorded the life stories of Puerto Rican women working in the garment industry in New York. She soon detected a pattern: the omission of testimony about victimization. Instead, the women gave her images of strength and combat. They sent to the younger generation of women a message to persevere. Erazo described the effect on her:

In our oral history work, we have acquired a renewed respect for the struggles of garment workers, for their steadfastness, ingenuity, and resolve in the midst of an alienating, oppressive, and often hostile environment. If these stories prepare a younger generation of listeners for anything, it is to understand how we have survived as a people: through persistence, perseverance, struggle, ingenuity, and hard work.[21]

A researcher can feel drawn to narrators and even inspired as in the examples just given or he or she may be repelled. Sometimes there arises real resentment about the way a narrator behaves with the interviewer. Daniels recalled the sexist manner in which the military psychiatrists treated her: "But, even without knowledge of the women's movement yet to come, I knew the responses I was getting had something to do with competition, resistance to taking instruction from a woman, resistance to a civilian and non-M.D., all combined in a general desire to minimize and neutralize my presence."[22] Their flirtatious overtures made her uncomfortable and put her on the defensive. Their tactics made her less effective as an interviewer.

I encountered something like this process of being rendered ineffectual when I interviewed the chair of the board of trustees and the head of a bank. He had been a crony and chief supporter of a president of the college I was writing about. The president was the man (discussed in Chapter 4) whose outrageous public behavior with a woman in a swimming pool had caused him to lose credibility at the college, and this did indeed adversely affect the history of the institution. When I requested an interview concerning his years as head of the college's board of trustees, the banker insisted that I fly to his summer home on an island off the New England coast—a kind of small kingdom where he felt very much in command. During the interview, he dealt with my questions by turning them into questions he then asked me. The interview was useless.

In both situations, the interviewer had to keep consciously reminding herself of the purpose of the research. Daniels reasoned that she needed to soften her style in order to seem less like a competitor to the military psychiatrists she was interviewing. Indeed, she was not their competitor, and she realized she needed to convey that fact. She was carrying on the research to get information, not to get the better of the narrator in some game. I decided that I would remain respectful to another human being no matter what his or her behavior: Whatever the other's purpose, mine was to write as honest a narrative as I could.

If you feel toward the narrator a rising dismay or increasing dislike, stay with your purpose to record a history. And be conscious that your proper role is that of listener, but that you also have feelings. It is all right to dislike the person—admit it to yourself and go on with your work. And as a compassionate human being, you do not have to give back what he or she dishes out. Remind yourself that the narrator has to live with the mistakes that he or she has made, while you do not—you live with your own. Look with compassion on this fellow traveler in the journey of life and pass on in search of your own destination.

The best effect on the interviewer has been saved for the last statement in this section: The process of interviewing can be an exhilarating experience, an epiphany. Paul Buhle, a social and cultural historian, described his interviews with Yiddish screenwriters for his project "An Oral History of the American Left." He said they gave him views of the making of popular culture from the inside, insights he could have gotten from no one else: "Seeing these people made me feel new again with oral history—I was both humbled and honored."[23]

Effects of Race, Gender, Age, Class, Ethnicity, and Subculture

In interviewing elites, the interviewer may feel that it is the narrator who is most in command and is just doing the interviewer a favor to grant a half hour of precious time. In interviewing working-class people, the interviewer may sense that the balance of power often is on the interviewer's side. It is the interviewer who knows all the questions to ask and, by implication, the answers. It is possible, of course, to have an equal balance of power. I had the feeling that "we're alike and we're in this together" was shared by the narrators and myself when I was interviewing other professional women about my age, coming from the same subculture. But even then, equality was not always the situation, and I would be reminded of this when the narrator would inform me that her husband was "chief of staff" in a local hospital and thus indicate her higher social status.

Race

Be aware of power relationships based on race and gender. When interviewers from the Works Progress Administration interviewed people who had been in slavery before the Civil War, research results depended on the race and gender of the interviewers. Black interviewers were not participants in the WPA project in the Southern states except in Virginia, Louisiana, and Florida. John Blassingame, in reviewing the life histories, concluded, "Generally, the stories are most revealing when the informant and the interviewer were of the same sex; black interviewers obtained more reliable information than white ones; and white women received more honest responses than white men."[24] When black scholars from Hampton Institute, Fisk University, and Southern University conducted nearly 900 interviews with ex-slaves between 1929 and 1938, the narrators talked much more freely than in the WPA project about miscegenation, hatred of whites, courtship, marriage and family customs, cruel punishments, separation of families, child labor, black resistance to whites, and admiration of Nat Turner.[25]

Racial differences impinged on the interviewing situation, but power and race were inseparable. Black narrators saw white males as having the power to hurt them if they said something those interviewers interpreted as criticizing the social order. White women were less threatening because they did not share in the formal power structure in the South in the 1930s and thus it was somewhat easier for a group that was powerless to identify with them. But white women, although they had no formal role in the power structure, were nevertheless intimately connected to those in power. This reality could not have escaped the former slaves. On the other hand, women are often easier to talk with because they tend to have a less authoritative manner, and so gender difference in styles of communication impinged on the interviewing situation as well as race and power.

Cultural Norms

Cultural norms also impinge. When I interviewed mill women in Carrboro, North Carolina, I received a very different description of sexual practices than did my male colleagues who interviewed the men. I heard from the women that there was no premarital or extramarital sexual behavior. The male interviewers were told about prostitution in the community. In this case, gender—and not power—affected the answers, but so did cultural norms. Men of that generation (those who came of age about the time of World War I) did not talk to women about sexual matters. (They could talk to other men about even risque sex, however.) And women did not talk about such things to other women unless they were their closest friends. At the beginning, my co-researchers and I decided it would be useless for me to ask male narrators about sexual practices or for them to ask women. But even the women I talked to were unable to discuss the topic.

On the other hand, interviewing farm families of a later generation (those who came of age during World War II) in a wealthy county in northern Illinois, I found that the men more readily talked to me about birth control than did the women. The men carefully chose the words to use, however, and never went into details. This was a later generation than the Carrboro narrators and there also was a difference in level of education: Cultural norms were different than in the earlier situation. Now men could talk in general terms about birth control to a woman.

Gender

Recent research on gender and communication indicates a difference in style in informal conversation that men and women use. In fact, some scholars argue that men and women come from different sociolinguistic subcultures.[26] Research findings are based on observation of casual conversation, and researchers stress that they are specific to the situation. The findings cannot all be applicable to the in-depth interview because of its formal nature, but some may be. And researchers use categories of male and female to show patterns of behavior. They are not assuming sex-linked traits; they base theory on speech behaviors learned in a sociolinguistic context. (Of course, individuals do not stay neatly in categories, and interviewing each individual is always a unique experience in some aspects.)

Consider some situations in which characteristics of casual conversation may not apply to the formal interview. In informal conversation men interrupt women more than women interrupt men.[27] In the formal situation of the recorded interview, the interviewer—no matter what the gender—is conscious of the rule that the interviewer does not interrupt (although the narrator might interrupt as soon as the question is understood). Sometimes, however, men use silence as a way of exerting power.[28] But the narrator knows the expectation is that he will answer or refuse to answer and use silences only to think. In informal conversation, women ask more questions than men, and women do more listening than men. In the interview situation, the expectation is that the interviewer—no matter what the gender—asks most of the questions and listens.

Speech communication researchers stress the asymmetry that is established between two speakers in informal conversation; for example, the one asking for information is requesting help that puts him or her lower than the person with information to give.[29] In the formal interview, the one asking for information is following the expectation for that activity and may not necessarily be viewed as "one-down" from the narrator. In casual conversation, men control the choice of topic more often than women;[30] but in the interview situation there is the clearly stated procedure that both interviewer and narrator will choose topics, but because the interviewer has a research plan, it is expected that he or she will introduce more topics than the narrator.

Nevertheless, some characteristics of gendered communication in casual conversation may carry over to the formal interview. Men often feel in interacting with another (or with a woman in their profession or at their rank) that the situation is competitive, that they must establish themselves in a higher position.[31] In the experience Arlene Daniels discussed, male psychiatrists in the military at first saw Daniels as a competitor. Oral historian Sally Hughes found that the male physicians and scientists she interviewed did not see her as a competitor even at the outset because she has a doctorate in the *history* of medicine, rather than in a physical science, and so they placed her in a different profession from theirs.[32]

On the other hand, these male elites were inclined to "talk down" to a woman. Research findings indicate that this is often the situation in male-female conversation because our society does not value women's work, expertise, or statements as highly as men's.[33] However, Hughes made sure she was thoroughly prepared for the interviews, which included familiarity with the history of the narrators' branch of science or medicine and a working knowledge of their key publications and professional contributions. Thus gender could have operated to her disadvantage, but her preparation made it obvious that she understood what was going on in their field.[34] Against their expectations, they became convinced that she was intelligent and informed (but not a competitor), and they stopped being condescending.

Also, as a woman, Hughes uses an interviewing style that is a "directed conversation, rather than a hard-boiled interrogation," which may help to put them in a nondefensive posture.[35] Because some men feel challenged when they are questioned and unconsciously "spar" with the interviewer, such a softening of style could mitigate the challenge whether the interviewer is male or female.

However, women in general may have an advantage in this kind of situation because women often learned as children to establish an ambiance of thinking things through together. Daniel Maltz and Ruth Borker summarized research on characteristics of women's cross-sex conversational behavior: Women are more likely than men to say things that encourage responses. Women are more likely to use positive minimal responses, such as "mm hmm," that indicate "I'm following you." And women are more likely to use the pronouns *you* and *we* to indicate awareness of and solidarity with the other.[36]

On the other hand, men may interpret a woman's "mm hmm" as agreement and are surprised when that is not the case.[37] Women may use "overlap" in speech—that is, before a sentence is finished, the listener says something that indicates she understands. Men may see this as an interruption. Or, a woman may express empathy. This is often interpreted by a man as condescension.[38] However, in general women have learned to interpret correctly nonverbal signals, and there is some safeguard in this.[39]

Whereas women hesitate to disagree, feeling that disagreeing or challenging might break the rapport they have built up, men see disagreeing in a different light. For men, this is an opportunity to exchange information, to have the satisfaction of a debate, to solidify a relationship rather than to disrupt it.[40]

Women seek to be supportive and feel empowered when they can be helpful. They try to discern if they have rightly understood the question and if they are making their meaning clear: The conversation is viewed as a way to establish connection. Men like to give information—this process establishes authority. Psychologist H. M. Leet-Pellegrini discovered in her research a "subtle interplay" between gender and expertise:

Women with expertise in the present study generally avoided responding in dominant ways. Particularly in the presence of non-expert men,
they responded with even more supportive, collaborative work
than usual. . . . Whereas the name of man's game appears to be
"Have I won?" the name of woman's game is "Have I been suffi-
ciently helpful?"[41]

In my own experience, however, most male narrators have genu-
inely wanted to be helpful—whether I was interviewing North-
eastern bankers or Midwestern farmers. Perhaps the definition of
the situation of the in-depth interview operates here: The stated and
mutually agreed on goal requires a helping role on the part of the
narrator.

Men in our culture learn as children to control expression of feelings.
However, "keeping cool" takes on other dimensions. Jack Sattel
argued that the problem "lies not in men's inexpressiveness per se,
but in the power and investment men hold *as a group* in the existing
institutional and social framework."[42] Men who are expressive may
incur the disrespect of others because they are not maintaining the
stance needed to reinforce power. Sattel offered the example of presi-
dential candidate Ed Muskie, who cried in public and afterward was
perceived by others as being unfit.[43] Therefore, the interviewer who
asks a male narrator about feelings is asking for more than this
particular bit of information: This is asking the narrator to make
himself vulnerable.

But again, my experience has been different; in interviewing men
in the later decades of their lives, I found that they wanted to express
feelings. I remember asking an 80-year-old Illinois farmer the standard question in our interview guide, "What do you consider the best
time in your life?" He replied with tears in his eyes, "When I was
courting Edith, of course." Edith, his wife of 50 years, was in the
kitchen; we were recording in the living room, so this was not said
for her hearing but for his pleasure in recalling and expressing this.
He was not ashamed of his tears. Possibly, because my interviews
with men have mostly been with narrators in their 70s and 80s, a
developmental need impinges. The published research does not
take into account developmental stages. Or another possible explanation is that by agreeing to be interviewed, these narrators are, by
definition, willing to talk about their lives, even their feelings.

In conversation, women often establish a quality of sharing. They exchange personal information and expressions of feeling as a way of creating a friendship bond.[44] There is not as much exchange of personal information in the formal interview situation because the narrator does most of the talking, but often an affinity between a woman interviewer and a woman narrator develops. This affinity may also develop between an empathic man interviewing and a woman narrating.

Women are pleased when the other person expresses interest in the routines of daily life. Men prefer to talk about politics or sports or intellectual subjects and may find "homey" topics inappropriate or boring. They feel most comfortable talking about personal topics in the abstract.[45]

What can the interviewer learn from this research on gender and communication? Although much of it may not be applicable to the formal interview situation, many interviewers have experienced aspects of these research findings while interviewing. Certainly, some research findings can suggest to us things to watch out for. Men interviewing can note and learn from the ways that women establish an ambiance of thinking things through together. They can soften the challenging stance of questioning. Both men and women as interviewers need to introduce the project as an opportunity for a collaboration in a mutually interesting endeavor. Similar to this, men and women may sense some jockeying for status in their interviews with men; the conversation may become a competitive situation. The interviewer should be careful to stop and in a friendly way define again the interview as "teamwork" and express appreciation for the narrator's contribution.

A male narrator may tend to talk down to a female interviewer; and a male interviewer may unconsciously talk down to a female narrator. A male interviewer, by acquainting himself with the research literature on gender and communication, becomes aware of this and changes his attitude. A woman interviewing can establish her own credentials and knowledge of the topic. But in the end, we women may have to just tolerate the situation, seeing it more as societal influence than individual arrogance.

Many women have learned to be amenable to an expression of feeling; however, men may be uncomfortable about expressing or hearing talk about feelings. Interviewers questioning men about feelings must take this into account. A sensitive interviewer listening to a male narrator talk about personal topics or domestic topics can be patient if the narrator is having trouble dealing with these. And women and men should maintain eye contact and nod to show interest. But women must be wary of overlap. And the interviewer should be watchful in expressing empathy—if the male narrator shows annoyance, he may be perceiving this as condescension. Generally, women like to be helpful, and this may carry over to the formal interview situation; men like to give information, and this may contribute to moving the interview along.

Sexual Attraction

Still another influence that may intrude is sexual attraction. I am reminded of the occasion when a 92-year-old man patted my knee and asked, "You're not married, are you?" Other women have heard the nuances in a conversation that indicate the male narrator is pleased to have a younger woman show interest in him. And probably many men have found that a woman narrator is flattered to have attention. Does this affect the course of the interview? Probably. But I suspect the ways that this sexual "chemistry" is manifested vary with the individuals. Again, be aware that this may happen and keep a professional attitude. Make it clear that this is not a friendship but a professional relationship. On the other hand, you may sense that you begin to feel attracted to the person you are interviewing. Admit this to yourself (even smile at yourself for being human) and do not let this attraction prevent you from asking the hard questions. Remind yourself of your purpose for being there.

Social Class

It is also possible that the effects of social class can impinge on the interpersonal relationship without the interviewer's being conscious of it. While interviewing millworkers in the village of Carrboro, I asked during a conversation about leisure activities among adolescent women workers: "What did you serve at the card parties?" The narrator replied, "Oh, we picked up hickory nuts and made fudge— we weren't such bad paupers." I knew immediately that somehow the issue of the level of their poverty had crept in. Did I cause that? Was it just inherent in the situation where a middle-class woman was asking a working-class woman about her life? (I had mentioned my own working-class upbringing, but my speech and dress and level of education marked me as middle class.)

When interviewer and narrator come from a different subculture, that fact also encroaches on the interpersonal situation. Rosemary Joyce found that early in her recording of Sarah Penfield's life story, she became aware of the "subtleties of connotative differences in culture—and correspondingly in speech." She told Sarah Penfield she was interested in learning about the "lives of women in our society." Sarah Penfield laughed and replied that she and her sister "weren't social people and never went to parties."[46]

Effects of Ethnicity

Interviewing in your own ethnic group may be easier than interviewing in a different one; but even so, habitual ways of relating that you take for granted, or are not conscious of, need to be examined critically. If you are interviewing in a different ethnic group, learn as much as you can about speech communication characteristic of this group. Researcher Deborah Tannen advised that conversational style is such an important aspect of ethnicity that only by understanding characteristics of the group can you be "on the same wave length."[47] For example, if your narrator is argumentative, you may wonder what is happening and ask yourself, "Have I done something wrong?" In that ethnic group, argument may be a way of developing sociability. Deborah Schiffrin found in studying conversations in a working-class, Eastern European Jewish group in Philadelphia that the speakers frequently disagreed with one another, a process that served to strengthen the bonds among them.[48] Other researchers, such as Mark Hansell and Cherryl Ajirotutu, have demonstrated that someone outside can detect different styles in speaking but miss their significance, that sometimes just figuring out whether a conversation is serious or humorous can be a problem.[49]

Conclusions About Differences Impinging on the Interview

I conclude that differences may be overcome to some extent, but you as researcher must give attention to the particular age group, gender, social class, race, ethnic group, and subculture. You must look at the interviews critically, asking yourself, Is there a possibility that the narrator is not comfortable here? How is the difference in age, race, gender, or class operating here to influence responses? Have I, coming from another subculture, missed the special meaning of a word or failed to understand the significance of an experience so different from my own?

Effects of the Interview on People Close to the Narrator

And last, be aware of the effects of the interviewing process and resulting publication on the people close to the narrator. Theodore Rosengarten found out that Ned Cobb's sons had a meeting to decide whether they would allow him to ask their father questions. Rosengarten understood their concerns: "When fathers talk about their lives, they must talk about their children; and what is social history to the outside reader is really Papa talking about family affairs."[50]

After the book was published, Rosengarten was surprised by the reaction of Ned Cobb's family. He remarked, "When I went back to see them, they told me straight out: they were deeply offended." He realized that, from their point of view, "Ned had told too much and I lacked the sensitivity to leave it out."[51]

Ned Cobb's son Wilbur especially objected because Rosengarten told family business, like his own quarrel with his father, that he believed should not have gone outside the family. Still, one daughter accepted the book because, although the ugliness was there, the "good is so overwhelming."[52]

Folklorist and ethnographer Jan Vansina recalled a student who wanted to study the history of two Russian Jewish immigrant families. The grandmother of one family had been murdered. The other branch knew who the murderer was, and the murderer belonged to their branch. The student delved into the tragedy and laid bare all the facts. She caused irreparable harm to the family members living now.[53] Thus intervention by means of the tape recorder can change relationships within a family and within a community.

Summary

The oral history interview can be rewarding for the narrator because there is an opportunity to make sense of events. In telling the story, the narrator gives her or his life meaning. The narrator may learn a different perspective from the interviewer. And in understanding anew things that have happened, there is the possibility of a resolution or at least acceptance. These positive effects are possible if the interviewer conveys a noncritical listening attitude and respect. When the interviewer communicates disdain, that affects the interviewing negatively. The narrator may lose interest in being helpful or may become defensive.

The interviewer has an opportunity to expand her or his knowledge and understanding of a different world of experience. The interviewer learns about himself or herself as the interviews go on because, as Cottle said, we watch ourselves as much as we watch others.

In the interpersonal relationship of the oral history interview, there is the danger of role confusion. The interviewer must keep in mind that a professional relationship is not a friendship and make that clear, if need be, to the narrator. When the interviewer has a negative reaction to what the narrator is saying or is distracted by some interpersonal chemistry, he or she must consciously keep in mind the purpose of the interview.

Interpersonal relationships are affected by age, race, gender, social class, status, ethnicity and subculture. Generally, there is more open communication when age, gender, class, and race are the same, but in any interviewing situation the interviewer must be conscious of the ways in which these basic social attributes impinge.

In our culture, behaviors for men and women in conversation are learned in the early socialization process and are maintained in a society where men expect to assert power. The interviewer must be watchful of possible effects of gender on the communication process in the formal interview. Awareness of conversational style in the particular ethnic group you are interviewing can make puzzling situations understandable.

The interviewer must also keep in mind that people close to the narrator may be affected by information from the interview that is made public. Sensitivity in interpersonal relations and respect create the climate most conducive to a productive interview.

Notes

1. James Olney, *Autobiography: Essays Theoretical and Critical* (Princeton, N.J.: Princeton University Press, 1980), 190.

2. Judith Modell, "Stories and Strategies: The Use of Personal Statements," *International Journal of Oral History* 4, no. 1 (February 1983): 5-6.

3. Robert Butler, "The Life Review: An Unrecognized Bonanza," *International Journal of Aging and Human Development* 12, no. 1 (1980-81): 35-39; see p. 36.

4. Ibid., 38.

5. Raymond L. Gorden, *Interviewing: Strategy, Techniques and Tactics* (4th ed.) (Chicago: Dorsey Press, 1987), 27.

6. William Foote Whyte, *Street Corner Society* (3rd ed.) (Chicago: University of Chicago Press, 1981), 365. For a debate on the methodology used for *Street Corner Society*, see the *Journal of Contemporary Ethnography* 21, no. 1 (April 1992), "Special Issue: *Street Corner Society* Revisited." For criticisms from some of Whyte's informants, see W. A. Marianne Boelen, "*Street Corner Society*: Cornerville Revisited," pp. 11-15 in the same special issue.

7. Theodore Rosengarten, "Stepping Over Cockleburs: Conversations With Ned Cobb," in *Telling Lives: The Biographer's Art*, ed. Marc Pachter (Washington, D.C.: New Republic Books, 1979), 115.

8. Ann Oakley, "Interviewing Women: A Contradiction in Terms" in *Doing Feminist Research*, ed. Helen Roberts (London: Routledge & Kegan Paul, 1981), 30-61; see p. 50.

9. Kristin M. Langellier and Deanna L. Hall, "Interviewing Women: A Phenomenological Approach to Feminist Communication Research" in *Doing Research on Women's Communication: Perspectives on Theory and Method*, ed. Carol Spitzach (Norwood, N.J.: Ablex Publishing, 1989), 193-220; see p. 207.

10. Oakley, "Interviewing Women," 49.

11. Arlene Daniels, "Self-Deception and Self-Discovery in Field Work," *Qualitative Sociology* 6, no. 3 (1983): 195-214; see p. 209.

12. Ibid.

13. Lynwood Montell, "Me 'n Ina: Dual Viewpoints on the Fieldwork Relationship," *Southern Folklore* 47, no. 1 (1990): 51-56; see p. 52.

14. Ibid., 53.

15. Ibid., 56.

16. Linda Shopes, communication to author, July 19, 1992.

17. Thomas J. Cottle, "The Life Study: On Mutual Recognition and the Subjective Inquiry," *Urban Life and Culture* 2 (1973): 344-360; see p. 351.

18. Daniels, "Self-Deception and Self-Discovery," 204.

19. Sherry Thomas, "Digging Beneath the Surface," *Frontiers* 7, no. 1 (1983): 54.

20. Daniels, "Self-Deception and Self-Discovery," 206.

21. Blanca Erazo, "The Stories Our Mothers Tell: Projections of Self in the Stories of Puerto Rican Garment Workers," *Oral History Review* 16, no. 2 (Fall 1988): 23-28; see pp. 26, 28.

22. Daniels, "Self-Deception and Self-Discovery," 202-203.

23. Paul Buhle, letter to author, November 14, 1992.

24. John Blassingame, "Using the Testimony of Ex-Slaves: Approaches and Problems," *The Journal of Southern History* 41, no. 4 (November 1975): 487.

25. Ibid., 489.

26. For popular presentation of research findings, see Deborah Tannen, *You Just Don't Understand: Women and Men in Conversation* (New York: William Morrow & Co., 1990); Barbara Bate, *Communication and the Sexes* (New York: Harper & Row, 1988);

Barbara Westbrook Eakins and R. Gene Eakins, *Sex Differences in Human Communication* (Boston: Houghton Mifflin, 1978). Robin Lakoff argued that men and women come from different cultures; *Language and Woman's Place* (New York: Harper & Row, 1975). See also Daniel N. Maltz and Ruth A. Borker, "A Cultural Approach to Male-Female Miscommunication," in *Language and Social Identity*, ed. John J. Gumperz (Cambridge, U.K.: Cambridge University Press, 1982), 196-216; see p. 196.

27. Don H. Zimmerman and Candace West, "Sex Roles, Interruptions and Silences in Conversation" in *Language and Sex: Difference and Dominance*, eds. Barrie Thorne and Nancy Henley (Rowley, Mass.: Newbury House, 1975), 105-129; see pp. 116, 123.

28. Ibid., 117-118, 123.

29. Pamela Fishman, "Interaction: The Work Women Do" in *Language, Gender, and Society*, eds. Barrie Thorne, Cheris Kramarae, and Nancy Henley (Rowley, Mass.: Newbury House, 1983), 89-101; Lynette Hirschman, "Male-Female Differences in Conversational Interaction," paper presented at annual meeting of the Linguistic Society of America, San Diego, Calif., 1973; both as cited in Maltz and Borker, "A Cultural Approach," which summarizes research findings on women asking questions; see p. 197.

30. H. M. Leet-Pellegrini, "Conversational Dominance as a Function of Gender and Expertise" in *Language: Social Psychological Perspectives*, eds. Howard Giles, W. Peter Robinson, and Philip M. Smith (Oxford: Pergamon, 1980), 97-104; see p. 98.

31. Zimmerman and West, "Sex Roles, Interruptions and Silences in Conversation," 125; Leet-Pellegrini, "Conversational Dominance as a Function of Gender and Expertise," 102.

32. Leet-Pellegrini, "Conversational Dominance as a Function of Gender and Expertise," 97. Tannen summarizes Elizabeth Aries's work in *You Just Don't Understand*, 130.

33. Sally Hughes, letter to author, October 19, 1992. See also a discussion by Alex Pang on interviewing scientific elites, "Oral History and the History of Science: A Review Essay with Speculations," *International Journal of Oral History* 10 (November 1989): 270-285.

34. Tannen, *You Just Don't Understand*, 125, uses research findings to show how men structure the asymmetrical situation by lecturing to the listening woman. See Maltz and Borker, "A Cultural Approach to Male-Female Miscommunication," 198, for a summary of the research on men's communication style in cross-sex casual conversation.

35. Hughes, letter, October 19, 1992.

36. Maltz and Borker, "Cultural Approach to Male-Female Miscommunication," 197-198.

37. Ibid., 202.

38. Research findings summarized by Maltz and Borker, "A Cultural Approach to Male-Female Miscommunication," 198.

39. Judith A. Hall, "Gender Differences in Decoding Nonverbal Cues in Conversation," *Psychological Bulletin* 85 (July 1978): 845-857.

40. Maltz and Borker, "A Cultural Approach to Male-Female Miscommunication," 198.

41. Leet-Pellegrini, "Conversational Dominance as a Function of Gender and Expertise," 98.

42. Jack W. Sattel, "Men, Inexpressiveness, and Power," *Language, Gender and Society,* 119.

43. Ibid., 120.

44. Maltz and Borker, "Cultural Approach to Male-Female Miscommunication," 209-210.

45. For a general discussion of this, see Tannen, *You Just Don't Understand,* 276. For comment on the research, see Sattel, "Men, Inexpressiveness, and Power," 122.

46. Rosemary O. Joyce, *A Woman's Place: The Life History of a Rural Ohio Grandmother* (Columbus: Ohio State University Press, 1983), 27.

47. Deborah Tannen, "Ethnic Style in Male-Female Conversation" in *Language and Social Identity,* ed. John J. Gumperz (Cambridge, U.K.: Cambridge University Press, 1982), 217-231; see p. 217.

48. Deborah Schiffrin, "Jewish Argument as Sociability," *Language in Society* 13, no. 3 (1984): 311-325; see p. 317.

49. Mark Hansell and Cherryl Seabrook Ajirotutu, "Negotiating Interpretations in Interethnic Settings," in *Language and Social Identity,* ed. John Gumperz, 85-94; see pp. 93-94.

50. Rosengarten, "Stepping Over Cockleburs," 115.

51. Ibid., 127.

52. Ibid., 128.

53. "It's Not the Song, It's the Singing," in *Envelopes of Sound: The Art of Oral History* (2nd rev. ed.), ed. Ronald Grele (Chicago: Precedent Publishers, 1985).

Recommended Reading

Effects of Interviewing on Interviewer and Narrator

Cottle, T. J. "The Life Study: On Mutual Recognition and the Subjective Inquiry," *Urban Life and Culture* 2 (1973): 344-360. This is a beautifully written, insightful essay on interpersonal relationships in the interviewing situation.

Daniels, Arlene. "Self-Deception and Self-Discovery in Field Work," *Qualitative Sociology* 6, no. 3 (1983): 195-214. Daniels presents a candid account of her own experiences as an interviewer—amusing, fascinating, and informative.

Goffman, Erving. *The Presentation of the Self in Everyday Life.* Garden City, N.Y.: Doubleday Anchor Books, 1959. Goffman analyzes the interaction of two people: "Together the participants contribute to a single over-all definition of the situation that involves not so much a real agreement as to whose claims concerning what issues will be temporarily honored."

Grele, Ronald. "It's Not the Song, It's the Singing." In *Envelopes of Sound: The Art of Oral History,* ed. Ronald Grele, 50-105. In this article, veteran interviewers discuss the effects of interviewing on themselves.

Langness, L. L., and Gelya, Frank. *Lives: An Anthropological Approach to Biography.* Novato, Calif.: Chandler & Sharp, 1981. Especially helpful in this book is the discussion of transference and countertransference in the interview situation and the effects of researcher intervention.

Olney, James. "Autobiography and the Cultural Moment: A Thematic, Historical, and Bibliographical Introduction." In *Autobiography: Essays Theoretical and Critical*, ed. James Olney, 3-27. Princeton, N.J.: Princeton University Press, 1980. This is an excellent introduction to autobiographical discourse.

Pang, Alex Soojung-Kim. "Oral History and the History of Science: A Review Essay With Speculations," *International Journal of Oral History* 10 (November 1989): 270-285. This article discusses, among other topics, responses of scientific elites to the interview situation.

Plummer, Ken. *Documents of Life*. No. 7 in the Contemporary Social Research Series. General ed. M. Bulmer. London: Allen & Unwin, 1983. This presents a sensitive approach to interpersonal relationships in the interview but especially to the struggle within the narrator as he or she composes the autobiography.

Popular Memory Group. "Popular Memory: Theory, Politics, and Method." *Making Histories: Studies in History Writing and Politics*. Ed. Richard Johnson et al. Birmingham, U.K.: University of Birmingham Center of Contemporary Cultural Studies, 1982. This is a serious search into the possibilities of exploitation of narrators by interviewers.

Gender and Ethnicity Impinging on the Interview Situation

Ardener, Shirley. "Gender Orientations in Fieldwork." In *Ethnographic Research: A Guide to General Conduct*, ed. R. F. Ellen, 118-129. London: Academic Press, 1984. This article discusses the influence of gender on the way researchers are perceived and on the ways they gather and analyze data.

Bennett, Adrian. "Interruptions and the Interpretation of Conversation," *Discourse Processes* 4, no. 2 (1981): 171-188. The author of this article analyzes different kinds of interruptions.

Henley, Nancy, and Cheris Kramarae. "Gender, Power, and Miscommunication." In *"Miscommunication" and Problematic Talk*, eds. Nikolas Coupland, Howard Giles, and John M. Wiemann, 18-43. Newbury Park, Calif.: Sage Publications, 1991. This is a thorough review of theories of male-female miscommunication.

Lakoff, Robin. *Language and Woman's Place*. New York: Harper & Row, 1975. This early, widely read book on gender and communication brought together many research studies and contributed insights that inspired much subsequent research.

Leet-Pellegrini, H. M. "Conversational Dominance as a Function of Gender and Expertise." In *Language: Social Psychological Perspectives*, eds. Howard Giles, W. Peter Robinson, and Philip M. Smith, 97-104. Oxford: Pergamon, 1980. The author contrasts the way men use expertise to gain power with the way women use expertise.

Maltz, Daniel N., and Ruth A. Borker. "A Cultural Approach to Male-Female Miscommunication." In *Language and Social Identity*, ed. John J. Gumperz, 196-216. Cambridge, U.K.: Cambridge University Press, 1982. This article summarizes research on this topic and integrates it to draw conclusions.

Sattel, Jack W. "Men, Inexpressiveness, and Power." In *Language, Gender and Society*, eds. Barrie Thorne, Cheris Kramarae, and Nancy Henley, 119-124. Rowley,

Mass.: Newbury House, 1983. Author argues that men's conversational style, although learned in early childhood, is maintained as a way of asserting power.

Schiffrin, Deborah. "Jewish Argument as Sociability," *Language in Society* 13, no. 3 (1984): 311-335. Speakers in this subculture frequently disagree with each other, but this is a form of talk and social interaction that actually increases solidarity.

Tannen, Deborah. "Ethnic Style in Male-Female Conversation." In *Language and Social Identity,* ed. John J. Gumperz, 217-231. Cambridge, U.K.: Cambridge University Press, 1982. The author's interesting observations stress that the "sharing of conversational strategies" creates satisfaction, a "sense of being understood."

Tannen, Deborah. *You Just Don't Understand: Women and Men in Conversation* (New York: William Morrow, 1990). The author draws on her own research as well as that of others in the fields of communication and gender studies. Popular and readable, but based solidly on research, this is important reading for any interviewer.

Zimmerman, Don H., and Candace West. "Sex Roles, Interruptions and Silences in Conversation." In *Language and Sex: Difference and Dominance,* eds. Barrie Thorne and Nancy Henley, 105-129. Rowley, Mass.: Newbury House, 1975. Discussion of "striking asymmetries between men and women with respect to patterns of interruption, silence, and support for partner in the development of topics."

Feminist Theory on Interpersonal Relationships in Interviewing

Recently, feminist scholars have raised questions about the nature of interpersonal relationships in fieldwork: An understanding of this dialogue is essential to an understanding of current theory and practice. Below are a few of the articles that I have found useful.

Anderson, Kathryn, with Susan Armitage, Dana Jack, and Judith Wittner. "Beginning Where We Are: Feminist Methodology in Oral History," *Oral History Review* 15 (Spring 1987): 102-127.

Lugones, Maria G., and Elizabeth V. Spelman. "Have We Got a Theory for You!" *Women's Studies International Forum* 6: 6 (1983): 577-581.

Oakley, Ann. "Interviewing Women: A Contradiction in Terms." In *Doing Feminist Research,* ed. Helen Roberts, 30-61. London: Routledge & Kegan Paul, 1981.

Patai, Daphne. *Brazilian Women Speak.* Rutgers, N.J.: Rutgers University Press, 1988.

Patai, Daphne. "U.S. Academics and Third World Women: Is Ethical Research Possible?" In *Women's Words: The Feminist Practice of Oral History,* eds. Sherna Gluck and Daphne Patai, 137-153. New York: Routledge, 1991.

Stacey, Judith. "Can There Be a Feminist Ethnography?" In *Women's Words: The Feminist Practice of Oral History,* eds. Sherna Gluck and Daphne Patai, 111-119. New York: Routledge, 1991.

Stanley, Liz, and Sue Wise. *Breaking Out: Feminist Consciousness and Feminist Research.* London: Routledge & Kegan Paul, 1983.

6

Varieties of Oral History Projects

COMMUNITY STUDIES

You may choose to interview with the objective of writing an individual's biography or you may choose to interview with the desired outcome being a study of an entire community. Although interviewing techniques will be the same, the overall design of the research project will be different for each kind of project. The special problems that biographies and family studies present are discussed in the next two chapters. In this chapter, you will find discussion on writing studies of communities—a group, a movement, a town, a particular kind of work, a company, or an institution.

When this kind of writing is historical in nature and commissioned, because its targeted audience is the community itself, it is often referred to as *public history*. Definitions of public history vary. Charles

Morrissey, an oral historian writing public history, defined its as scholarly history done by professionally trained historians in nonacademic environments.[1] Public history is based on the same research methodology that is used in noncommissioned studies. However, public history's aim is to inform the public rather than academicians; since about 1950, traditional histories have been written for academicians or at least a highly educated lay public. And yet the lines are not so sharply drawn in reality as on paper. The best academic histories have a wider audience than professors and students, and the best public histories have a wider audience, including academics, than the people written about. Nevertheless, public history's targeted audience differs from that of academic history.

Sociologists and political scientists have long had experience with commissioned research in special communities, and anthropologists are becoming more and more involved in such projects. As in public history, the targeted audience is the commissioner or the commissioner's chosen readers—not necessarily other scholars.

Such commissioned projects are often researched and written under contract in which the commissioners' objectives are spelled out. This situation presents special problems in ethics for researchers and writers in commissioned research. Although ethical problems specific to commissioned studies were examined in the chapter on legalities and ethics, some different kinds of pressure are presented in this chapter.

Preparation for Interviewing in Community Studies

Working in the traditional ways, we go into a project with a tentative list of topics we as scholars think are important and begin delving further into the subject by reading similar research. As historians researching a history of a community in which many members are still living, we would miss an opportunity to learn if we began with a set list of topics. We would tell them what is important in their history instead of learning what they think is important. We, the researchers and writers of contemporary history, can become the instrument through which a community gets its history told. In the same way, the ethnographic researcher can learn at the beginning how people view their lives, what they think is happening, what they see as important, and use this preliminary knowledge in conceptualizing the project.

The researcher is not just a passive recorder of information, however. He or she will pick up on topics informers mention that have relevance beyond the particular project. And the researcher will endeavor to get information on some topics narrators have not given much thought to before the interviewing process.

Historian Kenneth Kann, while engaged in an oral history project on the history of the Jewish community in Petaluma, California, found that he and the narrators differed in what they thought was significant in the history:

> Some called attention to a great community political battle in the 1950's, when the right wing kicked the left wing out of the Jewish Community Center, which left the community split in two. But virtually no one called attention to the social consequences of the displacement of family chicken ranches by corporate poultry production in the 1950's. Everyone recalled the economic trauma of that period, but few had considered how the disintegration of their common economic base had greatly accelerated ongoing changes in family and community life. It required an outside perspective to see.[2]

Thus both researcher and community members brought different interests to the project. Kann recorded information on their interests as well as his own.

The strategy for the oral history interviewing project can be more of a shared experience than the traditional approach to historical research where the informants cannot speak beyond the grave. It can be different from early anthropological and sociological research in which the "subject" was fitted into a category. This is a recognition that, in oral history research, members of the community who are experts on their own experience are natural resources for planning the topics to be covered. This can be a collaborative process in which everybody learns something.

The best way to proceed is to become informed as fast as possible by carrying out a literature review and then reading the relevant materials. At the same time, conduct informational interviews (no recording, just taking notes) with individuals who have been directly involved in the community. Questions to ask include:

- If you were writing this history, what events would you include?
- What persons stand out in your mind?
- If you were studying fishing here, what kinds of things would you cover?

Return to the written sources (or your notes from the first perusal) and scan the written work to see what informants have left out. Returning to the informants, mention some of these items to jog their memories and see what significance these have for them. Questions to ask in these informational interviews might include:

- Who knows a lot about this?
- Who would *you* interview?
- What do you think such a history should do?
- What would you like to learn from this study?
- Who has kept a scrapbook or a file on this?
- Where would I find the records I need?

At the conclusion of these preliminary talks, compose a list of topics to be covered in the recording process, then the first draft of the interview guide, and a list of possible narrators. You also have a list of possibilities for locating written documents or published records not yet deposited in archives.

After this preliminary period in the research has been completed, write a letter to prospective narrators, stating the goals of the project —the community members' and yours. (Although this procedure was discussed in Chapter 2, I will briefly review it here.) I have found that such a letter at the beginning of the research gets much better results than an out-of-the-blue telephone call to a narrator. Explain who you are and give any endorsements from members of the community that you have permission to give. State clearly what will happen to the taped histories and your written research. Then request the help of witnesses in the form of taped interviews. Explain why it is important to talk to people who lived through the experience. The letter should end with the notice that you will call.

The exception to this procedure is a situation in which the individuals have reason to distrust anything in print or to feel apprehension about such an invitation. Try to meet a friend of theirs to whom you can explain the project. Ask for help in making your purpose known and for an introduction. Then you can explain the research in person.

It is also important to explain your research project to groups in the community. John Fox, a historian at Salem State College who was conducting interviews for a history of the Parkers' Brothers games, delivered talks to the "brown bag luncheons" employees had. When I began the project on the history of the women's cooperative art gallery, I attended a meeting of the cooperative and explained what I was doing and how I would go about it. When I started working on the hospital history, the editor of the in-house publication wrote a little article about my project. By having this kind of advance publicity, people remembered something about the project and did not regard me as a complete stranger.

Knowing the significance of the project, narrators are more likely to take an interest. Tamara Hareven found when she was seeking narrators who had worked in the Amoskeag Mills in Manchester, New Hampshire, that people were puzzled and asked, "Why ask me? My story is not special." They consented to be interviewed because they wanted to help her. She and her co-workers organized a photographic exhibit of the mill buildings and workers. She commented on the difference this made:

> Attitudes changed drastically after the exhibit, "Amoskeag: A Sense of Place, A Way of Life," opened in Manchester. Although this exhibit was primarily architectural and was aimed at professionals and preservationists rather than at the larger public, it evoked an unexpected response from former and current textile workers in the community. It provided the setting for the former workers' public and collective identification with their old work place and it symbolized the historical significance of their work lives. . . . The sudden opportunity to view their own lives as part of a significant historical experience provided a setting for collective identification. Under these circumstances, interviewing ceased to be an isolated individual experience.[3]

The researchers found that the oral histories they recorded were of a different character than those recorded before the exhibit because the narrators were eager to talk to them. The narrators had assumed that everyone looked down on them because they were millworkers. Now they realized that others could be interested and see their work as part of the history of the nation. Hareven concluded, "The exhibit established our credibility as interviewers and laid the foundation for a continuing series of interviews with the same individuals."[4]

Let us say, then, that you are working on this introductory letter, getting to know people in the community, and preparing the advance educational events discussed above; meanwhile, you are searching the written sources and composing the interview guide. As you do this, ask yourself, "Who is being omitted? What is being neglected?"[5]

If you are a historian, the questions in the interview guide will be inspired by the community members you have spoken to, your own knowledge of similar historical events and of the historiography of the general topic, and your own interests. There will also be an awareness of the kind of history you want to write and the kind of history other involved people want. For example, you may want a social history of a craft and the craftspeople may want a history of technological changes in their work. One objective does not necessarily exclude the other, and you can structure the interview guide to reflect the different objectives of the completed history. If you are carrying out ethnographic research, the interview guide will reflect your own interests, the new insights gained from informational interviews, knowledge from your particular discipline, and research purposes—both yours and the people studied. As the interviewing goes on, however, you learn more and evaluate and change the guide.

As you work on the interview guide, do not underestimate the value of informal conversation. True, you should not use specific information of a personal nature or information told to you for your ears only for which you have no release form (unless you send the informant a note and receive permission), but you can use general information and find lines of questioning to pursue. Later you can correct some assumptions you might have made on the basis of guarded recorded testimony. Keep a notebook in which you can, as soon as you get a chance, write down the comments you hear that you suspect will prove valuable (and who said them in case you need to follow up later).

The procedure outlined above is the ideal. It is absolutely required for participant-observation research. In practice, it is not always possible for historians to live in the community they are researching or even to stay long enough to do this preparatory work. Paul Buhle, a social and cultural historian, has interviewed radicals from a wide variety of movements, Yiddish cultural activists to labor-movement veterans to Hollywood screenwriters. His objective has been to record their personal histories for the Oral History of the American Left, a national project centered at the archives of the Tamiment Library of New York University.

Buhle's narrators were members of a vibrant community or movement 30 to 60 years ago, but many individuals have moved in old age to different parts of the country. Buhle cannot live in the community—often it has been dispersed—and his interviewing time in a specific place is very limited. He must therefore rely on local people the narrators know and trust to spread the word about his work and his purpose for the interviews. He finds a guide-advisor who will personally introduce him. Before the interview begins, he shows the narrator work that he has done, such as his *Encyclopedia of the American Left* and *Oral History of the American Left Guide*. He explains again the project at the Tamiment Library and his reason for coming to record the life story. He gives the narrator leeway to talk about what is important to him or her, at the same time asking the questions he wants answered.[6] Under these conditions, he has depended on others for advance educational work necessary for productive interviews and on the fact that local people have recommended him as a trustworthy person. His own reputation as a scholar of social and cultural history as well as labor history also comes into play here. All of this illustrates that the ideal situation cannot always exist for the researcher, but it is still necessary within the real limitations to do some educating.

Choice of Narrators

The chapter on preparation for the interviewing project presents examples of how to select narrators for a community study. Historians will ask to record the memories of the individuals who held positions of power in the community or company or movement; but they will also need to interview individuals at every level to get a complete view. In researching the history of a Wurlitzer organ factory that was converted during World War II to a plant to manufacture gliders and guided bombs, the research team interviewed men who were the fine craftsmen, unskilled male and female workers who came into the plant to learn crafts, men and women who worked in the office, and floor managers. (We sought higher-up personnel, but they were deceased.) In interviewing for a history of a college, I recorded the testimony of maintenance workers, retired and current college presidents, secretaries, librarians, professors, students, laboratory assistants, public relations people, members of the board of trustees, bookstore employees, the heads of student life, advisors, and so on. I sought information about college life from people with different vantage points, of different levels of power, and with different experiences. I tried to get a variety of witnesses from different time periods. In the same way, ethnographers will search for narrators who offer different experiences and different vantage points.

You must prioritize when you draw up your final list of narrators. For historians, key decision makers are usually at the top (depending on the research topic), but it is also important for a historian to find out who was there the longest, who was in a position to observe developments, and who felt the effects of a decision most directly. Health considerations also play a part in the decision: First interview the oldest or those who have serious health problems.

Structuring the Interview Guide
to Show Connections to the Wider World

From the beginning, community studies present some special problems; anticipating this, you can structure the interview guide to help. In his review essay on seven community histories published in *The Oral History Review* in 1989, Michael Gordon discussed the pitfalls of this kind of research. About one project, he wrote that they "dangle brief anecdotes before us and aspire to nothing more than regaling local audiences with stories of bygone days."[7] He explained that "public memories that serve individual, institutional, and community needs do not always contribute to historical understanding."[8] On the other hand, he praised a book by Robert C. Hardy, *Hero: An Oral History of the Oklahoma Health Center,* as a "candid administrative history of the center" that provides "especially important insights about key administrative decisions, internal power struggles, and how people view their pasts and make use of public memory."[9]

Linda Shopes, discussing an oral history project in Baltimore neighborhoods in which she was involved, urged historians not to reflect the parochialism and ethnocentrism that characterize some oral testimony. Instead, she advised that "our popular histories ought to convey . . . an understanding of neighborhood not as an isolated collective experience, but as a collective experience that is part of, that has been shaped by, a larger urban process."[10]

In any community study, think in terms of the significance of it to outside researchers as well as to the people living or working there. General questions such as these can be a guide:

- What can be learned from this information about the connections between the community and the wider world?
- How did this community share in experiences common to much of the nation?
- How was this community unique?

In *Nearby History*, David E. Kyvig and Myron Marty presented a bibliographical essay on histories of cities and towns in their chapter titled "Linking the Particular and the Universal." This is a useful place to begin a study of local history, because the discussion of outstanding books will acquaint you with the kinds of questions historians have been asking since the 1960s. These questions include the following general approaches:

- How was modernization brought about?
- To what extent was there economic and social mobility?
- What were the patterns of migration into and out of the community?
- How, and in what ways, was assimilation of immigrants brought about?[11]

Also consider such questions as:

- How were gender roles changing?
- What were the effects of changes in technology on working lives?
- How was family structure changing?

Special Research Situations

Studies of Ethnic Communities

If you are an outsider beginning to research the history of an ethnic community, first learn as much as you can about the culture.

And even if you know the language and history, you may still have to build trust, as the following two examples illustrate.

As mentioned earlier, Kenneth Kann studied an immigrant community in which three generations still lived in the same place. He commented:

> Nothing happens fast in oral history, especially when the oral historian is not a member of the community he is studying. Communities, and their members, have all kinds of experiences and views that are not for outside ears. The Petaluma Jewish community was particularly interesting to me because it was such an intensely lived collective experience, and because there was unusual continuity over generations, but that also made it less acceptable to me as an outsider. Oral history, if nothing else, requires truckloads of patience and perseverance.[12]

Antonio T. Diaz-Roys, in collecting ethnobiographies of Puerto Rican migrants to the United States, had to learn again the traditional ways of building trust in that community although he was an insider. He found that, at the beginning, his university affiliation made his respondents cautious lest they say something to devalue themselves in his eyes. He put away his tape recorder. He began to participate in a pattern of visiting: They came to see his family and he visited theirs. Gradually, a relationship of trust developed. He shared his own life story and they began to see why he had become interested in their lives. Only then did he reintroduce the recorder.[13]

In the above examples the interviewer came from the same subculture but not the same community. Can the interviewer who is an outsider carry out productive interviews? In preparing for the Oral History of the American Left project, Paul Buhle learned Yiddish and read the newspapers that had been important to his narrators. These people recognized his deep interest in their lives, his sympathy for their idealism, and his scholarly expertise. The interviews were successful even though there were political and historical differences on specific issues.[14]

The outsider also may profit from reviewing the research on communication styles particular to a subgroup. Some subgroups have ways of communicating that the outsider may not be attuned to such as the excessive politeness shown to strangers in Southern home. For example, "Y'all come to see us" should not be taken literally until you know the speaker well enough to judge whether she means it literally. In some ethnic groups, an argumentative style is an indication that the narrator wants to establish a friendship on an equal basis with the newcomer. The outsider can be puzzled by behaviors characteristic of a narrator from an ethnic group. For example, in a study of intercultural encounters between Americans and Japanese, the Japanese hearing an American compliment were embarrassed because they were used to keeping personal references out of a conversation. The Americans interpreted this reaction to the compliment as denial.[15]

The insider knows the culture well, and the narrator will probably more readily trust the insider. But as Diaz-Roys learned, there is still work for the insider to do in explaining purpose and in becoming sensitive to nuances in personal relationships in the subculture he or she might have forgotten. The outsider can also carry out productive interviews if he or she is knowledgeable about and appreciative of the culture and is able to communicate the purpose (assuming that the purpose is agreeable to the community).

In addressing the issue of insider versus outsider, Linda Shopes reasoned that "neither is especially better; both have attributes that can both serve the purpose of the inquiry and work against it." She cautioned, "The point is to be aware of one's relationship to the culture being investigated and 'use' whatever strengths of the situation or relationship that there are."[16]

Neighborhood Histories

In researching the history of neighborhoods or small towns, make your purposes clear in your own mind from the start. Shopes, surveying common practices in researching neighborhood histories, concluded that there are several possible goals:

> While the specifics of these projects differ widely, most seem to share certain broadly humanistic goals: the encouragement of cooperation between professional historians and lay people in the community; the presentation of aspects of the community's history to the public; the use of history to build community identity and pride; and the development of appreciation and respect for the participation of nonelite groups in the community's history. In addition, some projects consciously adopt progressive social goals by trying to give [a] historical perspective on current issues in the community in the hopes of encouraging activism and change.[17]

She warned that unless these projects are rooted in the community or linked to important centers of community life, these goals will have little meaning. The question is then, How can the researcher involve the community? Or, rather, how can the researcher become the means by which a community gets its story told?

Shopes and her co-researchers received a grant to develop an oral history program at a senior citizens' center in a Baltimore neighborhood that was stable, well kept, multiethnic, and working class. They hoped they could interest the senior citizens in learning oral history methods and becoming interviewers themselves. They also hoped to locate written primary sources within the community. And they envisaged the publication of a popularly written local history. However, they found that at first people saw them as prying, did not share their enthusiasm for a community history, and were not interested in being interviewed or learning to interview. Much time was spent educating people about the project.[18]

Shopes and another project staff member began interviewing. These interviewees, some of their friends, and a few younger people in the community became interested. After months passed, Shopes began teaching a class to community residents in the skills of oral history interviewing. She found that they wanted to talk to each other, trading reminiscences, as much as they wanted to talk about interviewing methods. And although there was an interview guide, as interviewers they generally ignored the guide and let the interviewees talk only about what was important to them. A dominant theme was personal survival; larger social themes were not as prominent. They also wanted to talk about place (what was where and when) and tell stories of their mothers' heroism.[19] The emphasis on personal survival against odds is similar to the dominant theme in Studs Terkel's collection of oral histories in *Hard Times* and may be a familiar experience to many oral historians.

Shopes came to this conclusion: "What is at issue here is a tension between the kind of information historians think is important to recover about a community's history and what community residents, however unconsciously, think is important to record about that history."[20] Not trained as historians, the interviewers lacked the background knowledge that would have enabled them to delve deeper into topics of a wider historical significance than the neighborhood. She also saw a tension at the level of method: Neighborhood people interviewing their neighbors are careful not to challenge their interviewees' worldviews; nor are they willing to criticize their interviewees' interpretations of collective experience.[21]

Shopes gave a realistic view of the difficulties likely to be encountered, but she did not mean that neighborhood history projects fully involving the residents at every stage are impossible. She urged that historians first become closely allied with neighborhood groups. The researchers must become sensitive to what interests people in their own history. These interests themselves suggest themes in social history. "They are clues into the mind of a person or group of people," Shopes has written. "This kind of information can then be coordinated with the data gathered from the more traditional sources of the social historian to provide not a simple 'insider's view,' but a more powerful social analysis."[22]

Work Communities

Consider also special problems involved in researching work communities. I base my definition of an occupational community, or work community, on the definitions of theorists such as historian Trevor Lummis and sociologists David Lockwood and Robert Blauner, as well as on my own experience in researching the history of a textile mill, a hospital, a college, and a women's cooperative art gallery. A work community is a group in which members have a strong identification with a specific kind of work, commitment to the same general goal, reliance on a code of behavior specific to the occupation, and a sense of belonging to a special group.[23]

Usually, the researcher steps into these "little worlds" without firsthand information on the occupation and without understanding what it means to the participants to be a part of this work community. As discussed above, the best way to proceed is by asking the group's long-term members what they thought was important in their history and what is important about the present. Often you will have to make a list of technical terms used in that occupation and learn them as quickly as you can.

Find out which individuals who are now active in the occupation as well as those who are retired are considered the most knowledgeable. Charles Morrissey argued that the researcher can best conceptualize a project by interviewing former members of the work community—for example, former members of Congress as distinct from current members.[24] They have gotten some perspective with the passage of time. And their jobs are not at stake. In any case, glean as much information about knowledgeable individuals as you can and keep a file folder with information on each. Also maintain a card file on these potential narrators with addresses and telephone numbers.

Locate the places where people in the occupation go to talk—go there and listen. For the hospital history, I found it was the employee cafeteria. For the history of the women's cooperative art gallery, hanging around after gallery meetings and going to shows enabled me to learn a lot. For the college history, I discovered that the faculty dining hall was filled with stilted conversations of people who were wary of one another and that the "real talk" went on in small intimate groups meeting in private homes. Nevertheless, if I kept the conversation on the past—and far enough back in the past that a frank statement would not threaten their current situation—I could get general ideas about how people regarded a certain event or person. Wherever you go to listen, make sure people know you have an ulterior purpose: to record and write their stories. Let there be no misrepresentation of your role as researcher; you have to be honest with the people you want to be honest with you.

In recording the testimony of people in a work community, be cognizant of the fact that their jobs are at stake. In a small community, what someone says about someone else finds its way back to that person. Working relationships can be affected or company officials may judge a statement as proof of disloyalty and penalize the speaker. As usual, tell the narrator where the tapes will go and who will have access to them. Be aware that when they talk about the near-past and the present, they may have to be guarded.

John Fox, historian at Salem State College, talking about his history of an insurance company, remarked, "I'm certain that in the minds of some employees, I am an agent of the employer."[25] I found in interviewing hospital staff members that they talked frankly and enthusiastically about their research projects or work on the wards but steered clear of com- ments about the administration. The guardedness of this testimony was revealed by the things they were willing to talk about off-tape.

Historian Carl Ryant chose an industry in which the ownership was moving out of the community and workers felt a desire to tell their story.[26] This situation eliminated the problem of workers' vulnerability.

Most of us, however, are interviewing in ongoing companies or institutions. Respect workers' needs to protect themselves: Do not pressure them to reveal information that is potentially harmful to them. If they freely choose to reveal such information, knowing who will have access to the information, then record, of course. They want the information to be made known. In the case of a nursing home's abuse of patients, for example, employees knowingly risked their jobs to expose the violations. That was their choice. Otherwise, try to get usable on-tape information from people recently retired from the workplace. But even in this situation, people may be afraid that their frank discussions may put their pensions in jeopardy.[27]

Robert Byington, who studies workers and organization of work, advised seeking endorsement from the union, not management.[28] Of course, this is not possible if you have been hired by management to write the history; but if you are a free agent, it is advisable to seek union approval, knowing that you still have to get permission from management to observe in the plant itself.

Commissioned Studies

When you are commissioned to write a history, those who pay the bill have ideas about what kind of history they want. As a scholar, you know what you want, and that is based on your interests and your knowledge of the research history of the topic. Ideally, the two approaches are similar; in reality, they may sometimes be antithetical.

Sociologist Maurice Punch, who was commissioned to write the history of a school in Britain, found that even after several revisions the narrative and analysis could not please the school's administrators. He cautioned:

> Most sponsors, I would suggest, may find it painful to have their protective myths pierced. This should be borne in mind by inexperienced researchers who might learn the subtle art of not treading too irreverently, and too unnecessarily, on institutional corns. Furthermore, research students might learn that the research process from original aim to successful publication is not always a harmonious progression but can be beset with fieldwork difficulties and with struggles to have the findings accepted.[29]

The public is used to a superficial account. This so-called study delves into no problems and offends no one—for example, a history where, to use David Henige's phrase, "seldom is heard a discouraging word."[30] The truth is that if you are writing with the intention of publishing research on a company or institution for which you work or a town in which you live, then start thinking about how much adverse reaction you can stand. Carol Kammen described the questions she had as she began to write the history of her town:

> Was it a history I could tell? This question really is, do we tell the truth? Do we point to reverses in the past when we know that this is not the public's perception of what local history has been and should be? Do we examine unfavorable episodes along with more positive themes when a community generally expects that its local history will be promotional and make the community feel good about itself? Do we expose prejudice, stupidity, bad judgment, errors, or criminal behavior in the past? They are certainly topics dealt with in our newspapers today, yet I have rarely seen a local history that admits these things could have happened or were commonplace.[31]

Sometimes you suspect that the book will never see daylight if you are completely honest and that all your labor will be of no use to anyone. Still, even with these second thoughts, we face the fact that a less than honest account of the research findings profits no one. Often, however, it is possible to avoid trouble around the issue of the commissioners' desire to protect their image. Educate the commissioners and the lay public about the difference between a public relations document and a serious research study. And the public *needs* to be informed about the way that a professional works. Much information is transmitted through the mass media where careful research is not necessarily valued, so you cannot assume that most people understand the nature of scholarly research.

David Lewis and Wesley Newton, who wrote *Delta: The History of an Airline,* said that no company has gone through a long history without making mistakes. Not to confront and evaluate the effects of the mistakes is to produce a "puff job" that enlightens no one. They advised oral historians to make sure corporate executives understand this "risk of laying bare [the company's] past to objective scholarship."[32]

Carl Ryant, a historian at the University of Louisville, was commissioned to write the history of the L&N Railroad. He was determined to record witnesses at every level in that work community. In an interview for Australian public radio, he explained:

We wanted to know how the change had taken place from passenger to freight, what had happened when steam engines disappeared and diesel engines came in their place, what it was like if you were a minority on a railroad (and in America most of the people who had what we would have called menial jobs, the porters, the workers in the dining cars, were Blacks). And we wanted to know what happened to women. . . . The railroad, I think, were a little suspicious of this. They never said no but they could not quite understand why we wanted to deal with such specific groups, whereas, they would have preferred us to talk only about nostalgic things, what the station was like.[33]

When Ryant asked for pictures, the railroad executives sent him pictures of past presidents. He replied, "This is very nice but I'd like pictures of Blacks and women working in the cars." They said, "We'll send them to you, but why do you want them?" He answered, "This illustrates a theme I want to deal with." He convinced them that that was part of the story, too.[34]

From the beginning, in talking to members of the community, make clear the goals of the professional. Charles Morrissey suggested that historians can state at least three purposes:

(1) [He or she] can underscore obvious factors in the institution's past performance, but because they are obvious they merit emphasis; (2) [he or she] can remind the institution of forgotten aspects of its history which have passed from collective memory as the institution changed staff or turned in directions away from its earlier experiences; and (3) [he or she] can elucidate the unexamined and often unarticulated premises upon which policy decisions were made.[35]

Ethnographers can stress that they want to help the community they study by providing information useful to its members.[36] Once the commissioners understand that these goals will be helpful to them, they may see that obscuring the truth will defeat this purpose.

To further educate the public at the beginning of the project, Morrissey urged oral historians to conduct a one-day seminar in the company to educate managers on the purpose and methods of history.[37] In the Wheaton College Oral History Project (Norton, Massachusetts), I offered to conduct six two-hour workshops on oral history interviewing for staff and faculty, and a dozen people took me up on it. My purpose was to engage the members of the work community in active participation in the researching of their own history. I soon discovered another benefit: When I recorded the life histories of these participants, they were especially helpful, understanding the questioning process and the importance of the recorded tapes for the college archives and the written history.

Another way to structure a project so that you have some help educating the public about the purposes of the research and the nature of ethnographic research is to have an advisory committee or board. Ann Moyall, author of *Clear Across Australia,* the history of Telecom Australia, the national telecommunications company, had a board set up. She insisted that the members include not only Telecom executives but also a professor of political theory who was an expert on communications and a historian respected for his work on technology. She also included an editor employed by an external organization. The board proved to be a great help. When one Telecom executive took chapters and rewrote them according to his view of history, the board was able to persuade Telecom that this would not produce the "scholarly and popular history" the company desired.[38]

I also see an advisory committee as a group of people with expertise who can give other kinds of help. Jeremy Brecher said that his community and labor advisory panel during the research project on brass workers helped locate interviewees and find photographs and documents. They publicized the project and encouraged the research.[39]

Although board members can become valuable resources in educating the public, putting the researcher in contact with narrators, and consulting in the design of the research project, some caution is advised. A board with different kinds of expertise is needed. In his *Oral History Program Manual,* William Moss suggested issues that an advisory council should consider at the outset, such as institutional affiliation and disbursement of funds as well as office space and depository facilities. But the researcher must make it clear that the advisors' role should be to "advise and facilitate, not direct or obstruct."[40] The problem is that a much-involved board can take over the project.

Ultimately, in researching and writing public history our purpose is to help people look at their past again and learn something valuable to them in the present. As ethnographers, we seek an understanding of how individuals participate in, live, and change a community culture. And for us, as researchers and human beings, we learn the answers to some of our questions about our collective past and present.

Summary

Educate the group commissioning the study in purpose and research methods. Make sure these individuals understand that the best research study is an honest one, that it is poor public relations to publish something that omits truths and presents a false picture. This destroys the institution's credibility and the entire project backfires. Furthermore, the community about whom the project will be written needs educating: Advance publicity about the project evokes greater interest and willingness to help.

Devising topics for the interview format and a list of narrators can be a shared experience. Begin the project by conducting informational interviews. Find out where community members gather for informal conversation and avail yourself of these informal small-group discussions to ask questions about the topics in which you are interested. Find out what they think is important. Continue to read secondary sources and scan primary sources such as newspapers.

Compose a list of topics for the interviews. For histories of communities, neighborhoods, institutions, and businesses, construct an interview guide that will enable you to write a history that presents not just the unique event but also the ways the local history shares in and differs from the history of the region and the nation.

In researching histories of ethnic communities, reflect on your own relationship to that subculture. Learn about the subculture before you begin the project and become knowledgeable about social expectations, communication styles, and values. In any neighborhood study be sensitive to people's interests and become allied with neighborhood groups so that you have a network. In researching work communities, be aware that employees' jobs are at stake, and the employers may see the company's interests as being at stake.

Notes

1. Charles Morrissey, communication to author, March 11, 1993.

2. Kenneth Kann, "Reconstructing the History of a Community," *International Journal of Oral History* 2 (February 1981): 4-12; see p. 8.

3. Tamara Hareven, "The Search for Generational Memory," in *Public History Readings*, eds. Phyllis K. Leffler and Joseph Brent (Malabar, Fla.: Krieger Publishing, 1992), 270-283; see pp. 277-278.

4. Ibid.

5. Morrissey, manuscript notation, March 11, 1993.

6. Paul Buhle, letter to author, November 14, 1992.

7. Michael Gordon, "Seeing and Fleeing Ourselves: Local Oral Histories of Communities and Institutions," *Oral History Review* 17, no. 1 (Spring 1989): 117-128; see p. 118.

8. Ibid., 119.

9. Ibid., 120. Also Robert C. Hardy, *Hero: An Oral History of the Oklahoma Health Center* (Oklahoma City: Oklahoma Health Sciences Foundation, 1985).

10. Linda Shopes, "Baltimore Neighborhood Heritage Project: Oral History and Community Involvement," *Radical History Review* 25 (1981): 26-44; see p. 38.

11. David E. Kyvig and Myron Marty, *Nearby History: Exploring the Past Around You* (Nashville, Tenn.: American Association for State and Local History, 1982), 223-224.

12. Kann, "Reconstructing the History of a Community," 7.

13. Antonio T. Diaz-Roys, "Maneuvers and Transformations in Ethnobiographies of Puerto Rican Migrants," *International Journal of Oral History* 4, no. 1 (February 1983): 21-31; see p. 21-23.

14. Paul Buhle, letter to author, November 14, 1992.

15. D. Barnlund and S. Araki, "Intercultural Encounters: The Management of Compliments by Japanese and Americans," *Journal of Cross-Cultural Psychology* 16 (1985): 6-26. Quoted in Stephen P. Banks, Gao Ge, and Joyce Baker, "Intercultural Encounters and Miscommunication," in *"Miscommunication" and Problematic Talk*, eds. Nikolas Coupland, Howard Giles, and John M. Wiemann (Newbury Park, Calif.: Sage Publications, 1991), 103-112; see p. 111.

16. Linda Shopes, letter to author, July 20, 1992.

17. Linda Shopes, "Baltimore Neighborhood Heritage Project," 27.

18. Ibid., 30.

19. Ibid., 32.

20. Ibid.

21. Ibid., 33.

22. Ibid., 37.

23. Robert Blauner, "Work Satisfaction and Industrial Trends in Modern Society," in *Labor and Trade Unionism*, eds. Walter Galenson and Seymour Martin Lipset (New York: John Wiley, 1960), 351; Trevor Lummis, "Occupational Community of East Anglian Fishermen," *British Journal of Sociology* 28, no. 1 (March 1977): 58-61; David Lockwood, "Sources of Variation," in *Working-Class Images of Society*, ed. M. Bulmes (Boston: Routledge & Kegan Paul, 1975), 17.

24. Charles Morrissey, letter to author, March 11, 1993.

25. John Fox, paper delivered at the session "The Historian as Hired Gun," Oral History Association Conference, October 10, 1991, Salt Lake City, Utah.

26. Carl Ryant, interview with Bill Bunbury for Australian Public Radio, Oral History Association Conference, October 10, 1991, Salt Lake City, Utah.

27. *Brass Valley: The Story of Working People's Lives and Struggles in an American Industrial Region,* eds. Jeremy Brecher, Jerry Lombardi, and Jan Stackhouse (Philadelphia: Temple University Press, 1982), 277.

28. Robert H. Byington, "Strategies for Collecting Occupational Folklife in Contemporary Urban/Industrial Contexts," *Western Folklore* 3 (1978): 43-56.

29. Maurice Punch, *The Politics and Ethics of Field Work* (London: Sage Publications, 1986), 75.

30. David Henige, "Where Seldom Is Heard a Discouraging Word: Method in Oral History," *Oral History Review* 14 (1986): 35-42.

31. Carol Kammen, *On Doing Local History: Reflections on What Local Historians Do, Why, and What It Means* (Nashville, Tenn.: American Association for State and Local History, 1986), 86.

32. David Lewis and Wesley Newton, "The Writing of Corporate History," *Public Historian* 3, no. 3 (Summer 1981): 68.

33. Carl Ryant, interview with Bill Bunbury for "Talking History," weekly national radio program of the Australian Broadcasting Corporation, recorded at the Oral History Association Conference, October 10, 1991, Salt Lake City, Utah.

34. Ibid.

35. Morrissey, "Public Historians and Oral History," p. 26.

36. R. M. Keesing, "Anthropology in Melanesia: Retrospect and Prospect," in *The Politics of Anthropology: From Colonialism and Sexism Toward a View From Below,* eds. G. Huizer and B. Mannheim (The Hague: Mouton, 1979), 276-277, as quoted in *Ethnographic Research: A Guide to General Conduct,* ed. R. F. Ellen (London: Academic Press, 1984), 137.

37. Morrissey, "Public Historians and Oral History," 27.

38. Ann Moyall, interview with Bill Bunbury in 1991, for "Talking History."

39. *Brass Valley,* 273.

40. William Moss, *Oral History Program Manual* (New York: Praeger, 1974), 20.

Recommended Reading

General Discussion of Public History

Allen, Barbara, and Lynwood Montell. *From Memory to History: Using Oral Sources in Local Historical Research.* Nashville, Tenn.: American Association of State and Local History, 1981. See especially the chapters on uses of oral history, ways to interpret conflicting accounts, and tests for validity in oral sources. The authors are folklorists, and the text is helpful in pointing to ways to handle legend and myth.

Benson, Susan Porter, Steven Brier, and Roy Rosenzweig. *Presenting the Past: Essays on History and the Public.* Philadelphia: Temple University, 1986. This collection of essays on public history raises methodological issues.

Frisch, Michael H. *A Shared Authority: Essays on the Craft and Meaning of Oral and Public History.* Albany: State University of New York Press, 1990. See especially "The Memory of History," pp. 15-27, a thoughtful essay on how public history can convey a sense of the past that can "enhance our ability to imagine and create a different future."

Gerber, David A. "Local and Community History: Some Cautionary Remarks on an Idea Whose Time Has Returned," *History Teacher* 13 (November 1979): 7-30. The author considers the new element in local history: the converging of academic and popular interests. He discusses the questions we ask about ethnicity and suggests goals such as researching local history to analyze "the interaction between various social processes, such as urbanization, industrialization, social mobility, or immigrant assimilation."

Gordon, Michael. "Seeing and Fleeing Ourselves: Local Oral Histories of Communities and Institutions," *Oral History Review* 17: 1 (Spring 1989): 117-128. This provides an excellent review of recent work published in community history.

Grele, Ronald. "Whose Public, Whose History?" *Public Historian* 3 (Winter 1981): 40-48. The author considers questions raised about public history, "questions that go to the heart of the uses of history in the culture and processes by which historical consciousness is formed and expressed." He gives a brief history of the public history movement and discusses the role that public history may play.

Kelly, Robert. "Public History: Its Origins, Nature, and Prospects," *Public History Readings.* Ed. Phyllis K. Leffler and Joseph Brent, 111-120. Malabar, Fla.: Krieger Publishing. 1992. This is a brief and useful history of the development of the movement in public history in this country.

Kyvig, David E., and Myron Marty, *Nearby History: Exploring the Past Around You.* Nashville, Tenn.: American Association for State and Local History, 1982. This is a resource for locating the written sources as well as suggestions for questions for oral history research.

Morrissey, Charles. "Public Historians and Oral History: Problems of Concept and Methods." *The Public Historian* 2, no. 2 (Winter 1980): 22-29.

Samuel, Raphael. "Local History and Oral History," *History Workshop* (Great Britain) 1 (1976): 191-208. This is a provocative essay on the uses of oral history in studying communities.

Guide to Use in Teaching Local History

Metcalf, Fay D., and Matthew T. Downey, *Using Local History in the Classroom.* Nashville, Tenn.: American Association for State and Local History, 1982. This work is brief on oral history, but the information on other primary sources is helpful.

Studies of Neighborhoods, Cultural Groups, and Towns

Broussard, Albert. "Oral Recollection and the Historical Reconstruction of Black San Francisco, 1915-1940," *Oral History Review* 12 (1984): 63-80. Broussard discusses the ways in which he used oral history to recover the history of a black community in San Francisco, especially to discover leaders and organizations that had been forgotten.

Buckendorf, Madeline, and Mercier, Laurie. *Using Oral History in Community History Projects*. OHA Pamphlet Series No. 4. OHA Executive Secretary, P.O. Box 3968, Albuquerque, NM 87190-3968.

Diaz-Roys, Antonio T. "Maneuvers and Transformations in Ethnobiographies of Puerto Rican Migrants," *International Journal of Oral History* 4, no. 1 (February 1983): 21-31. This has excellent suggestions for learning about the culture before undertaking interviews for a project.

Di Leonardo, Micaela. "Oral History as Ethnographic Encounter," *Oral History Review* 15 (Spring 1987): 1-20. This is an account of experiences interviewing in a California Italian-American community. The book on which this research is based is *The Varieties of Ethnic Experience: Kinship, Class and Gender Among California Italian-Americans* (Ithaca, N.Y.: Cornell University Press, 1984).

Kann, Kenneth. "Reconstructing the History of a Community," *International Journal of Oral History* 2 (February 1981): 4-12. Kann uses his experience in writing the history of an ethnic community—the Jewish community in Petaluma, California—to illustrate problems and solutions.

Myerhoff, Barbara. "Telling One's Story," *Center Magazine* 13 (March 1980): 22-40. The author discusses her work among Jewish retirees in a community center. The book based on this research is *Number My Days* (New York: Dutton, 1978).

Okihiro, Gary. "Oral History and the Writing of Ethnic History," *Oral History Review* 9 (1981): 27-46. Okihiro raises important questions about the use of oral history research in ethnic communities.

Serikaku, Laurie R. "Oral History in Ethnic Communities: Widening the Focus," *Oral History Review* 17, no. 1 (Spring 1989): 71-88. This is a very useful article on the ways oral history can inform a study of ethnic communities.

Shopes, Linda. "Baltimore Neighborhood Heritage Project: Oral History and Community Involvement," *Radical History Review* 25 (1981): 26-44. Shopes, in the context of her specific project, raises questions about researching community history in general, focusing especially on the involvement of the community itself.

Studies of Work Communities

Bodnar, John. "Power and Memory in Oral History: Workers and Managers at Studebaker," *Journal of American History* 75 (March 1989): 1201-1221. This work discusses the way workers remembered important events in labor struggles.

Brass Valley: The Story of Working People's Lives and Struggles in an American Industrial Region. Eds. Jeremy Brecher, Jerry Lombardi, and Jan Stackhouse. Philadelphia: Temple University Press, 1982. This provides a skillful interweaving of text and oral history.

Friedlander, Peter. *The Emergence of a UAW Local, 1936-1939: A Study in Class and Culture*. Pittsburgh: University of Pittsburgh Press, 1975. Friedlander discusses his use of repeated in-depth interviews with a principal narrator.

Hareven, Tamara. "The Search for Generational Memory," *Public History Readings*. Eds. Phyllis Leffler and Joseph Brent, 270-283. Malabar, Fla.: Krieger Publishing,

1992. This is an account of research among former workers in the Amoskeag Mills in Manchester, New Hampshire. The author's research strategy is interesting.

Lummis, Trevor. "Occupational Community of East Anglian Fishermen," *British Journal of Sociology* 28, no. 1 (March 1977): 51-77. The author discusses the selection of narrators to include a broad range of people who speak about the experience, including those who chose not to fish.

Comments on Using Oral History to Write Business History

Lewis, David, and Wesley Newton. "The Writing of Corporate History," *Public Historian* 3, no. 3 (Summer 1981): 63-74.

Ryant, Carl. "Oral History and Business History," *Journal of American History* 75, no. 2 (1988): 560-566. This work describes the state of the field at the end of the 1980s and presents important considerations.

7

Varieties of Oral History Projects

BIOGRAPHY

Oral history research methods are especially appropriate for writing biographies. In biography, the time is long past when the writer could just recount the deeds of the dead person, extolling the accomplishments of the public life. As biographer Leon Edel remarked, "The public facade is the mask behind which a private mythology is hidden—the private self-concept that guides a given life, the private dreams of the self."[1] Now readers want to understand the way the individual sees himself or herself, the inner struggles and motivation, the way psychological makeup influenced the subject's interpersonal relationships, the interpretation the subject gave to life's events. Evidence for these concerns do not often appear in written documents unless the researcher has access to private correspondence and personal journals. And even when such written sources are available, they do not always contain passages in which the subject has described such reflections. Oral history techniques of questioning about motivation, feelings, and meaning making are an effective way to get this information. The in-depth interview is, in fact, the research method that enables you, the researcher, to ask the person to think out loud.[2]

In this chapter, techniques for using oral history to research biography are explored. Agenda that both interviewer and narrator may have are examined. The importance of asking the hard questions and not creating a plaster saint is explained. And problems such as dealing with family members are discussed.

Life History and Biography

A *life history* has been defined as the account by an individual of his or her life that is recorded in some way, by taping or writing, for another person who edits and presents the account.[3] Examples of written life histories are those edited and published by John Burnett in *The Annals of Labour: Autobiographies of British Working Class People, 1820-1920.*[4] Burnett searched archives all over Britain for accounts by working people of their lives, accounts often written at someone else's suggestion or request. *Life as We Have Known It,* edited by Margaret Llewelyn Davies, is a collection of life stories written by working women.[5] They were encouraged by the Women's Co-Operative Guild in Britain to write. In this guide, however, *life history* refers to a taped oral account.

This is not simply the recording of testimony because the interviewer has agenda. Alex Haley pointed out in his introduction to *The Autobiography of Malcolm X* how the interaction of narrator and interviewer changed the narration. Malcolm X was trying to project an image of a critic of society, a thinker. Haley asked him questions about his childhood, his mother, his emotional life.[6] In short, the interviewer's influence is unavoidably present in the recording because the questions affect the direction of the conversation and the answers.

Presenting the life history to the public is another aspect of intrusion. In *All God's Dangers: The Life of Nate Shaw,* Theodore Rosengarten presents only the words of black sharecropper Ned Cobb (Nate Shaw in the book).[7] He transcribed the words as he heard them, placed discussions on the same topic together, and arranged accounts in a chronological order. Although Cobb needed neither prompts nor questions, Rosengarten had questions, although they are omitted in the published text. In *A Woman's Place: The Life History of a Rural Ohio Grandmother*, Rosemary O. Joyce interspersed her text with long quotations from the narrator Sarah Penfield. She explained, "The long block quotations enabled me to present Sarah with far less intrusion of me as editor."[8] Studs Terkel cuts, arranges, omits his questions, and usually gives no information on the interview situation. It is clear, then, that no matter how long the direct quotation from the narrator, the interviewer-editor manipulates the written text, just as he or she has already to some extent guided the oral account. Thus the final product of a life history is the result of a collaboration.

I distinguish this literary form from biography in which the subject is quoted, but which seldom presents long blocks of testimony from his or her life account. The main part of the text is the author's words. Although the author has been helped by various narrators, this is not a collaboration.

Nevertheless, oral history research will go on in much the same way for life histories as for biographies. If the subject is alive and willing to talk, the researcher will spend as much time as possible recording the individual's discourse. If the subject of the biography is unavailable for whatever reason, then oral history taping with friends, associates, family members, and enemies is still necessary in writing contemporary biography.

In this chapter, I will discuss oral history techniques applicable to research in preparing to present both life histories and biographies. And I will draw on the research and writing concerning autobiography. Sections of the recorded life history are autobiographical in that the speaker chooses to present accounts of his or her life not prompted by the interviewer's questions. In many cases, the account has been forming in the narrator's mind long before the interviewer appears at the door. But prompted or not, the narrator presents a view of the self, and this process is close to that of an autobiographer. Both have an audience in mind, although in an interview situation the audience—the interviewer—is immediate and most questions come from the interviewer. Nevertheless, the act of composing a self in the process of telling one's life story is happening in both forms, and this makes critical writings on auto-biography useful to the in-depth interviewer.

Initial Contact With the Subject

Famous people expect that someone will want to write their biographies. On the other hand, Ned Cobb, a simple farmer without education, understood that his movement, the Sharecropper's Union of the 1930s, deserved to be known to history. He remarked to historian Theodore Rosengarten, "I knew someday you'd come."[9] But Sarah Penfield, an Ohio farm woman who had known Rosemary Joyce for several years, was puzzled when she realized Joyce wanted her to be the subject of a book.[10]

Usually, the person will want to know why you have chosen him or her to study. Researcher Raymond Gorden suggested thinking about the answers to these questions before approaching the individual: How should I introduce myself? What is the purpose of this research? Do I have a sponsor or will I work on my own? Why have I selected this person? Is it feasible for me to promise anonymity if the person desires this? Can I offer any extrinsic reward? How open are we going to be?[11]

You may know with certainty that you are going to present a life history or write a biography of a famous person. But with an unknown person, you do not know during the first or second interview that you have chanced upon a natural *raconteur* whose memory for details and vivid language warrant a full life history. Rosengarten went to Alabama to research the history of the Sharecropper's Union and had no idea he would publish a life history. Joyce knew Sarah Penfield for years before she decided that she would work on her life history. Sometimes it takes a while to realize that the temptation to work on the life story of an extraordinary narrator is too compelling to resist. When the goal is clear to you, then discuss the work with the narrator. Gorden's suggestions will be useful to reflect on as you clarify procedures in this collaboration.

Why would an individual agree to work with a researcher, revealing intimate details of a life? Sociologist Gordon Allport listed the following reasons:

- They sense an opportunity to provide justification for the way they have lived.
- They desire to create order from disparate events.
- They seek redemption and social reincorporation through confession.
- They are pleased to be helpful in increasing knowledge of human lives.
- They enjoy the aesthetic pleasure of expressing their thoughts in a unique way.
- They like to give their own perspective on life.[12]

Sometimes the narrator is pleased to have an account of his or her life to leave to grandchildren. Sometimes the narrator wants to set the historical record straight. But the reason may also be simply that people enjoy the opportunity to talk about their experiences with an attentive listener. There is a need to reminisce in individuals from age 50 on.

When the narrator understands your intentions and agrees to work with you, then you should settle on a work schedule. Researcher Ken Plummer advised deciding together on time and place of meetings, kinds of questions that will be asked, whether the person will receive a list of topics before the session begins, what leeway the subject has to talk about what interests him or her, what the final product might look like, and what control the person will have over the contents of the publication.[13]

Again, you may not know at first what work schedule will be best. Work out the arrangements together. Rosengarten recorded Ned Cobb's testimony as Cobb made oak baskets in a shed. Joyce recorded Sarah Penfield's words as Penfield worked in her home. One narrator I went back to many times preferred to talk when work was over, and we could sit in the yard during summer in the late afternoons and drink ice tea and spend periods of time thinking silently. Another liked for me to sit at the huge dining room table in her apartment above her son's funeral parlor. Her dining room was a neighborhood meeting place, so there were interruptions, but I learned to just turn off the recorder and "hang out" when other people came in. In each of these situations, the recording went on at a time and in a place most conducive to the narrator's relaxed mood and ability to concentrate.

Although you do not know what the final product will be, you should discuss possibilities with the narrator. You may have to make some compromises, such as granting the narrator the right to review information you give in detail about her or his personal life or information implicating someone else. Do not, however, give anyone the right of veto over the entire manuscript.

Thoughts on Recording
a Life History: Constructing a Self

To begin with the most obvious, oral testimony is selective. Of course, nobody tells another person everything. The available collection of written sources also is selective. What letters remain to the researcher? Only those the receiver chose to keep and chooses to reveal. And what information is in the letters? Only that which the writer chose to include. However, with oral accounts of events long past, there is in addition the problem of forgetting. (Mercifully, we do not remember everything.) Human beings tend to remember the things that are important to them. And although you cannot ask a letter to recall, your questions will prompt memory in a narrator.

Furthermore, accounts—written and oral—are biased in the way the events are presented. Just as the letter writer has an agenda, so the narrator has his or her own agenda. However, with a retrospective life review you encounter the fact that impressions change over time because the narrator is affected by subsequent events.

These limitations of the research data are valuable indicators in themselves. A scholar who has written about the autobiographical form, Georges Gusdorf, argued that the retrospective autobiographical account is more valuable than the present-centered interview because the present is "only a fragmentary cutting from my personal being without guarantee that it will continue."[14] The oral history interview, by requiring the narrator to discuss developments over time, can elicit information on the subjective interpretation of a life. The interviewer can get a window on the narrator's changing world by asking outright such questions as, "You see this now as a test of courage. How did you see it then?"

Furthermore, Gusdorf insists that the process of composing an autobiographical account facilitates a discovery of the self:

> In recounting my history I take the longest path, but this path that goes round my life leads me the more surely from me to myself. The recapitulation of ages of existence of landscapes and encounters, obliges me to situate what I am in the perspective of what I have been. My individual unity, the mysterious essence of my being—this is the task of gathering in and of understanding in all the acts that have been mine, all the faces and all the places where I have recognized signs and witness of my destiny. In other words, autobiography is a second reading of experience, and it is truer than the first because it adds to experience itself the consciousness of it.[15]

Although Gusdorf is referring to the writing of one's life history, this process is also going on in the speaking of one's life history.

What the interviewer is privileged to witness is a process by which the narrator constructs a self or an identity. It is, of course, an endeavor in which we are all constantly engaged, but in the formal interview this is a focused action. Agnes Hankiss, a researcher who uses the life history approach in gathering data, described this process: "Human memory selects, emphasizes, rearranges and gives new colour to everything that happened in reality; and, more important, it endows certain fundamental episodes with a symbolic meaning, often to the point of turning them almost into myths, by locating them at a focal point of the explanatory system of the self."[16]

What narrators choose to discuss, how they treat the topic, the meaning they attribute to it, and the conclusion they draw—all give a continuity to the story. For them the answers they give to your questions and the topics they choose to interject fit into the picture they have of their life so that it remains a comprehensible whole, with a limited number of themes. From this wholeness of recounted experience, an identity—a feeling of "I am this kind of person"— emerges.

It is important, then, that you as interviewer permit the narrator to offer topics other than those you have in the interview guide. Oral history, like other kinds of qualitative methodology, is a quest in which the unexpected turns up. Part of the pleasure is in its serendipity. You will get around to asking for information directly pertaining to topics you want to know about, but even the discussion of topics that seem far afield from your interests at first may offer clues on the personality of the speaker—and maybe evidence for a subject that will interest you as you reflect on all the information later.

Motivation, Bias, and Strategies in
the Narrator's Testimony

I have touched on initial reasons the narrator may have for beginning the project. Once under way, you may sense that there are motivations that are not so conscious. Both narrator and interviewer have
biases, and an awareness of them will enable you to understand
what is happening in the interpersonal relationship, to critique the
oral document, and to look at your own interpretations critically.

Sometimes the narrator struggles to reconcile evidence from the
past with present needs. Doris Kearns described several versions
Lyndon Johnson gave of his relationship with his mother. While
Kearns was researching the Johnson biography, he would call her in
the early morning hours when he could not sleep. This occurred
frequently during the last year and a half of his life. He would re-create
moments with his mother in the distant past:

> As he described her to me, she was not the same model mother he
> had praised two years before. . . . Before, Johnson had pictured his
> mother as loving, sensitive, and spiritual. Now she was the demand-
> ing, ambitious, frustrated woman who had loved him when he suc-
> ceeded for her and scorned him when he failed. . . . The next morning
> he would sound guilty for blaming her; he would try to take his tale
> back, saying, "Now I didn't mean anything bad about my mother, she
> was the most wonderful, beautiful woman, and she loved me no mat-
> ter what." Soon he would offer another episode of her darker side,
> but his slow exorcism seemed as painful as it was now irrepressible.[17]

Johnson's contradictions in his testimony revealed to his biographer
what was troubling him. His identity was that he had been a loved
son and he needed to support that; on the other hand, he wrestled
with painful memories that revealed the complexity of his relationship with his mother. Loved? But in what way? For Kearns, learning
about this was more important than acquiring factual information
about his mother.

Gusdorf advised, "One should not take the narrator's word for it,
but should consider his version of the facts as one contribution to
his own biography."[18] Johnson described for Kearns his great-great-
grandfather's heroic death at the Battle of San Jacinto in Texas. Later
Kearns discovered that the ancestor had never been at the battle. A
real estate dealer, he had died at home in his bed. Probably Johnson

had not meant to lie, but he had wanted a heroic ancestor; after telling the story many times, he himself had come to believe it.[19] By telling the story to Kearns, he revealed an important aspect of his personality to his biographer: He needed to believe that he had not just a respectable, but a heroic family history. This was possibly a foundation for his own belief that his destiny was leadership.

Perhaps Johnson needed this "shoring up" in the last years of his life more than at any other time. Indeed, an important fact impinging on the in-depth life study is the phenomenon of developmental stages. At different stages of life, human beings have specific emotional needs and life tasks to complete that differ from those at other stages. On this topic, two excellent studies to consult are Daniel Levison's *Seasons of a Man's Life* and George Vaillant's *Adaptation to Life*.[20] Erik Erikson's work on stages remains the classic study to read, while Gail Sheehy's *Passages: Predictable Crises of Adult Life* is a popular version of the research data.[21] Knowing the literature on human development will enable the researcher or writer to place the subject in the context of emotional needs of others of the same age group.

Unfortunately, researchers have concentrated on life stages of men in our society, ignoring gender differences. The long-term naturalistic studies of stages in women's lives have yet to be done. Carol Gilligan at the Harvard Graduate School of Education studied girls at age 11.[22] Her study of moral development in women, *In a Different Voice: Psychological Theory and Women's Development*,[23] is a landmark. Other studies of women's lives, although not longitudinal, may be helpful, such as *Women's Ways of Knowing* and *Educated American Women: Self-Portraits*.[24]

Indeed, developmental issues differ for men and women, and so do other aspects of living a life. Feminist biographers have made an important contribution in insisting on a consideration of the question, "What difference does gender make in a life?" The ways in which women may be seen and permitted to act have been defined by society; images of women are socially constructed. In the introduction to *The Challenge of Feminist Biography: Writing the Lives of Modern American Women*, the editors stated this concern:

> When the subject is female, gender moves to the center of the analysis. Feminists contend that women's lives differ from men's, often in profound ways. Because society tends to value male models of achievement and behavior more than it values female models, a woman's

gender may exercise greater constraints on the way her life evolves. Failing to consider this difference distorts, if not falsifies, any account of a woman's life. No matter how "free" of gender-specific conditions she may think she is, these conditions nonetheless affect her.[25]

The influence of gender on the way a life is lived is true for men as well. Images of men are also socially constructed. The biographer researching the life of a man would do well, the editors argued, to ask what constraints have forced him to make a certain choice and not another, to behave in a certain way and not another. They insisted that with a heightened gender consciousness, the biographer would explore "the nature of his family and work relations with individuals of both sexes." They advised that "a gender consciousness in men's biographies would lead to a greater recognition of the tensions men often feel, but seldom publicly acknowledge, between their private and public selves."[26]

Apart from gender and developmental issues, the narrator will have agenda unique to him or her—sometimes this soon becomes apparent, but often the interviewer comes to understand it only after some time. Just as Johnson needed in his past a mother who loved him unconditionally, another may need to impress you with the social standing of his family (especially if the family later fell on hard times) or with the parental expectation that she be both daughter and son, thereby justifying her ambitions. Or, an old emotional wound may be unconscious motivation for the narrator to present a significant individual in his or her life as a cad.

There are also cultural expectations involved. In "Woman Remembering: Life History as an Exemplary Pattern," Elaine Jahner described the process of recording the life history of a Lakota Sioux woman, Ann Keller. She found group traditions affecting the narration. Keller would eliminate certain things and place events in an order so that she could compose a distinctive kind of narrative—the kind she was most familiar with in the Lakota culture. She would find traces of the past in contemporary events and comment on them; this process was also a part of her cultural heritage. She emphasized positive outcomes and eliminated what, in her view, could not be useful to others. Jahner discovered why:

> We could assume that her concentration on the positive is a personal preference with no particular relation to her cultural tradition, but a careful reading of similar Lakota women's autobiographical accounts

collected under comparable conditions shows the same tendency on the part of women to use events of their own lives to sketch a model or a pattern that can permit the audience to use experiences as a positive example.[27]

As you critique the oral history, consider the narrator's culture, especially its influence on selection of details and narrative construction and its characteristic ways of interpreting certain experiences.

Because the narrator is human, he or she can be expected to have biases. Sometimes these reveal themselves in omissions, evasions, or outright lies. In his chapter, "The Doing of Life Histories," in *Documents of Life,* social scientist Ken Plummer gave a checklist for judging the credibility of a narrator's testimony. Among the questions he suggests should be asked of the testimony of the life history informant are the following:

- Is unintended misinformation being given?
- Has there been any evasion?
- Does evidence suggest direct lying or deception?
- Has a "front" been presented?
- What might the informant take for granted and thus hence not reveal?
- How much is the informant seeking to please you?
- How much has he or she forgotten?
- How much of what is or is not revealed self-deceptive?[28]

Interviewer's Motivations, Strategies, and Biases

In the process of selecting topics and questions and in the rearranging of segments of an oral history, the researcher's own ideas intrude. He or she decides what is important enough to ask about. The writer of a biography is present in the life story in an even more direct way because of the necessary selectivity of information and interpretations. The researcher or writer must make conscious his or her own motivation in undertaking the work and in selecting as well as in interpreting the life story.

Thoreau's biographer, Richard Lebeaux, insisted that a biographer seeks a subject in part on the basis of unconscious fulfillment of needs. He or she then changes the interpretation during the course of the research as his or her own life changes.[29]

Certainly, in researching textile workers in the mill village of Carrboro, North Carolina, I sought to understand my own roots. And in choosing to interview the women only, I gave as a conscious motivation the fact that women talk more readily to another woman about some issues than they do to men. That was true, but unconsciously at the time, I created an opportunity to experience the pleasure of entering the world of women, of re-creating the warmth and sense of "We are women together" I had known as a child in my mother's kitchen. As the project went on, I sought reassurance in the way each woman saw her life as a whole, integrating the crises, putting them into perspective, at a time when I was confronting crises in my own life. But possibly my unconscious agenda biased my questioning (like not asking questions that embarrassed them), and the resulting written account may have been skewed in the direction of presenting too positive a picture—something I was not aware of at the time.

We, as oral historians and biographers, however, feel some hesitation in exposing a human being we have come to like and who has trusted us. In *A Woman's Place*, Rosemary O. Joyce said she first wrote about her subject, Sarah Penfield, as an ideal woman, not as a real woman. She then tried to achieve a middle ground by including the inconsistencies and shortcomings, coming closer to a very human portrait rather than the idealized one. Sarah Penfield's daughter acted as an advisor, reading and commenting on the final draft, and apparently she was willing to let the biographer present the "real" woman.[30]

On the other hand, in the interviewing process, you may hear some things that make it difficult for you to hold back your disdain. Try not to reveal your negative feeling at this stage of the research: just listen. For some reason, not clear to you yet, the narrator feels a need to tell you this. In writing the biography, if you believe that the words or deeds are not distorted in this version and reveal something of importance about the individual, then leave them in. In researching her biography of General Joseph Stillwell, Barbara Tuchman said she found he had referred to Franklin Roosevelt as "Rubberlegs." She admitted, "He had a talent for inventing wicked nicknames, I knew, but to make fun of a physical infirmity seemed to me unforgivable." She researched among people who were Stillwell's peers the nicknames used and found his to be "run-of-mill." She decided to include the term although "it felt like picking up a cockroach."[31]

In discussing the writing of political biography, Kenneth Morgan advised the historian or biographer to observe the following, using Lloyd George as an example: "What he should rather try to do is . . . convey the essence of Lloyd George's rebelliousness, and his urge for dynamic change, the short-cuts and sharp practice this sometimes meant, and the constant interaction between his dynamic, creative personality and a somewhat slower-moving world."[32] By discussing the "sharp practices" within the context of a complex personality and the times in which Lloyd George lived, Morgan presented a rich, full biography.

A hero-worshipping account soon becomes tedious because the reader senses that this is a six-foot paper doll the writer has drawn, not a human person. Everyone knows the biographer should not "create" facts, but some writers think it is acceptable to omit them. Sometimes this is done consciously as the writer weighs consequences. Sometimes this is done unconsciously by slanting an account because the interviewer-writer did not ask the hard questions or skipped over topics in the writing. Leon Edel, Henry James's biographer, insisted, "We must not flinch from the realities we have discovered; we must realize that beyond the flesh and the legend there is an inner sense of self, an inner man or woman, who shapes and expresses, alters and clothes, the personality that is our subject and our art."[33]

I have learned to try to ask the troubling questions. I do not want my sympathy for the subject to lead me to create a half-story. Only if the narrator could be seriously hurt by recording something from the past—information that would be available when the tape is deposited or the biography is written—do I hesitate. I have to make a judgment. (Chapter 4 discusses ethics, legalities, and criteria for deciding to record the difficult topics, and Chapter 3 discusses interviewing methods and ways to ask difficult questions, so I will not elaborate on these here.)

On the other hand, it is tempting to judge the narrator. After all, you have probably seen more of the evidence than anyone else since you are the one who has done the research. Step back; look at the reasons within yourself that make you inclined to condemn. Historian Joyce Antler described the research process for her biography of Lucy Sprague Mitchell, a pioneer in early childhood education. Antler said that when she first read an article about her subject's opposition to the passage of the suffrage amendment in California, she reacted "with visceral disappointment." She soon realized, "To separate my own feminist convictions from my subject's historical place and point of view was difficult but essential."[34]

Above all, be aware of your own assumptions when you begin to make sense of the various kinds of information you are collecting. If you assume that something cannot be so, then you will not ask for or recognize evidence to the contrary in the interviews. Once having become conscious of your own assumptions, you deliberately hold them tentatively, expecting change.

Gather the details in the in-depth interviews that give the total picture of the personality. Include the information that is pertinent to all sides of an issue. Lawrence Watson cautioned in his article "Understanding a Life History," that a life history is "a source of information about subjective experience that cries out for understanding."[35]

You have a framework, but it is very tentative. This limbo is a troubling but creative period. In her article on biographical method, "Lies and Silences," Victoria Glendenning remarked that when she works on someone's life, she piles up a mass of materials that are unrelated or downright contradictory. Her old model of what the subject's life was all about has to be thrown out and for a while no new model takes its place.[36] But by being open to new ways of thinking about the individual, you are receptive to hearing new things in the interview situation.

To test for the interviewer's bias, Plummer suggests asking these questions of oneself:

- How has the interview been shaped by my age, gender, class, race?
- How has it been shaped by my appearance and body language?
- How has it been shaped by my personality—for example, need for approval, hostility, anxiety to get the interview finished?
- How have my own attitudes impinged—my religious values, political views, general assumptions, my theories and expectancies? (I also ask here, by my conscious and barely conscious reasons for choosing the subject in the first place?)

And the interaction needs to be scrutinized: Did it make a difference that the interview was held in one place and not another? That we knew each other before the project began? That there was a certain kind of nonverbal communication going on?[37]

Interviewing Associates and Enemies

In the same critical way, in interviewing your subject's associates, take into account that impressions also change over time for them. In comparing interviews with Lyndon Johnson's associates to those with John Kennedy's associates, Doris Kearns found that there was a marked difference: "The tendency of President Johnson's associates is to be critical, while the tendency of President Kennedy's associates is to be admiring." She surmised that this was not just a reflection of the different personalities of the two men. She wrote, "The central figures in the Johnson circle seem to be trying to break free of the intimacy and the fusion they experienced with Johnson, trying to live a life of some detachment, proving that they deserve their liberty by criticizing their former master."[38] On the other hand, John Kennedy kept his political associates at some distance. Kearns wrote, "The Kennedy men, in my judgment, are often seeking through the written word to tie bonds that they never had to the president."[39]

Beware, too, of associates and family members who create and sustain myths about the dead individual. Possibly we all do this to some extent: only listen to the testimony at funerals. We have been taught not to speak ill about the dead. And missing the individual, we tend to think of the good times. But in addition to this, our association with "greatness" lends drama to the story of our own lives. The biographer must listen critically and be aware of the process of mythmaking.

If the subject of the biography is still living, you hope to have many recording sessions with the individual. But if the person is not available, you still want to interview the people who knew him or her. You may be tempted to interview only those you see as important in the life story. Consider interviewing some of those who are not so important. Newspaper reporters know that they should seek out maids, servants, and chauffeurs to the famous if they want information on what the person was like on a daily basis.

Reporters also find out how the individual handled crises when he or she got back to the office by asking the "not-so-important people" there. Interview the subordinates in the subject's organization. Beatrice Webb insisted that the "mind of the subordinate in any organization will yield richer deposits of fact than the mind of the principal."[40] They are the ones who implemented your subject's decisions and are knowledgeable about the consequences.

There also are people who knew your subject only briefly at one stage of the career, but the glimpse they give you of the individual's actions at that time and place are revealing. When historian Dee Garrison was researching her biographical study of Mary Heaton Vorse, a journalist and labor organizer, she went to Vorse's favorite home in Provincetown, Massachusetts. She interviewed many people—those who had liked and disliked Vorse. Garrison began to get a picture of her subject's effects on this little town. One ex-minister, recalling the opposition of townspeople when he marched in a local demonstration against the Vietnam War, said, "The emotional support she offered me was very, very important to me at the time."[41]

Of course, you have to make choices; but like a detective, explore as many leads as you think may prove informative. Follow your hunches.

Interview the opponents. They will be biased, just as loyalists and defenders are, but underlying the account there may be deeds the subject's friends did not experience, and you will get a different perspective on your subject. In critiquing John Toland's biography of Hitler, David Mitchell noted that Toland had interviewed mostly Hitler's associates. Toland said he interviewed Hitler's deriders, as well; but Mitchell argued that the emphasis was on the other side. Mitchell observed, "If he had interviewed primarily opponents and victims of the German tyrant, the emphasis of the biography would most certainly have been altered."[42]

Another good reason to interview opponents is that you can better understand what your subject faced. You can place your subject's writings or political opinions, for example, in the context in which they were produced. You can know whose writings she or he was reading, whose arguments needed to be answered, or the kinds of personalities with whom he or she dealt.

Revealing Details of Private Life, Family Reactions

As a historian and biographer, you would like to avoid the content of the gossip column. The private details of a person's life can be titillating to an audience, but whether they are necessary to the biography will be for you to judge. And there is the matter of invasion of privacy. If your subject means to tell you, that is one thing. If someone else tells you details about your subject, that is something else again. First, check the evidence: An often-quoted rule is, "A biographer is an artist who is on oath."[43] If true, consider whether these are necessary to adequately convey the personality of the individual or the context in which he or she acted.

When Victoria Glendenning was doing the research for a biography of poet Elizabeth Bowen, she visited a woman whose deceased husband had had a love affair with Bowen. The widow had invited Glendenning, saying she had Bowen's love letters to him. She gave Glendenning a choice: The writer could quote from the letters and not name him or she could say Bowen had the affair with the named man and not quote from the letters. Glendenning chose to quote from the letters and not name him. The choice of words, the writing style, the details so revealed an important aspect of Bowen's life at the time and her state of mind then that they needed to be included. The name of the man was not as necessary to the understanding of Bowen.[44]

Historian Sara Alpern decided to reveal the fact that her subject, Freda Kirchwey, an editor of *The Nation*, and her husband, Evans Clark, had open extramarital relationships. But she also made the decision not to disclose the names of the persons involved. No problem about that judgment. However, she agonized over including— in a discussion of the effects of the death of a young son on Kirchwey —the subject's statement that this son was her favorite. Alpern did not want to hurt the feelings of a surviving son. When he read the manuscript, he asked Alpern to put the quotation back in, saying that she owed the reader that information.[45]

Often, however, the inclusion of details about private experience gets the researcher or writer into trouble with the subject or the subject's family. One consideration is based on how well known the subject was or is. Ulick O'Connor stated the problem clearly:

> A question however which must always concern the biographer is to
> what extent does he have to take into account the matter of living rela-
> tives and their susceptibilities. It seems fair to say that this decision
> can have something to do with the sort of person who is the subject of
> the biography. The great statesman, writer or artist has after all placed
> himself in the public domain to an extent that in order fully to compre-
> hend his position in relation to the circumstances and age that bred
> and shaped him, it can be necessary to deal with material that many
> relatives and friends would prefer to see left alone.[46]

As an example, O'Connor said he had discussed in a page and a half in his biographical study of Brendan Behan the attraction Behan felt toward both sexes. O'Connor believed that it was necessary to discuss Behan's unusually active sex drive because that was part of his ferocious appetite for pleasurable experiences in life. And Behan himself talked about this openly. After publication of the biography, some family members were angry, but Behan's mother's comment was, "Aren't we all human?"[47] Often, however, family members will take offense because you have a different view of the life than they have, and they are not likely to be as tolerant as Behan's mother.

Legal Difficulties in Researching and Writing Contemporary Biography

Sometimes the differences over interpretation or inclusion of a detail can make relationships bitter indeed. The lawsuit that Jacqueline Kennedy brought against William Manchester is an example of this. Honored by the Kennedy family's choice of him to write the story of the president's assassination, Manchester agreed that Jacqueline Kennedy and Robert Kennedy would have the right of censorship and veto over publication if they did not like his account. When Manchester presented the manuscript to the people designated by the Kennedy family to read it, he was advised to go ahead with publication. Mrs. Kennedy then read it, found it objectionable, and the family began a lawsuit to stop publication. The editor of the publishing company judged the writing to be fair and judicious; however, Manchester deleted portions of the manuscript to please the Kennedys. The case was settled out of court.[48] The biography was published.

Researching and writing a biography on your own does not necessarily make you freer. Letters and other personal documents deposited in public archives may have restrictions on use. And individuals who lend you letters from your subject or consent to be interviewed sometimes do so with strings attached.[49] If you have to sign a legal document concerning use of a restricted collection, read the fine print. If a narrator wants you to promise him or her something that prevents you from using essential information, refuse—even if you lose the interview.

Whether you are considering writing an authorized or an un-authorized biography, you may have to do some educating with narrators about why a biography that presents a plaster saint cannot be credible in our times. You may have to make some compromises, but try to limit the amount of change and kind of change that you must do. At the end, invite commentary on the text and consider all criticisms, but stick to your guns if you are convinced your version is best. It is difficult, if you are writing a commissioned biography, to get a contract that does not give the commissioner the ability to veto publication, but make it clear that you cannot work when some-one else has right of censorship or veto over the entire manuscript. Think long and hard before agreeing to any kind of restriction, and get a lawyer if necessary.

Representativeness of the Life

In writing a biography or presenting a life history, you will encounter the question, Why tell this individual's story? Barbara Tuchman justified her biographies on the grounds that the characters were present at pivotal events in history and the life story helps the reader understand the context for an important event. Rosengarten justified his book in which Ned Cobb speaks as the vehicle by which the deeds and life of a black sharecropper in the South become known in history. Rosemary O. Joyce explained that in many ways Sarah Penfield's life showed the reader what it was like to be a farm woman in Ohio in the early part of the century. Sara Alpern began her study of *Nation* editor Freda Kirchwey because, she admitted, "I wanted answers to all the questions I faced as a woman, historian, and mother." She concluded that the biographical study had revealed that women today had "accepted impossible standards against which to measure current efforts to combine private and public lives."[50] It became important for her to share this study with other women. Bette Weidman, in her article "Oral History in Biography," wrote that oral histories reveal the life of a larger community, and in this way "the oral sources contribute most richly." She added, "Frequent reference to other people and relationships by the oral sources give the reader the sense of participation of a community in the life being recorded."[51] In each of these explanations, the relationship of the individual to the larger history at the time is central to the research and writing.

The interviewer-biographer must of necessity become well informed about the social and cultural milieu in which the individual lived and the history that was occurring both on a local and national level. In the interview guide, include the questions that will give you information on the ways that historical events impinged on this life. Not to place the individual in a historical context is to wrench the life from its meaningful place, to isolate the person in a strange way.

Ask yourself, "How is this individual typical for his or her gender, race, social class, cultural group? How does living in this historical moment affect the life? How is this individual different from what would be expected? In what ways is the person unique?"

Summary

Whether the goal is to present a life history or write a biography, oral history interviewing is an effective method because it allows us to ask questions not only about events but also about motivation, reflections, interpretations, and feelings.

It is important to discuss with the narrator the reasons why you want to present the life history or write the biography. And the narrator must be consulted about arrangements: where you will record and for how long, what topics will be discussed, what rights the narrator has to offer topics or refuse to discuss. But in the end, do not let anyone have a veto over publication of the entire manuscript.

Both narrator and interviewer have agenda—conscious and unconscious. It is necessary to tease this out of the discourse so that you can evaluate the questions you have pursued as well as the content of the narrator's answers. Give the narrator leeway to discuss topics you have not thought of: If they are important to the narrator, they will be important in some way to you.

Beware of creating an unbelievably "good" character by avoiding the questions that trouble the narrator or by omitting information that is unpleasant. Present the real woman or man by getting information on needed questions—even when these are difficult to ask— and by including the details that give a full account in the context of the interaction of the individual personality and the times.

Be open to the possibility of different ways of framing the life experiences. Seeking to understand the narrator's view of the life, contrasting it with your view of the life, and presenting different ways to interpret the meanings of the evidence result in a rich biography, not a one-dimensional account.

In constructing the interview guide, include questions that probe the individual's reactions to the historical events of the times. Find out how the person fit into his or her community or movement, how the values of the group affected him or her, and how he or she fulfilled expectations based on gender, race, class, and social status. The individual biography or life history has much to say to the reader beyond the fascination of the unique aspects of the person.

Notes

1. Leon Edel, "Biography and the Science of Man," in *New Directions in Biography*, ed. Anthony M. Friedson (Honolulu, Hawaii: Biographical Research Center, 1981), 1-11; see p. 9.

2. This sentence was suggested by this Weidman statement: "The interview is the one historical document that can ask people what they mean." Bette S. Weidman, "Oral History in Biography: A Shaping Source," *International Journal of Oral History* 8 (February 1987): 41-55; see p. 50.

3. L. L. Langness, *The Life History in Anthropological Science* (New York: Holt, Rinehart & Winston, 1965), 4-5.

4. John Burnett, *The Annals of Labour: Autobiographies of British Working Class People, 1820-1920* (Bloomington: Indiana University Press, 1974).

5. *Life as We Have Known It*, ed. Margaret Llewelyn Davies (London: Hogarth Press, 1931; New York: W. W. Norton, 1975).

6. Alex Haley, *The Autobiography of Malcolm X* (New York: Ballantine, 1964), 390.

7. Theodore Rosengarten, *All God's Dangers: The Life of Nate Shaw* (New York: Avon, 1974).

8. Rosemary O. Joyce, *A Woman's Place: The Life History of a Rural Ohio Grandmother* (Columbus: Ohio State University Press, 1983) 10.

9. Theodore Rosengarten, lecture, University of Rhode Island, fall 1978.

10. Joyce, *A Woman's Place*, 48.

11. Raymond L. Gorden, *Interviewing: Strategy, Techniques and Tactics* (4th ed.) (Chicago: Dorsey Press, 1987), 165-173.

12. Gordon Allport, *The Use of Personal Documents in Psychological Science* (New York: Social Science Research Council, 1942), 69-74.

13. Ken Plummer, "Doing of Life Histories," in *Documents of Life*, no. 7 of the Contemporary Social Research Series, ed. M. Bulmer (London: Allen and Unwin, 1983), 93.

14. Georges Gusdorf, "Conditions and Limits of Autobiography," in *Autobiography: Essays Theoretical and Critical*, ed. James Olney (Princeton: Princeton University Press, 1980), 38.

15. Ibid.

16. Agnes Hankiss, "Ontologies of the Self: On the Mythological Rearranging of One's Life History," in *Biography and Society*, ed. Daniel Bertaux (Beverly Hills, Calif.: Sage Publications, 1981), 203.

17. Doris Kearns, "Angles of Vision," in *Telling Lives: The Biographer's Art*, ed. Marc Pachter (Washington, D.C.: New Republic Books, 1979), 90-103; see p. 101.

18. Gusdorf, "Conditions and Limits of Autobiography," 36.

19. Kearns, "Angles of Vision," 98.

20. Daniel J. Levison, *The Seasons of a Man's Life* (New York: Alfred A. Knopf, 1978); George Vaillant, *Adaptation to Life* (Boston: Little, Brown, 1977).

21. Erik Erikson, *Childhood and Society* (New York: W. W. Norton, 1963); see Chapter 7 for the "Eight Stages of Man." Gail Sheehy, *Passages: Predictable Crises of Adult Life* (New York: E. P. Dutton, 1976).

22. Carol Gilligan, *Making Connections: The Relational Worlds of Adolescent Girls at the Emma Willard School* (Cambridge, Mass.: Harvard University Press, 1990).

23. Carol Gilligan, *In a Different Voice: Psychological Theory and Women's Development* (Cambridge, Mass.: Harvard University Press, 1982).

24. Mary Field Belenky et al., *Women's Ways of Knowing: The Development of Self, Voice, and Mind* (New York: Basic Books, 1986); Eli Ginsberg, *Educated American Women: Self-Portraits* (New York: Columbia University Press, 1966). See also Nadya Aisenberg and Mona Harrington, *Women of Academe: Outsiders in the Sacred Grove* (Boston: University of Massachusetts Press, 1988); although not a developmental study, the oral history testimony does point to connections between life stages and an academic woman's thinking about career.

25. Sara Alpern, Joyce Antler, Elisabeth Israels Perry, and Ingrid Winther Scobie, *The Challenge of Feminist Biography: Writing the Lives of Modern American Women* (Urbana: University of Illinois Press, 1992), 7.

26. Ibid., 7-8.

27. Elaine Jahner, "Woman Remembering: Life History as an Exemplary Pattern," in *Women's Folklore, Women's Culture*, ed. Rosan A. Jordan and Susan J. Kalcik (Philadelphia: University of Pennsylvania Press, 1985), 214-233; see p. 218.

28. Plummer, "Doing of Life Histories," 103.

29. Richard Lebeaux, "Thoreau's Lives, Lebeaux's Lives," in *Introspection in Biography: The Biographer's Quest for Self-Awareness*, eds. Samuel Baron and Carl Pletsch (Hillsdale, N.J.: Lawrence Erlbaum, 1985), 225-248.

30. Joyce, *A Woman's Place*, 22.

31. Barbara Tuchman, "Biography as a Prism of History," in *Telling Lives: The Biographer's Art*, ed. Marc Pachter (Washington: New Republic Books, 1979), 144.

32. Kenneth Morgan, "Writing Political Biography" in *Troubled Face of Biography*, eds. Eric Homberger and John Charmley (London: Macmillan, 1988), 33-48; see p. 47.

33. Leon Edel, "The Figure Under the Carpet," in *Telling Lives: The Biographer's Art*, ed. Marc Pachter (Washington: New Republic Books, 1979), 16-34; see p. 34. See also Leon Edel, "Biography: A Manifesto," *Biography* 1, no. 1 (1978): 2.

34. Joyce Antler, "Having It All, Almost: Confronting the Legacy of Lucy Sprague Mitchell," in *The Challenge of Feminist Biography*, 97-115; see p. 109.

35. Lawrence C. Watson, "Understanding a Life History as a Subjective Document: Hermeneutical and Phenomenological Perspectives," *Ethos* 4, no. 1 (Spring 1976): 95-131; see p. 98.

36. Victoria Glendenning, "Lies and Silences," in *Troubled Face of Biography,* eds. Eric Homberger and John Charmley (London: Macmillan, 1988), 49-62; see p. 51.

37. Paraphrase of Plummer, "Doing of Life Histories," 103.

38. Kearns, "Angles of Vision," 98.

39. Ibid.

40. Beatrice Webb, *My Apprenticeship* (London: Longman, Green, 1926), 409.

41. Dee Garrison, "Two Roads Taken: Writing the Biography of Mary Heaton Vorse," in *The Challenge of Feminist Biography,* 65-78; see p. 73.

42. David Mitchell, "Living Documents: Oral History and Biography," *Biography* 3 (April 1980): 283-296; see p. 291.

43. Quoted in Ulick O'Connor, *Biographers and the Art of Biography* (Dublin: Wolfhound Press, 1991), 7.

44. Glendenning, "Lies and Silences," 57-58.

45. Sara Alpern, "In Search of Freda Kirchwey: From Identification to Separation," in *The Challenge of Feminist Biography,* 159-176; see p. 173.

46. O'Connor, *Biographers and the Art of Biography,* 76.

47. Ibid., 77-78.

48. C. Peters, "William Manchester: Old Pro and the Comeback Kid," *Washington Monthly Review* 11 (March 1979): 32-35. John Corry, *The Manchester Affair* (New York: Putnam, 1967).

49. Steve Weinberg, *Telling the Untold Story: How Investigative Reporters Are Changing the Craft of Biography* (Columbia: University of Missouri Press, 1992). See especially Chapter 6, "The Promise and Peril of Investigative Biography," pp. 201-223.

50. Alpern, "In Search of Freda Kirchwey," 162.

51. Weidman, "Oral History in Biography," 54.

Recommended Reading

Alpern, Sara, Joyce Antler, Elisabeth Israels Perry, and Ingrid Winther Scobie. *The Challenge of Feminist Biography: Writing the Lives of Modern American Women.* Urbana: University of Illinois Press, 1992. This collection of 10 essays by feminist biographers presents a discussion of how their research and writing evolved; it argues that private and public life are inextricably intertwined and that the biographer cannot ignore the pervasive influence of gender in both men's and women's lives.

"Book Review Symposium: Oral History and Biography," *Oral History Review* 18, no. 1 (Spring 1990): 93-109. This symposium contains an introduction to biography by Linda Shopes and reviews of six recent biographies. It is informative for the connections between biography and oral history and for characteristics of effective biographical writing.

Clifford, James L. *From Puzzles to Portraits: Problems of a Literary Biographer.* Chapel Hill: University of North Carolina Press, 1970. This offers an account of how the author tracked down leads and followed hunches; it is both fun to read and informative.

Cohler, Bertram. "Personal Narrative and Life Course." In *Life-Span Development and Behavior,* Vol. 4, eds. P. Baltes and O. Brim. New York: Academic Press, 1982. See pp. 205-241. This essay uses psychoanalytic theory to explain how transitions are accommodated in the telling of one's life.

Cottle, Thomas J. *Private Lives and Public Accounts*. Amherst: University of Massachusetts Press, 1977. See the first chapter, pp. 3-26, for a thoughtful introduction to research for a biography.

Crapanzano, Vincent. "Life Histories," *American Anthropologist* 86, no. 4 (1984): 953-960. This essay stresses that "when we analyze a life history, we are analyzing a text, not social reality, and this text is itself the product of a complex collaboration."

Erikson, Erik. *Childhood and Society*. New York: Norton, 1963. See Chapter 7, "Eight Stages of Man," pp. 219-234, for a brief explanation of each of Erikson's stages.

Geiger, Susan N. "Women's Life Histories: Method and Content," *Signs: A Journal of Women in Culture and Society* 2 (Winter 1986): 334-351. This review article offers instructive commentary on several recently published life histories.

Glendenning, Victoria. "Lies and Silences." In *The Troubled Face of Biography,* eds. Eric Homberger and John Charmley. London: Macmillan, 1988. This essay deals with such gritty issues as what the biographer leaves out.

Gusdorf, Georges. "Conditions and Limits of Autobiography." In *Autobiography: Essays Theoretical and Critical,* ed. James Olney. Princeton, N.J.: Princeton University Press, 1980. This is a brilliant discussion of the relationship of past events to the present in the narrator's mind.

Hankiss, Agnes. "Ontologies of the Self: On the Mythological Rearranging of One's Life History." In *Biography and Society,* ed. Daniel Bertaux. Beverly Hills, Calif.: Sage Publications, 1981. This essay shows how a narrator may create a mythological system about the past that enables him or her to justify the present condition.

Hunt, David. *Parents and Children in History: The Psychology of Family Life in Early Modern France*. New York: Basic Books, 1970. For an overview of Erik Erikson's theory of human development, see Chapter 1, "The Psychological Background: Erik Erikson's Theory of Psycho-Social Development," pp. 11-17.

Kaufman, Sharon. *The Ageless Self: Sources of Meaning in Late Life*. Madison: University of Wisconsin Press, 1986. The author shows "in detail the process by which individuals integrate and accept the diverse experiences of a lifetime, so that they achieve the final stage of development outlined by Erikson."

Langer, Elinor. "Coming to Terms," *Pequod: A Journal of Contemporary Literature,* nos. 223-224 (1987): 209-240. The author discusses omissions in her subject's memoir as well as her relationship to her dead subject. She confronts the question, "Do you keep the secret your subject kept?"

Langness, L. L., and Gelya Frank. *Lives: An Anthropological Approach to Biography*. Novato, Calif.: Chandler & Sharp, 1981. See especially the section "Biography and the Structure of Lives" for a discussion of the way individuals have a "unity of some kind" that helps them select and make sense of memories.

Lebeaux, Richard. "Thoreau's Lives, Lebeaux's Lives." In *Introspection in Biography: The Biographer's Quest for Self-Awareness,* eds. Samuel Baron and Carl Pletsch, 225-248. Hillsdale, N.J.: Lawrence Erlbaum, 1985. This offers an account of how a biographer seeks a subject to fill his own needs and then changes the interpretation as his own life changes.

Mitchell, David. "Living Documents: Oral History and Biography," *Biography* 3 (April 1980): 283-296. This article discusses the uses of oral history in writing biography and presents outstanding biographies based on oral history.

O'Connor, Ulick. *Biographers and the Art of Biography.* Dublin: Wolfhound Press, 1991. This has several interesting chapters, but see especially the discussion on dealing with untrue accounts written by the subject (pp. 90-98).

Pachter, Marc. "The Biographer Himself: An Introduction." In *Telling Lives,* ed. Marc Pachter, 2-15. Washington, D.C.: New Republic Books, 1979. This is an incisive essay on the effects of the writing of biography on the biographer.

Quilligan, Maureen. "Rewriting History," *The Yale Review* (Winter 1988): 259-286. This is a review of five biographies of women and a discussion of the way "prominent women have a double burden: not only to be unique . . . but [also] to be representative."

Schwarz, Ted. *The Complete Guide to Writing Biographies.* Cincinnati, Ohio: Writer's Digest Books, 1990. The chapter on ethics, "How Can You Say That About Them?" offers specific examples.

Shore, Miles. "Biography in the 1980's," *Journal of Interdisciplinary History* 12, no. 1 (Spring 1981): 89-113. The author presents a brief history of approaches in biographies and sets forth criteria for judging the use of concepts from clinical psychology to analyze life history data.

Thompson, Paul. "Life Histories and the Analysis of Social Change." In *Biography and Society,* ed. Daniel Bertaux. Beverly Hills, Calif.: Sage Publications, 1981. See pp. 289-306. This article offers an account of the ways individual biographies can be used for a study of social change.

Watson, Lawrence C. "Understanding a Life History as a Subjective Document: Hermeneutical and Phenomenological Perspectives," *Ethos* 4, no. 1 (Spring 1976): 95-131. This describes the ways in which the biographer brings his or her own background, intellectual interests, commitments, sensitivity to dialogue, and ability to re-create insights to the interpretation of the subject's life.

Weidman, Bette S. "Oral History in Biography: A Shaping Source," *International Journal of Oral History* 8 (February 1987): 41-55. This article discusses the ways oral history influences the presentation of the life in a biography.

8

Varieties of Oral History Projects

FAMILY RESEARCH

Oral history can be like the light that shines on a family in a 17th-century Dutch painting as they go about their daily tasks. Indeed, it is the daily life of the family—experiences that no one thought important enough to write down—that can be illuminated in the oral history interview.

Relationships among family members, motivations, fears, strong feelings, the vivid memories about an individual's words or actions at some important moment can be sought in oral history questioning, as well. Scholars who study the family emphasize the importance of family stories that contribute to the shaping of individuals' lives. Usually, these are not written down but simply told by one generation to the next. Oral history facilitates the taping and preservation of stories unique to a family.

Family history, when you research your own family, can be richly rewarding. A student in my class, a woman of Italian-American heritage, decided to write a three-generational history of herself, her mother, and her maternal grandmother. The grandmother, whom she at first saw as an old woman whose values differed in important ways from her own, became to her granddaughter through the interviewing process a young woman—in photographs looking much like her granddaughter—with many of the same hopes and fears. She drew closer to her grandmother in a way she had not thought possible.

This is one reason, creating a bridge across generations, that teachers assign oral history projects on family history to students. Another reason is to give students the opportunity of increasing appreciation of their own cultural heritage. Another is to offer a project that makes students aware that history is something that happens to them, that it is not just in a textbook. Still another reason is to give students in social science an opportunity to observe and analyze interaction in this small unit of society that influences social interaction on other levels, as well. It is an effective way for students to learn the methodology of historical research or to gain experience in ethnographic research.

Many of us, no longer students, undertake family history projects involving extensive interviewing because we seek answers to questions about our own families that we were vaguely aware of as children but which pique interest or trouble us in adulthood. In these wider research projects with many families, we ask the questions that give us insight into our own.

Individual family history has been looked at sometimes with disdain by professional historians. There are good reasons for this: Too often in the past such publications have been mere laudatory accounts, skimming the surface of serious issues, masking the unpleasant events, whitewashing the less-than-respectable deeds. And the scope has been narrow because there was little concern with how the individual family was affected by and participated in the history of the wider world. But family history, thoroughly researched, that confronts and deals with serious concerns, presents an honest account, and places the individual family in a wider historical context can be enlightening. Because there are recently published family histories that do just that, critics in the historical profession have become interested in individual family histories. Psychologists, sociologists, folklorists, and anthropologists have also begun to take an interest in individual family history. In a public lecture in 1949, Oscar Lewis talked about the need for sociologists and anthropologists to study individual families. He had been thinking about the best way to "study the individual and understand his relationship to the culture." He argued that a study of the family could help "bridge the gap between the conceptual extremes of the culture at one pole and the individual at the other." The researcher could see in this social unit how individuals work together or refuse to do so, and defy, carry out, or change wider societal norms and create behavioral expectations characteristic of that unit. Lewis concluded, "It is in the context of the family that the interrelationships between cultural and individual factors in the formation of personality can best be seen."[1]

In this approach to the study of the family, a dynamic model is required that involves delving into a history of the family. Anthropologist Christie Kiefer, in researching and writing an ethnographic study of three generations in Japanese-American families, aimed at "viewing personality as a lifelong process that dynamically interacts with cultural and historical change."[2] Using the in-depth interview and also observing community life, she inspected her "respondents' perceptions of their own past" to find out how "these perceptions affect relations between the generations."[3] She described her general approach: "I show how intellectual habits related to age, sex, culture, and social class affect the way people see their history and how they act toward each other."[4]

Family history has been referred to as a "high-risk endeavor."[5] To get the honest, well-researched account that will make the effort worthwhile requires understanding and sensitivity. In writing this chapter, I have been conscious of the fact that the readership may vary from the historian reconstructing a social history of the family, to the sociologist or anthropologist using a limited number of families as case studies, to the family member seeking to understand his or her own personal history. Whatever the purpose, each of us must be aware of what our intervention into this small group can do. On a more specific level, differing purposes at times require different considerations, and I try to address these. However, each of us has a family, and I make the assumption that information about researching one's own family will be of some interest to every reader. On the other hand, those of us researching our own families can learn from social scientists studying families from a different vantage point.

Finding Families
for Social Science Research

For your own family history, you will probably interview all interested relatives, but social scientists do not have such an easily defined and accessible research population. Some researchers have contacted heads of agencies in a targeted community and asked these individuals to introduce them to families they think might be interested.[6] Others have asked clergy or physicians to recommend them to families, but according to the nature of the project, this may put the minister or doctor in an awkward position because of the relationship of trust and confidentiality he or she often has with families.[7] Often family members are reluctant to commit themselves to such a project, believing that they must have some special problem that has caused them to be singled out or fearing that they will have to reveal intimate details of their lives. Reuben Hill obtained consent from the director of the Minnesota Family Study Center at the University of Minnesota to write a letter telling families who had had contact with the center how important the research was to an understanding of families. The director stressed that this was a study of three generations in the same family, that it was difficult to find three generations in one geographical area, and that the help of these families would be greatly appreciated.[8] Interviewers found that this letter from a respected organization resulted in goodwill toward the research and a willingness to participate.

British sociologists J. M. and R. E. Pahl, studying the impact of a man's managerial career on the family, contacted the men during the time they were in a program at Cambridge and later when they had been in their careers several years.[9] By sending questionnaires to both husbands and wives early on (before they even planned to conduct in-depth interviews), the Pahls aroused interest in the project. I suspect that the purpose of the research—which did not imply that the families were chosen because they were in trouble—made this less threatening. And because the researchers invited everyone who had been in the course to participate in the research, the narrators could assume that they were like everybody else—a comfortable feeling when family matters are going to be discussed.

Introduction
of the Project to the Family

Although I have been referring to "the family" as if it were a monolithic entity, nothing could be further from the truth. Each family member is an individual with his or her own thoughts about a family history or participation in a study of families. At the very beginning of a family interviewing project, it is advisable to take into account the feelings of differing personalities. Folklorist and family historian Margaret Yocum thinks that introducing the project to one's own family is "the biggest emotional hurdle for a field-worker." She advised the researcher to consider three issues: (1) What do you already know about different family members' reactions to recording and writing a history? (2) How do members react when you talk about your desire to write such a history? (3) Is it better to propose the project to the whole family at a gathering or to small groups of individuals?[10]

You must discuss the purpose and research strategy fully with family members. Yocum suggests clarifying the following: (1) what your purpose is, what you want to learn; (2) how each member can help you in the interviewing, research, and editing; (3) whom you will record; (4) how you will deal with sensitive family issues; and (5) what you will do with the material.[11]

The last consideration is of utmost importance for the social scientist. This will require an explanation of the ways that anonymity and confidentiality will be maintained. Also, the social scientist usually does not involve subjects in the editing of research studies, but with this kind of research in which you use extremely personal information from in-depth interviews, such involvement of narrators may be warranted. Although you disguise the individuals for outsiders, those talked about may recognize themselves. If at all possible, let them see the manuscript before publication. Give them this reassurance at the beginning.

Inspiring Narrators' Interest in
Participating in the Research

If you are researching a history of your own family, in explaining your project, you may want to do as Yocum suggests and compare the family history to a genealogy, simply because genealogy is something most people are familiar with.[12] You can point out that a family history or a study of the contemporary family will give a more detailed picture than a genealogy. Explain, for example, that genealogy gives important information, such as birth dates, marriage partners and dates, births of children, deaths—but not how anybody felt about those events. You might also show members other family histories or studies of families to give them specific examples of what you want to do.

Understanding may not be achieved easily, however. Micaela di Leonardo, not intending to write her own family's history, but to do some practice interviews with the aim of saving the tapes for the family, approached her uncle Tony. He consented to be interviewed but never understood her purpose. She described the encounter:

> Tony, an interviewer's nightmare, began as soon as I turned on the tape recorder—"All right, I'm just gonna give you one chapter and you better get it down"—and proceeded to discourse as he pleased, about what he pleased, for hours, refusing to answer my questions. He then called all my aunts and told them I was going to make thousands of dollars from his interview and that he wanted his share.[13]

Di Leonardo's experience is a reminder that even when you think an individual in the family understands what you are doing, that might not be so. You have to explain once again.

Yocum advised the family researcher to ask to see the family Bibles; poems and stories members wrote or loved; crafts such as carvings, quilts, and gardens; and possessions such as scrapbooks, photograph albums, and personal collections.[14] Ask the person to talk about these artifacts and take notes. More problematic are legal papers: Most people will show a birth certificate but might be reluctant to bring out a divorce decree. Do not insist: Get the record from the appropriate county government office. If you take a photograph, get it copied immediately and return the original.

The research activity discussed above has a double purpose: The family members' interest in their own history is awakened, and the researcher learns a lot through artifacts and discussion about them. Researchers must not take without giving something back, however. If you are writing a history of your own family, Yocum suggests making holiday greeting cards with quotations from the members or making for each a photograph album of family history. You might write a paper on the family's folklore and give each member a copy.[15] Another gift is a booklet of family recipes with anecdotes about them. By doing this, you show that you value the preservation of family traditions.[16]

If you are a social science researcher, you will need to interest family members enough so that they will devote time and effort to the interviews. Celia Deschin found that family members in her study of a suburban community became intensely involved "only when questions in the interview touched upon aspects of the individuals' lives about which they felt concern, conflict, or other emotional involvement."[17] In explaining the research questions that you have, you could show how the information gained will be useful to the families interviewed as well as to the wider community.

As in researching one's own family, it helps rapport to make a gesture of respect. If you are able to make photographs—for example, of the original family home—make a copy for each family member. Send the families a letter telling them how the research is coming along and what conclusions seem to be emerging.

Research Strategies

When you are introducing the project, a meeting with all family members eventually is needed. And in researching your own family history, an informal meeting of several family members, listening to them reminisce and spark one another's memories as you record or take notes can be valuable. The in-depth interview is different from the focused interview in a small-group setting, however. The intensely personal nature of the in-depth interview requires one-on-one interaction. Both family historians and social scientists can profitably use a combination of focused interviews and individual interviews.

However, I argue against interviewing just husband and wife together, because the responses of one spouse are influenced by the presence of the other. More important, conjoint interviews are at the top of the scale for high-risk endeavors, because some things may be articulated by one spouse that hurt the other's feelings. Sociologist Richard Gelles found that conjoint interviews in his study of domestic violence exacerbated the enmity between two marriage partners.[18] Only if the research purposes require observation of family interaction would such a research design be warranted.[19]

Sensitivity to Members' Feelings Versus Need to Present Evidence

Inevitably, you will encounter the skeleton in the closet. In researching the biography of her grandmother, Ruth Hanna McCormick, Kristie Miller found that her mother's father had committed suicide. The physician had been induced to list cardiac infarction on the death certificate, and the family had kept its secret for 40 years. By the time Miller began to do the research, family members had accepted the fact of the suicide and the harmlessness of telling the truth about it.[20] Miller was saved by the passage of 40 years.

Indeed, passage of time is an important consideration: You may feel freer to bring the skeleton out if the members of that generation are deceased. When your family history deals with recent events, you have some alternatives. The preferred one is to discuss the skeleton with family members, deciding on wording that is acceptable. Another is to promise to withhold public distribution for a stated length of time. But obscuring the truth is not an alternative if your goal is a credible history. If, as a social scientist, you are presenting a limited number of case studies, you should discuss with family members ways to convey the information in a general way while maintaining confidentiality in specific matters.

Another problem is antagonism between two members. Kristie Miller was bent on interviewing her mother's sister even though her mother had not spoken to this sister for years. She found that reestablishing contact with the aunt and interviewing her at length brought back to her a valuable personal relationship she might never have reclaimed otherwise.[21] Presumably, her valid excuse—the writing of the grandmother's story—made this acceptable to her mother. You have to trust, and hope, that your impartial interviewing of all family members of a certain generation will show that you are just interested in recording each person's story—rather than wanting to record evidence to support one side. However, you may have to make that explicit.

Often family members have different memories of the same event, and almost always they have different interpretations. The challenge is to present these different views in a way that no one feels slighted. When you write the study, use the oral history testimony so that each narrator's individuality is appreciated. Show that diversity in interpretation is expected and enriching. Consider the situation and point of view of each one. Although the following example is simple, it shows an approach that can be used:

> John accompanied his father to the office each day and observed him interacting with businesspeople and associates. His judgment was that he was a hard man to deal with. Ellen, then 10 years old, ran to meet her father when he came home in the evenings. To her, he was affectionate and teasing.

Also, the passage of time and subsequent life experiences influence testimony. When Joyce Antler was researching the life of Lucy Sprague Mitchell, a leader in early childhood education, she was surprised to hear Mitchell's adult children disparage her parenting. One son, then 65, admitted that it was in his adulthood, when he was disappointed in the way his career had gone, that he became resentful of his mother.[22] In researching a biography of Jessie Daniel Ames, a leader in interracial reform organizations in the South in the 1920s and 1930s, Jacquelyn Hall found written evidence of the love Jessie Daniel Ames felt for her sister in their youth. This was corroborated by family members' testimony. But Ames's writings in middle age emphasized resentment against her sister. Part of this stemmed from Ames's memory that her sister had been their father's favored child, and part came from her adult rejection of a model of femininity she identified with her sister.[23]

This kind of highly problematic situation has to be dealt with gingerly if one or both parties is living: One possible way is to indicate that you understand that lives and relationships changed over time, that some family members drifted apart as they encountered their own separate challenges, that because of different experiences over time they cannot now see things in the same way.

Confronting Differences in
Interpretation With the Narrator

Another situation that may arise is when you as researcher-writer accurately record and present an event in the manuscript but the narrator strongly opposes your interpretation. Folklorist Katharine Borland recorded the life history of her grandmother, Beatrice. One event took place in the grandstand at a horse race in Maine in which the young Beatrice, attired in frilly dress, gloves, hat, and carrying a purse, bet on a horse against her father's advice. Her horse won and won again in the second heat while the men around her grew more and more dismayed. When her horse won for the third time, she threw hat, gloves, and purse to the wind.[24]

Her feminist granddaughter analyzed the situation as one in which women were granted only "partial participant status." Beatrice had defied this and bet—"the narrated event takes on the dimension of a female struggle for autonomy within a hostile environment." Beatrice's throwing away gloves, hat, purse—the trappings of femininity—symbolically acted out her rejection of encumbrances placed on women's behavior.[25] The grandmother was shocked by this interpretation and accused her granddaughter of reading into the story her own values.[26]

Borland said that in retrospect she wished she had played that segment of the tape for her grandmother and asked her what meaning she gave it. She also suspected that in part her grandmother's strong feeling about the interpretation came from "loss of authorial control." Borland regretted that she "assumed a likeness of mind when there was in fact a difference."[27] Later, grandmother and granddaughter went over the manuscript again; and the grandmother admitted that although she had not thought about the events in her life in that way, some of what Borland had said was "very true."[28]

This experience points to the danger of the researcher presenting an interpretation of an event in a family history as the only one, of reading into a situation in the past a present view. This does not mean the researcher should keep silent about her or his own interpretation. Borland rightly advised checking with the narrator about meaning and distinguishing the narrator's from the interviewer-writer's interpretations.

Social scientists studying many families can also check interpretations. Chaya Piotrkowski, in preparing the manuscript for *Work and the Family System: A Naturalistic Study of Working-Class and Lower-Middle-Class Families,* discussed a draft with most of the research families. He explained his reasons for doing so:

> Although it was costly, the benefits of such a collaboration for the research investigation cannot be overestimated. Sociocultural bias in interpretation becomes much less problematic, as does the danger of misunderstanding. Such a process also helps guide the course of research, and there is less chance of emerging with a description that is not grounded in the experience of those it purports to represent.[29]

Interviewing Techniques With Family Members

Interviewing in one's own family is different in an important way from other kinds of oral history interviewing. The interviewer has a lifelong relationship with the narrator and a mutual identification with the same family. The good or bad reputation of one family member affects the other family members. The emotional hurt that one member sustains has consequences of some sort for others. You, as interviewer, must be especially sensitive to the difference in interviewing family members from other kinds of interviewing.

There is already a level of trust, but you can give further assurance of your determination to maintain confidentiality. In his book *Recording Your Family History,* William Fletcher advised giving the narrator in a family history the tape to keep. This is not the usual practice, but in this situation it may be advisable, as he explains:

> It helps build trust and emphasizes by direct action the confidentiality that exists between the two of you. You want to stress that the tapes are for your narrator first, and that you want him or her to feel completely sure that feelings of privacy come first where the duplication and distribution of a person's life are concerned.[30]

The narrator may want you to delete a part. You could offer the alternative of deleting the part in the copy but not in the original that the narrator keeps. But if he or she insists on deletion, you must delete. Several weeks later, the narrator may be feeling differently about telling you the same story and say it on tape again and not request deletion. In any case, when the interviews are completed, ask for the tapes, duplicate them, and return the originals to the narrator. Do not discuss the content of the tapes with anyone until the family member has signed a release.

However, I do not advise letting a narrator keep the tape if you are a social scientist researching others' families: In this situation, stress your professional role and define the tape as necessary to your research.

Do as much research as you can in the records before you start interviewing. If this is your family, it is a good idea to interview your favorite relative first, because you will be more relaxed as you become familiar with your interview guide.[31] If this is a social science research project, choose someone who seems most amenable to the project. In either case, you need a goodwill ambassador vis--vis the other members of the family.

Begin the interview with nonthreatening questions, such as date and place of birth, people significant in childhood, favorite games. Wait until the individual reveals confidence in his or her ability to respond and trust in you before you attempt the hard questions. Even then, you may not be inclined to ask a hard question, and the narrator may not feel like answering it. Tell the narrator how you feel about asking; give him or her a chance to describe to you feelings about discussing the matter. Discuss with the narrator the significance of the topic in the overall study.

Also, there will be times when the narrator is evasive. A gentle phrasing of a "why" or "how" question is appropriate. I have said, "Help me to understand this." Probing will not necessarily wreck the relationship if this is done sensitively and in the spirit of collaboration in an important endeavor. Anthropologist Karen Fields's experience in recording and publishing a life history of her grandmother, Mamie Garvin Fields, *Lemon Swamp and Other Places: A Carolina Memoir*, is a good example of this process. The memoir begins with childhood in a black community in Charleston, South Carolina, in the 1890s and ends with her retirement from teaching in 1943. There were several subjects in which Karen Fields and her grandmother did not see eye to eye:

> As we drew chapters from transcripts, we discussed some matters vigorously. Upon rereading certain passages, Grandmother Fields would say, "We *must* add to this"—if, for example, we had neglected the accomplishment of some respected local person. Or she would write, "Let's leave this out"—if, on mature reflection, a comment

seemed too strong, or if an observation threatened to resurrect some long-dead sentiment that she deemed well dead. "Why?" I would demand. Discussing the reasons why showed me aspects of belonging to a Southern community that would not have occurred to me to ask about, while showing us both differences between our standpoints. These discussions deepened our understanding of the human context in which we were working and of each other. Needless to say the arrival of deepened but unsought understanding caused us to dismay at times, for it meant rewrapping packages we had thought already tidy.[32]

At the beginning of each session, ask if there are things about the last interview the family member would like to add. The questions you asked in the session before stimulate memory as the narrator reflects on them later. At the end of each session, suggest topics you will discuss in the next session: "Next time, let's talk about the first years in Brooklyn, what your aunts and uncles were doing then and what family get-togethers were like, experiences with the first baby, etc." Encourage the narrator to add the topics she would like to discuss. These general hints will get the narrator to start thinking and remembering, looking for photographs and letters.

Ask also for the names of people in the community who knew family members well—the customers who regularly came into the family shop over the years, teachers who taught individuals in the family, and so on. By talking to them, you can get not only information but also a sense of how people outside the family thought of various family members. A clearer picture of relationships between family and community members emerges.

Use of Artifacts in Interviewing

In interviewing family members, use of photographs and artifacts is especially helpful. This became clear to me when my brother, Robert Yow, a genealogist, and I went to visit a distant relative, then in her 90s. She mentioned that she still had our great-great-grandfather's New Testament, the one he had carried in his hip pocket when he was fighting in the Civil War. We were curious, because most of the family were Quakers and pacifists. How did this man feel about going against family values? She brought out his New Testament for us to hold. My brother asked if the ancestor had ever talked about his feelings about fighting. She replied that seeing the book reminded her, "Yes, he always said that was wrong and he wished he hadn't done that." She then remembered that as an old man, he refused a pension because he said it was wrong to take arms against a brother. This artifact might have led us to another. By not asking to see this correspondence with the government, we missed an opportunity to see still another important source.

Photographs are the kinds of records that most people keep. The narrator will likely tell you who is in the photograph and where the picture was taken. Ask questions, such as, "Why was the photograph taken at this time? Why does the big sister hold the little sister—were they very close when they were children? After they grew up? Why does this son stand beside his mother while this son stands beside his father? Were these their best clothes? What were their everyday clothes like? The house looks different in this picture from the way it looked in the earlier one: How did the house change over the years?"

Although Bibles and photographs are kept and people define them as important, be alert to other possibilities—such things as a scrap of paper with a grocery list found at the bottom of a trunk or a faded paisley shawl or a broken toy or a mildewed account book or a diagram of a garden. Artifacts not only can be a powerful stimulus to memory and but also lead you to ask questions you had not thought of. Ask about a grocery list: "Are these the only things people usually bought at a store? What did they raise themselves or make at home?" About a wooden toy: "Who made this? Who was it made for? Was this a special relationship in the family? Why do you think this was kept in the family when other toys were not?" About a diagram of a garden: "Whose garden was this? I see only flowers here—does this mean that the woman had a vegetable garden somewhere else or that she did not have to worry about raising her own vegetables? Where did she get her seeds? How did she learn to garden? Who worked with her?"

Also important is the way that family members helped one another. Ask how they survived when there was no cash, what limits were set and who set them, how goods were shared, how services were offered or asked for, how payment was made—in delayed payments of cash, services, or goods?

Those slides and home movies you slept through as a child—look at them again with family participants. Ask them to explain why they took the shots that particular day. Find out if there were family members who refused to be filmed and why. Get them to talk about their feelings on seeing themselves at that period of their lives. This is a window on what their life was like then.

Family Folklore

Smithsonian colleagues Steven Zeitlin, Amy Kotkin, and Holly Cutting Baker collected family folklore and presented types in *A Celebration of American Family Folklore*. They were particularly interested in family sayings, which they described as "the poetry of everyday life."[33] These convey family values and indications of feelings about individuals. One family recalled the origins of a saying: The family drove down to a river where the boys were getting ready to begin a boat trip. Just as they were leaving, one son kissed his sister on the cheek and said, "Goodbye, Sis. Tell Ma the boat floats." From then on whenever a family member called home to assure others that things were all right, he said, "Tell Ma the boat floats."[34] The saying expresses the confidence that individuals in the family care and will want to know what is happening to a family member. This is an example of an important family value lived and carried on from one generation to the next.

Storytelling is another indication of family values or interaction. In *A Celebration of American Family Folklore*, the authors reminded readers that often people remark after a harrowing experience, "At least it will make a good story." They analyzed this process: "Our family stories make it possible to laugh over incidents that were anything but funny at the time, and the laughter signals that the trauma has been incorporated into the daily round of family life."[35] The story will have a meaning in the context of the particular family. Ask each narrator after he or she tells the story, "What do you think is the meaning of this story?"

Often a story will characterize an individual in one broad stroke. For example, family members tell the upcoming generation a story about the grandmother who realized that the granddaughter had not done that day's chore of collecting eggs from the henhouse. The grandmother swore at her, "May ye never have a hen." That granddaughter left the farm and lived in cities all her life. Was the interaction between grandmother and granddaughter a liberation from the hard work of a farm? Perhaps, but in that family, it was an indication of the personalities of the two individuals.[36] Zeitlin, Kotkin, and Baker commented, "[The family stories] enable us to simplify the complexities of a family member's personality into an easily remembered, easily communicated narrative."[37]

The pitfall is that these brief glances simplify too much. The complexity of a character is not revealed. It will be up to you, the interviewer, to get the details that present more complete evidence about an individual.

Family myths serve a purpose, such as to reinforce a distinguishing characteristic of the family, to teach a family value or to save a reputation. "We were rich then." Or, "Your grandfather was known as the smartest man in town—why, he invented the washing machine." Or, "We were always known for our hospitality." Or, the one in my family, "Your grandmother never let a person leave her house hungry." (I've spent a lot of time cooking and nurturing others, believing on the basis of this myth that I, as a woman in this family, am expected to do this.)

You may unconsciously accept the myths in your own family because they are a part of your way of thinking about the world or because they stimulate family pride that you also feel. Or you may be a social scientist studying a particular family from a greater emotional distance. In any case, check these myths out. They may contain a kernel of truth that you can corroborate with other kinds of evidence. On the other hand, they may present an account that is demonstrably false yet revealing of a family need and therefore true in an important way.

Consider family rituals such as the gatherings at weddings, funerals, reunions, and special holidays as evidence of some special kinds of interaction among members. In *A Celebration of American Family Folklore,* religious and secular rituals are described as ways that "real emotional business is transacted." The authors explained: "Stories are told, nicknames bantered, photos taken and perused. For some families these may be their only way of expressing kinship."[38] Go and be both participant and observer. Take field notes on questions you want to ask your narrators about these rituals. Look for all of the ways that kinship is expressed, and ask the participants when you get to the interview what the rituals mean to them.

The family historian and any ethnographic researcher would thus do well to consider folklore as evidence. Distinguish this from factual information about an actual event, however. Here the emphasis will be on meanings. To be meaningful, a story does not necessarily have to be true in its details. For factual information about events, look for corroborating evidence in written records; compare the oral accounts with other kinds of evidence, such as letters, photographs, official documents, and newspaper accounts. Check dates for accuracy.

Ruth Polk Patterson, in her family history, *The Seeds of Sally Good'n: A Black Family of Arkansas,* relied on oral history interviews in which family stories of her ancestors were told to her. She sought to corroborate this information with other sources, such as interviews with neighbors, letters, official records, artifacts, excavation of the family home (with the resulting drawings of the layout), and remains such as pieces of china cups. All of these became clues in the detective work of finding the evidence for the family history.[39]

Suggested Questions to Ask in Family History Research

Patterson's family history is an informative one for the public, because the individuals, although caught up in family aspirations and their own desires, are always seen against the background of national events and local customs. You will need to consider broad themes as you plan the interview guide. William Fletcher in *Recording Your Family History* suggested organizing questions about family history into three broad categories: (1) typical life cycle and "life crisis" events—courtship and marriage, births of children, work and career experiences, decisions in middle age, retirement; (2) historical events and your narrator's experience of them—for example, the two world wars, the Depression, war in Korea and Vietnam, rapid change in technology; (3) personal values, experiences, and life philosophy—for example, religious experiences, affiliations, community, life experience lessons, generational differences.[40]

Linda Shopes suggested a slightly different organization in that it emphasized social relationships and community: (1) the impact of major historical events and trends; (2) relationship of various aspects of social life such as work, religion, community life, or class status and mobility to individuals within the family; (3) structure and dynamics of family life; and (4) folklore by which a family preserves and uses its experiences.[41]

Often a roughly chronological approach is the most useful way to organize an interview. When the narrator is remembering a certain time, living in a certain place during that time, living with certain people, then the researcher can ask the appropriate questions within the broad themes selected. If the narrator has her or his own organization, however, you, as researcher, can fit your questions into it. Because recollections often spring from the way people associate one thing with another in their minds, memoirists often abandon chronological sequences in choosing what to remember. A woman may want to concentrate on the life stages of each child rather than on her own, and she may see herself in the context of interaction with the child. A man may want to discuss first the highlights of his career and return to discuss childhood second because he sees childhood as serving the career.

If you are researching your own family, specific questions such as the following probably have come to mind: "Why did my great-grandparents come here? How did they survive those first years? What did they want for themselves and for their children? What were their decisions and their values that went into the process of making my parents the people they were? How was a family culture built up? Where did it come from? In what ways did family members communicate with one another? What behaviors were expected of a man and of a woman? How have such influences affected my life?"

William Fletcher's *Recording Your Family History* and Jim Watts and Allen F. Davis's *Generations: Your Family in American History* both offered suggestions such as these: In talking about people and events in any life situation, ask, "What was a typical workday like?" Or, "What was a typical Sunday like?" Probe with specific questions: "When did you get up? What did you do? Who prepared the food? Was this the big meal of the day? What did you eat? Who was there?"[42] Such specific questions as "How were people seated at the table?" can be very useful. Seating arrangement is an indication of status within the family: Sometimes women did not sit at all. And headship indicates level of power or, at least, the person to which the group makes a show of respect.

Discover the roles each family member would be expected to take. In discussing the adolescent years, ask such questions as "What were your chores around the house as a girl? What were your brothers' chores? What were you allowed to do for fun? What were your brothers allowed to do? Did your mother and your father indicate to you what they expected you to do in your adult work? Did you think about what you wanted to be? What did you see as the possibilities? Were there other family members who talked to you about what you might do in adulthood?"

The influence of outside institutions can be explored. In our secular times, we may discount religious experience, for example, but this was a part of the lives of older generations. I asked people who had been children in a North Carolina mill village before World War I what they had gotten out of Sunday school attendance. One woman remarked of her minister, "He made me feel important." This was no small feat in a mill village population where the saying in the nearby town about millworkers was, "Don't get close—you'll get lint on you."[43]

Questions about games and stories are productive of many kinds of revelations. In the same project discussed above, I was struck by the narrators' ingenuity and originality in childhood. They made their own games from natural materials. For example, they covered rocks with moss and made "stuffed sofas" for doll furniture. They made their dolls from corn cobs. They then invented life dramas that these dolls played out. They had marriages and funerals for the corncob families in which they practiced the behavior that would be expected of them as adults—for example, someone would deliver an eloquent sermon, someone would cry.[44] I learned much about the norms of this group from asking questions about children's play. And questions about childhood play revealed things about family relationships and the personalities of individuals, such as which aunt let children play in her house and dress up in adult clothes and shoes, which one let the children jump up and down on the beds, which one insisted on silence and obedience.

When the discussion focuses on childhood and adolescence, you have an opportunity to discover family expectations about acceptable behavior and appropriate gender roles. Ask questions such as, "What would have been your mother's attitude toward premarital sex or teenage sex? How did she let you know these things?"[45] Watts and Davis suggested asking, "How important was it in your generation to become a father? A mother?" And inspired by Piri Thomas's account of growing up in *Down These Mean Streets*, they offered this question: "What does 'becoming a man' mean to you?"[46]

Information about family survival is important to all family members. Ask who took care of sick family members, how the family got along during periods of unemployment, what effects there were when a wage earner left the family. In this context, ask how the family survived the Depression. Did the family lose a home? a farm? How did this affect the women? the men? Find out how the two world wars (or others) affected the family.

Many families in this nation have experienced immigration. For a history of black families, find out how the individual family members accomplished the move from South to North, who helped them in this transition, what kinds of experience were different in the new setting, what their hopes were, how they survived.

For immigrant groups, get as much background information on the particular group as you can. Studies such as these will give you clues about specific questions to ask. In your questioning, search for motivation. Find out how the immigration was accomplished and what their expectations were as well as the details of the encounter with the new culture. Watts and Davis suggest asking, "For your grandparents, what did 'making it' in American society mean? What did it mean to your parents? What does it mean to you?"[47]

And ask the hard questions about social injustice, such as, "Was your family ever under attack by another group—for example, the Ku Klux Klan?"[48] And even harder, "Do you know if he ever joined the Klan?" Or, "Were you denied that job because you were not a man (or the right color or attended the right church or had the right kinship ties or spoke the right kind of English)?"

The questions suggested here do not even begin to cover all the possibilities. In your background reading of the particular culture the family comes from and in your reading of other family histories, biographies, and manuals on family history mentioned here, you will find questions applicable to your own study. Search and be open to all kinds of areas to explore; then write out an interview guide with the broad themes significant to you and, within them, the specific questions you need answered. Decide how you will vary the guide to make it appropriate for each family member you interview.

Evaluation of Family Members' Oral Histories

As you ask these questions, there will be times when something does not ring true or contradicts another narrator's testimony. You may also find contradictions in the narrator's statements on the same subject. In writing your own family's history, even though you love these narrators—each of them significant in some way in your life—you must carefully evaluate the oral history. It is a document, a primary source to be approached critically. Of course, you compare one narrator's testimony to others', and you search for other kinds of evidence to dispute or corroborate statements that you suspect may not be true. Akemi Kikumura, from her experience in writing a biography of her mother, advised using direct observation and comparing what you observe with what is being told to you. She also suggested repeatedly asking the same question of a narrator over a long period of time.[49] The narrator may think things through or check on him- or herself and arrive at a more accurate answer. Or something may happen that will make the narrator decide to answer your question more candidly.

There is the phenomenon that Mario Puzo calls *retrospective falsification*.[50] Social scientists sometimes use the term *biography reconstruction* or *retrospective interpretation*. The motivation for this reconstruction of experience to suit the narrator stems from the desire of family members to paint a picture of family life that teaches what they want the next generation to learn. This way of presenting the past in such a way that it satisfies current need is not a characteristic unique to family history, of course. But if it is essentially a picture that other evidence does not support, then you must beware of perpetuating it. Sometimes you, as a member of the family, share its values and want to believe the "retrospective falsification." Be conscious of this possibility as you evaluate the oral history testimony. What the narrator says is true for him or her at that moment or is what he or she wishes were true. You must find out if the evidence bears it out before you present it as a true picture for everyone in the family, generations to come.

Advantages of Studying Family History

I have pointed out potential problems as roads to avoid or choose with caution, but the journey is worth taking. Consider the advantages in researching your own family: Family members will tell you things they would never tell an outsider (and vice versa). Kikumura, an American-born woman from a Japanese family, described her mother as "a woman of Meiji Japan, born in an era when Confucian ethics tenaciously gripped the moral fabric of that country."[51] She found that both generational and cultural differences separated her from her mother, and she felt that she was both "outsider" and "insider." Still, her mother's biography could not have been written by anyone else:

> Given the purpose of my research and the kinds of data I wanted to collect, I firmly believe that my study could not have been completed by anyone other than a member of my immediate family. When I asked my mother if she would have revealed her life experiences to anyone other than a close family member, she replied, "No! You don't disclose your soul to a *tanin* (a nonrelative)."[52]

Certainly the rewards for this research are rich. This is a journey into your family's past, but it is also an exploration of yourself—of the stories, rituals, relationships, values that influence your own way of looking at the world. And the process itself of going over a life together is a means of coming to understand family members and drawing closer to them. Kikumura commented on the effects of this process for her:

> The Life History turned out to be a very transformative experience for me, for in the process, I was able to reshape many of the negative images that society had ascribed to people of color and I was drawn closer to my mother, my family, and my community.[53]

Collecting the tapes that compose an oral history of the family or writing a history is a gift to the generations that come after us. It is a personal, intimate gift. And in this sense, the advantage of doing this kind of historical research is unique.

For the social scientist who has studied by means of in-depth interviews a limited number of families, the work is also rewarding. As Oscar Lewis pointed out, "In the description of the various family members we see real individuals as they live and work together in their family group rather than as averages or stereotypes out of context."[54]

Summary

Family relationships are forever (just a reminder). Therefore the family researcher must be highly sensitive to each member's feelings and motivations in this kind of project. It is crucial that introduction of the project is done so that cooperation or at least acceptance is achieved, but you cannot sacrifice honesty about your purpose to get cooperation. Education of family members about the uses of the family history and research methods is necessary whether you are researching your own family history or carrying out a research project involving several families.

In questioning during the interviewing, defer the hard questions until the narrator is used to the process of being interviewed. Discuss the feeling surrounding the hard question.

Do not hesitate to ask for explanations when something is not clear. Work in the spirit of collaboration on a project of mutual importance when you are researching your own family history. If you are a social scientist studying families, express your appreciation for the time and effort the narrators give to the project. Thank them for helping you learn and keep them informed about the progress of the research.

In planning the project, think in terms of broad categories to be explored. In composing the interview guide, be as specific as possible in formulating the questions so that you get information within the categories or major themes you have chosen. Plan the interview format so that the family history is not wrenched out of the context of the general history of the period. Ask the questions about the impact of depression and unemployment, of war, of immigration that will promote understanding of the family's relationship to the history of the world outside.

With any primary source, a critical approach is necessary, and a family member's recorded testimony is no exception. Stand outside the family in imagination and try to discover the family myths that you yourself accept. Be aware that some members may consciously or unconsciously present a false picture as they teach future generations about the family.

The advantage of researching your own family is that you will have access to information an outsider cannot obtain. The rewards are that you will learn about yourself, gain greater understanding of individuals significant in your life, and leave a priceless heritage. The social scientist gains an appreciation of the ways the general culture interacts with the unique family culture and how both impinge on individual members' psychological development.

Notes

1. Oscar Lewis, "An Anthropological Approach to Family Studies," in *The Psychosocial Interior of the Family* (3rd ed.), ed. Gerald Handel (Chicago: Aldine, 1985), 119-128; see pp. 120-123.

2. Christie W. Kiefer, *Changing Cultures, Changing Lives: An Ethnographic Study of Three Generations of Japanese Americans* (San Francisco: Jossey-Bass, 1974), ix.

3. Ibid., xx.

4. Ibid.

5. Judith Worth, "The Use of the Family in History," *New England Social Studies Bulletin* 34 (1976-1977): 19-22.

6. Elizabeth Bott, *Family and Social Network: Roles, Norms, and External Relationships in Ordinary Urban Families* (London: Tavistock, 1957), 16.

7. Ibid., 13-14.

8. Reuben Hill, *Family Development in Three Generations: A Longitudinal Study of Changing Family Patterns of Planning and Achievement* (Cambridge, Mass.: Schenkman, 1970), 122.

9. J. M. and R. E. Pahl, *Managers and Their Wives: A Study of Career and Family Relationships in the Middle Class* (London: Penguin, 1971), 6-7.

10. Margaret R. Yocum, "Family Folklore and Oral History Interviews: Strategies for Introducing a Project to One's Own Relatives," *Western Folklore* 41 (October 1982): 251-274; see p. 255.

11. Ibid.

12. Ibid., 260.

13. Micaela di Leonardo, "Oral History as Ethnographic Encounter," *Oral History Review* 15 (Spring 1987): 1-20; see p. 10.

14. Yocum, "Family Folklore and Oral History Interviews," 260.

15. Ibid., 262.

16. Yocum, "Family Folklore and Oral History Interviews," 265.

17. Celia S. Deschin, "Some Further Applications and Suggested Principles," *Social Work* 8 (April 1963): 14-18; see p. 17.

18. Richard Gelles, *The Violent Home* (Newbury Park, Calif.: Sage Publications, 1987), 37-38.

19. Linda A. Bennett and Katharine McAvity, "Family Research: A Case for Interviewing Couples," in *The Psychosocial Interior of the Family,* ed. Gerald Handel (New York: Aldine, 1985), 75-94; see pp. 82-87. See also J. Collins and B. Nelson, "Interviewing the Married Couple: Some Research Aspects and Therapeutic Implications," *British Journal of Psychiatric Social Work* 8, no. 3 (1966): 46-51. Graham Allen, "A Note on Interviewing Spouses Together," *Journal of Marriage and Family* 42 (February 1980): 205-210.

20. Kristie Miller, "Ruth Hanna McCormick: A Life in Politics," paper presented at annual meeting of the Oral History Association, October 17, 1992, Cleveland, Ohio. See Kristie Miller, *Ruth Hanna McCormick: A Life in Politics* (Albuquerque: University of New Mexico Press, 1992).

21. Kristie Miller, discussion during the session on biography, annual meeting of the Oral History Association, October 17, 1992, Cleveland, Ohio.

22. Joyce Antler, "Having It All, Almost: Confronting the Legacy of Lucy Sprague Mitchell," in *The Challenge of Feminist Biography*, eds. Sara Alpern, Joyce Antler, Elisabeth Israels Perry, and Ingrid Winther Scobie (Urbana: University of Illinois Press, 1992), 106.

23. Jacquelyn Dowd Hall, "Lives Through Time: Second Thoughts on Jessie Daniel Ames," *The Challenge of Feminist Biography*, 139-158; see pp. 150-151.

24. Katharine Borland, " 'That's Not What I Said': Interpretive Conflict in Oral Narrative Research," in *Women's Words: The Feminist Practice of Oral History* (London: Routledge, 1991), 63-75; see pp. 65-67.

25. Ibid., 67.

26. Ibid., 67-69.

27. Ibid., 69-72.

28. Ibid., 73-74.

29. Chaya S. Piotrkowski, *Work and the Family System: A Naturalistic Study of Working-Class and Lower-Middle-Class Families* (New York: Collier, 1978), 26.

30. William Fletcher, *Recording Your Family History* (New York: Dodd, Mead, 1986), 11.

31. Alan J. Lichtman, *Your Family History* (New York: Vintage, 1978), 49.

32. Mamie Garvin Fields with Karen Fields, *Lemon Swamp and Other Places: A Carolina Memoir* (New York: Free Press, 1983), xii.

33. Steven Zeitlin, Amy Kotkin, and Holly Cutting Baker, *A Celebration of American Family Folklore* (New York: Pantheon, 1982), 150.

34. Ibid.

35. Ibid., 19.

36. Ibid., 16.

37. Ibid., 14.

38. Ibid., 164.

39. Ruth Polk Patterson, *The Seed of Sally Good'n: A Black Family of Arkansas, 1833-1953* (Lexington: University Press of Kentucky, 1985).

40. Fletcher, *Recording Your Family History*, 2.

41. Linda Shopes, "Using Oral History for a Family History Project," in *Oral History: An Interdisciplinary Anthology*, eds. David K. Dunaway and Willa Baum (Nashville, Tenn.: American Association for State and Local History, 1984), 238-247; see pp. 240-241.

42. Jim Watts and Allen F. Davis, *Generations: Your Family in American History* (New York: Alfred A. Knopf, 1978); Fletcher, *Recording Your Family History*, 48.

43. Valerie Yow (listed as Valerie Quinney), "Childhood in a Southern Mill Village," *International Journal of Oral History* 3, no. 3 (November 1982): 167-192; see p. 186.

44. Ibid., 168.

45. Fletcher, *Recording Your Family History*, 26.

46. Watts and Davis, *Generations*, 27.

47. Ibid.; see Section 3, "The American Dream," pp. 34-68.

48. Ibid., 51.

49. Akemi Kikumura, "Family Life Histories: A Collaborative Venture," *Oral History Review* 14 (1986): 1-7; see pp. 5-6. The biography of her mother is published as Akemi Kikumura, *Through Harsh Winters: The Life of a Japanese Immigrant Woman* (Novato, Calif.: Chandler and Sharp, 1981).

50. Quoted in Watts and Davis, *Generations*, 48-49.

51. Kikumura, "Family Life Histories," 4.

52. Ibid., 3.

53. Ibid., 7.

54. Lewis, "An Anthropological Approach to Family Studies," 123.

Recommended Reading

Overviews of Family History

Bate, Kerry William. "Family History: Some Answers, Many Questions," *Oral History Review* 16, no. 1 (Spring 1988): 127-130. In this brief review essay, Bate raises questions about two recently published family histories—one, *The Seed of Sally Good'n: A Black Family of Arkansas, 1833-1953*, is mentioned in this chapter.

Hareven, Tamara K. "The History of the Family as an Interdisciplinary Field," *Journal of Interdisciplinary History* 2, no. 2 (August 1971): 399-414. This article reviews major work on family history and treats each approach, for example, demographic, developmental, and sociological.

Hareven, Tamara K. "The Search for Generational Memory." *Public History Readings.* Eds. Phyllis K. Leffler and Joseph Brent, 270-283. Malabar, Fla.: Krieger Publishing Company, 1992. This is an excellent essay on the need individuals have for "vicarious linkage with the historical group experience"; it presents an analysis of the appeal of the *Autobiography of Malcolm X* and *Roots.*

Saveth, Edward. "The Problem of American Family History," *American Quarterly* 21 (1969): 311-329. Saveth provides an informative overview of what had been done in the history of the American family up to the late 1960s.

Vinovskis, Maris A. "American Families in the Past," *Ordinary People and Everyday Life: Perspectives on the New Social History.* Eds. James B. Gardner and George Rollie Adams. Nashville, Tenn.: American Association for State and Local History, 1983; see pp. 115-137. This article is an overview of scholarly works on the family, with a bibliography pointing to specific studies.

On Using Oral History in the Classroom to Research Family History

Cuthbert, David. "Undergraduates as Historians: Family History Projects Add Meaning to an Introductory Survey," *The History Teacher* 7 (1973): 7-17. In this specific and helpful article, Cuthbert includes the handout he gives to his classes, the release form he uses, and questions his students ask.

Jeffrey, Kirk. "Write a History of Your Own Family: Further Observations and Suggestions for Instructors," *The History Teacher* 7 (1974): 365-373. Jeffrey points out in brief essay form the difficulties of assigning a family history in a one-semester course but includes reasons for having students write a family history nevertheless.

Metcalf, Fay D., and Matthew T. Downey. "Teaching About Families With Local History Sources," in *Using Local History in the Classroom*. Nashville, Tenn.: The American Association for State and Local History, 1982; see pp. 129-149. This could be termed "using the history of a family to teach local history." The chapter includes some specific information on using such sources as federal census data.

Suggestions for Family History Projects

Fletcher, William. *Recording Your Family History*. New York: Dodd, Mead and Company, 1986. Fletcher suggests several hundred questions. My qualm is that some of these as phrased are "leading questions," but the ideas behind them are still useful.

Greven, Philip. *Four Generations: Population, Land, and Family In Colonial Andover, Massachusetts*. Ithaca, N.Y.: Cornell University Press, 1970. The book provides an introduction for the broad themes he pursued in a history of the family in Andover during the 17th and 18th centuries, pp. 1-18, and may suggest themes you can use.

Kikumura, Akemi. "Family Life Histories: A Collaborative Venture," *Oral History Review* 14 (1986): 1-7. This article deals mainly with the interpersonal relationships of interviewer and family members but also contains some suggestions on interviewing strategies.

Kyvig, David E., and Marty, Myron. *Your Family History: A Handbook for Research and Writing*. Arlington Heights, Illinois: AHM, 1978. This is a very useful guide. See especially questions to ask on pp. 27-32 and look at the model Family History Deposit Agreement and the Summary Data Sheet.

Oblinger, Carl. *Interviewing the People of Pennsylvania: A Conceptual Guide to Oral History*. Harrisburg, Penn.: Pennsylvania Historical and Museum Commission, 1978. In this helpful guide, refer especially to Appendix C, "Family and Work Interview," pp. 70-80.

Martin, P. et al. "Family Stories: Events (Temporarily) Remembered," *Journal of Marriage and Family* 50 (May 1988): 533-541. The authors' research indicated that family stories are mainly about personal events rather than historical events of a broader nature; 75% of stories their subjects told were about grandparents, only 20% about great-grandparents, and farther back, only about 4%.

Shopes, Linda. "Using Oral History for a Family History Project," *Oral History: An Interdisciplinary Anthology*, eds. David K. Dunaway and Willa Baum. Nashville, Tenn.: American Association for State and Local History, 1984; see pp. 238-247. Shopes provides a brief, but helpful, introduction to the use of oral history in researching family history.

Watts, Jim, and Davis, Allen. *Generations: Your Family in Modern American History*. New York: Knopf, 1978. The authors present selections from family histories with introductions and suggested questions.

Yocum, Margaret R. "Family Folklore and Oral History Interviews: Strategies for Introducing a Project to One's Own Relatives," *Western Folklore* 41 (October 1982): 251-274. The article contains specific information on this important step of introducing the project to family members.

On the Use of Artifacts

Kyvig, David E., and Marty, Myron. *Nearby History: Exploring the Past Around You.* Nashville, Tenn.: American Association for State and Local History, 1982.

Taft, Robert. *Photography and the American Scene.* New York: Dover, 1964 (first published 1938). This is a history of photography that gives the characteristics of photographs at different times in history. If you are trying to date a photograph, this may help.

9

Conclusion of the Project

This last chapter presents information on evaluation of the interview, possibilities for analysis, provisions for retrieval of information, and instructions for depositing tape and transcript in archives.

Technical concerns are discussed, such as how to write the face sheet, information sheet, and index a tape (see also samples in Appendix C). How to compile a master index from the indices in the total collection is demonstrated. Techniques for transcribing are shown, and transcribing problems are considered. Finally, the necessity for making the tape and transcript available to other people is explored as well as criteria for choosing the place to deposit a collection.

These are the finishing touches to the project: To leave these undone is like leaving the Mona Lisa without a head, not to mention a smile—just putting your brush down and wandering off, muttering, "Finished."

Evaluation of the Interview

This book has offered much discussion on ways that interpersonal relationships, personal agendas, setting, memory, and interviewing techniques affect the quality of the interview. After the interview is completed, the interviewer needs to listen to the taped memoir objectively and evaluate it, asking questions about how the influences mentioned above have made a difference in the taped document.

Consider these approaches to evaluation: Try to corroborate the information on the tape with other documents, written and oral. Listen closely to the testimony to determine if there is consistency within the testimony. If there is a lack of consistency on some point, try to find the reason for this. Ask of the document: What has been omitted? Suppressed? Distorted? Consider also, in the light of what happened afterward, whether this testimony makes sense. Check on facts where you think memory may have been faulty.

Look at the narrator's credentials for the testimony on specific issues: Does he know what he is talking about? Is this firsthand information? How close was he to the events recounted? Think about the recorded testimony in the context of the life. How does the purpose of the narrator affect the testimony? How are reflections on the past influenced by the present situation? Are events or feelings remembered in such a way that they show the influence of present feelings—such as a feeling of abundance and well-being so that harder times in the past are minimized in the telling?

This kind of "filtering" occurred when my students and I were interviewing farm families. We heard much about loneliness and lack of social contacts from the older generations. We wanted to accept their conclusion that the present is a time of social isolation; however, in looking at the list of social activities in the community, it seemed there were plenty of chances for socializing. The older generation may not, in fact, have had as many organized groups in their young adulthood. Other reasons for their loneliness, which they did not emphasize, were that their children had grown up and many activities had involved the children, and their health and age did not permit them to stay up as late as many activities required. Therefore, we had to consider their current situation as they idealized the past in their lives when they went to Grange meetings, danced at the schoolhouse, and played cards with other couples late on Saturday nights.

Ask of the taped memoir how the relationship between interviewer and narrator affected the course of the conversation. First, were they both aware of the historical significance of the document they were recording? Did social norms impinge on the interviewing situation and influence the testimony? (Taboos against discussing sexual experience with a stranger, for example, will certainly influence an answer.) Did interviewing conditions—the environment, others in the room, the narrator's health—affect the testimony? How did phrasing of the question influence the answer? How did the interviewer's skills— such as clarifying, following up on a topic, challenging—make a difference in the information offered?

Looking at the in-depth interview objectively, evaluate its usefulness. Does this taped memoir offer a unique perspective? Does it contribute some insight or some richness of detail not found elsewhere? Is this the best means of acquiring this information? Finally, ask how the information in this interview might be of consequence and importance to people outside the project interested in the general research topic. (See the Oral History Association's "Oral History Evaluation Guidelines" in Appendix B.)

This critique will be invaluable to you as you sift evidence for your own writing. The information should also be written as "Interviewer's Comments" and accompany the tape when it is deposited with the transcription. Whoever listens to the tape or reads the transcript will find your evaluation of it very helpful, indeed. (If you have promised confidentiality, however, you must take care not to include information identifying an individual.)

Face Sheet and Information Sheet

The interviewer's comments go on an information sheet that accompanies the tape. At the top is the information any listener will need to know: the title of the project, the general topic of the interview, the narrator's name (or pseudonym if required), birthplace, date of birth, occupation, and family members if you are using the narrator's real name. In addition, there is the interviewer's name, the date, and the place of the interview. A face sheet is placed over this as a title page. All of this gives information necessary to orient the listener to the situation of the interview. (See Appendix C.)

Content Analysis

As you are evaluating the oral history document, studying the text closely, and indexing the tape, you begin to be aware of how the narrator is recounting experiences—how he or she is selecting, organizing, and constructing. Because this is a guide for collecting information, I do not treat analysis in any depth. However, as you begin to make notes to yourself and discern patterns, this is a good time to consider analytical approaches across disciplines. This is a most creative period for the researcher-writer. John and Lynn Lofland used the terms *surrender* and *discipline* to describe the process of analyzing:

> The surrender entails opening yourself up to your personal sensibilities, insights, and proclivities, as these interact with the data. The discipline entails channeling and evolving these personal interactions with the data in terms of relevant units of analysis, appropriate questions, and the constraints of what is interesting.[1]

Often scholars using the in-depth interview as a research method look for recurring themes, use of symbols and original imagery, and rhetorical devices. Examples of intensive analysis of the individual testimony can be found in folklorist Patrick Mullen's book *Listening to Old Voices: Folklore, Life Stories, and the Elderly.* Mullen showed how a narrator talked about beginning his career as an auctioneer at age 11. In that year of his life he also witnessed an exhumation of a grave and looked down into the visage of a man dead 10 years—an unforgettable confrontation with death. In the closing years of his own life, he chose these two incidents to recount, symbols of his beginning his adult life and of his awareness of its end.[2]

If you have several in-depth interviews with one person, you may take additional approaches. Discussion on analyzing a life history using concepts from clinical psychology was presented in an article by Miles Shore in the *Journal of Interdisciplinary History.* Shore cautioned that psychological interpretation can be considered when (1) otherwise inexplicable events can be explained by psychological factors, (2) enough information is given in the document to warrant this kind of interpretation, (3) the researcher has a degree of mastery of psychological matters, and (4) psychoanalytic concepts can be applied to the specific life history so that it enhances understanding. He suggested considering such occurrences as developmental crises, loss, disappointment, life change precipitating emotional distress, and manifestations of physical and psychological illness. He called attention to the "personal myth," explaining this as "the set of less-than-conscious motivations" that influence attitudes and behavior that form a pattern as the individual goes through life stages.[3]

For writing biography, David Mandelbaum, drawing from his study of the life of Gandhi, suggested considering the parameters of a person's life, the principal turnings, and the person's characteristic means of adaptation. These should be seen in the context of the sociological and cultural structures within which the life unfolded.[4] Another way is to analyze a life history in terms of roles the individual played. L. L. Langness and Gelya Frank presented a discussion about this in a review of anthropologists' analyses of life histories in *Lives: An Anthropological Approach to Biography*.[5] Feminist biographers showed the importance of analyzing life histories in terms of the limitations of gender for both women and men.[6]

Another model to consider is the historian's. If the researcher is using a collection of life histories, usually gathered around a theme such as a particular occupation or movement, then it is the common meanings of the shared experience that are sought. Alessandro Portelli showed how individuals used symbols held collectively that conveyed the meaning of their struggles together.[7] In Ronald Grele's analysis of two oral histories of working-class people, he searched for themes concerning their history. In both accounts the narrators organized and interpreted events, shared by a wider group, to articulate its history, and each found a place for him- or herself within that history. Their interpretations differed, but they were both involved in a "process in the construction of a usable past."[8]

If you are working with life histories from several individuals, looking for recurring concepts and hoping to develop theory from your data, consider still other models. Sociologists Leonard Schatzman and Anselm Strauss suggested taking theoretical notes during the process of data collection. They see this as leading to a process whereby data are placed in categories: for example, "Probably the most fundamental operation in the analysis of qualitative data is that of discovering significant *classes* of things, persons and events and the properties which characterize them."[9] The researcher then finds the links between these classes and begins to form organizing schemes. The example Schatzman and Strauss gave was drawn from research on a hospital. The researchers started with a class of scheduled encounters among hospital staff; they found, however, that most encounters occurred incidentally and around the time of the occurrence of a new or problematic event. They then set up a new class termed "incidental encounters."[10]

In *The Research Act,* Norman Denzin uses the work of sociologists such as Kimball Young and anthropologists such as L. L. Langness to describe an *objective approach* to analyzing life histories. Researchers examine the life histories in the project in terms of the individuals' developmental history—that is, life stages—and life experiences. (Young looked also at the inner life, for example, self-concept and values.) Each life history is viewed as a complete world, but there is much working back and forth between life histories in the collection, comparing the case specific and the general. Denzin contrasted this approach to the *interpretive approach* in which the researcher concentrates on discovering the "meaning of that life as it has been lived by the subject."[11]

Although you need not analyze the oral history in terms of categories, recurring myths, themes, symbols, rhetoric, and so on to prepare it for deposit in the archives, keep in mind possibilities for analysis as you work with the document. Jot down these thoughts for later development as you begin to use the information in your writing.

Index to Each Tape and Master Index

You need an index to the tape. Without an index, any listener, yourself included, will have to guess where a certain conversation begins and then play with the fast forward and reverse buttons on the machine until it can be located. With an index, for example, you know that on side one, around tape counter number 450, the narrator begins to discuss your topic of interest. (Counter tapes vary from recorder to recorder, so the number is approximate.) Any time that you spend indexing the tape will save you much more time as you begin to use the information.

Indexing requires patient and careful listening. Make four headings: narrator's initials (or pseudonym if this is ethnographic research), tape side, tape counter number, and topics. Start your tape counter number exactly at zero as you begin to play the tape. As the narrator begins to discuss a different topic or takes a different slant on the topic, write down the tape side and counter number and the new topic heading. I like to write in some detail what the narrator discusses under the topic heading. In some cases, where I expect that I may quote the narrator directly, I transcribe the sentence. If you do not expect to transcribe the entire tape, then you can save time by transcribing now the sentences you expect to use later. (I have usually not had money for transcription later, but if you do, it is not necessary to transcribe anything at this stage.) (See Appendixes C and D for sample tape index and sample master index to a tape collection.)

There are computer programs for compiling a master index from the indices to individual tapes in a project. I have always done the master index manually, but if you have access to a program that will do this, by all means avail yourself of this convenience. To compile a master index manually, I first make two photocopies of each index so that I have two copies I can cut up. Here you will see the usefulness of having the narrator's initials beside the tape side and counter number on the index: As you cut out these horizontal slivers, each one describing a topic discussed with side and number and narrator's initials, you separate them from the others on the page—and you lose no pertinent information. Cut out each entry and place it in the appropriate subject category. (These are the categories that you had composed for the interview guide.) There will be categories that you did not anticipate, of course, and you make up the titles that fit the subjects the narrators discussed.

You will end up with 15 to 20 or more piles. Look more closely at the items within the piles of cut out slips of paper. Decide which need to be divided along more specific lines than the general topic allowed. For example, I had a heading "Opening of the Gallery" when I was working on the master index for the collection of tapes from the project on the women's cooperative art gallery. Under this heading, I had slips of paper from some 15 narrators who had described the opening preparations. I had another dozen slips from oral histories that gave accounts of the opening celebration itself. I realized that even though these were closely related, they were different subjects that required two piles. Some conversations may appropriately go under another heading; here your extra photocopy can be cut up so that the other heading will have this slip in its pile as well. Alphabetize the headings. You are ready to type a master index to the tape collection.

Later, as you use the information from the project and you want to know who said what on a topic, you have only to look at your master index to see under that topic the names of the narrators who talked about this, with the tape side and tape counter, and brief description of what was said. Within a few seconds, you know which tapes and which segments to review. What a time-saver!

Transcription

A transcription is the written form of a taped interview. There is much debate about whether a transcription is truly a primary source. Surely, the written version of a conversation is not the same as the spoken version. David Dunaway, in considering the relationship of transcription to tape, remarked, "The oral interview is a multilayered communicative event, which a transcript only palely reflects."[12] The transcription is thus at best a step removed from the original. An analogy I use is the difference between a copy in someone's writing (other than the author's) of a 12th-century document: For research purposes you use it, but if you ever get the chance to see the original, you study it and check the copy. For 20th-century history, if it is possible to listen to the tape, that is preferable. And it is necessary in some projects: People studying oral language usage must hear the tape. But often for research purposes, a scholar in history, education, anthropology, sociology, and so on will find that a transcription suffices. Certainly I have been grateful to libraries that sent me photocopies of the transcriptions when I could neither travel miles to listen to the tapes nor afford the cost of having a taped collection duplicated for me. And for my purposes, the transcription was easier to handle because I did not have to put a tape on the machine to play back, hunt for the counter number, and transcribe. In archives, it often is easier to let the scholar read a transcript first so that the tapes are not put under stress from continuous rewinding, fast-forwarding, and so on. Once he or she identifies the crucial tapes, then these are made available. And in some cases, where the tapes are not stored properly, the sound fades and the transcript saves the document from being lost entirely.

Transcribing Techniques

The problem is that accurate transcription is painstaking and time-consuming. It takes a high level of skill and good judgment to force an oral document into a written form that has the degree of truthfulness necessary for research. However, good transcribing techniques can be learned, as well as good judgment.

There is a benefit when the interviewer is also the transcriber, because he or she is familiar with the narrator's speech and the interviewing situation. If you are the transcriber, but not the interviewer, then you will find it helpful to listen to the entire tape first to get a feeling for the speech patterns. Then listen ahead a bit so that you know what comes after the sentence you are working on: You get an idea of where it ends and where the meaning changes. Then rewind the tape to the beginning of the sentence, listening to the phrase, writing it down. When you have finished copying the sentence, listen again, making sure the word order is correct.

A transcribing machine is a godsend, of course. Earphones and a footpedal make this a much easier process than struggling along, using your right hand to rewind and play while also writing or typing. A word processor contributes to the ease of making corrections as you listen, and you end up with a clean copy. If there are mistakes that an auditor or the narrator finds, these are easy to fix without typing the entire transcript again.

Reproducing Speech

The goal is to reproduce as closely as possible the speech of the narrator. In doing this, one of the problems that arises is how to represent speech that is not standard English, the speech we are accustomed to reading.

In *A Woman's Place,* Rosemary O. Joyce discussed "tidying up" (my phrase) a narrator's speech: "Because faithful reproduction takes us one step closer to actual data, any deviation becomes an error." She added:

> It seemed to me a heightened form of snobbery *not* to use the vernacular, a subtle way of saying, "Your speech is strange, and, rather than embarrass either of us, I shall make it proper—like mine." Pure ethnocentrism! Better by far that we quote the bank president, and all of us, with accent intact.[13]

Stay as close as possible to the sound you actually hear. You may be writing down "goin' " and "havin' " many times as well as "ain't" and bad grammar in such phrases as "spoke to him and I." If that was what was said, write it. And the narrator might have said, as Ned Cobb did in *All God's Dangers*, that someone was a "low-down, half-assed scalawag." Leave it in and spell it as closely to the way it sounded as you can.

In her article "Resisting the Editorial Ego" in the *Oral History Review*, Susan Allen expressed this adherence to the spoken version most forcefully:

> Oral history is what comes out of people's mouths, and it has to be captured accurately on paper; or else you violate the integrity of the interviewee, who has been kind enough to give you his or her time, and you violate the integrity of the medium. What is on the tape is what happened in the interview. What is on tape is what was actually said. It is history already written on the wind, and if you feel any responsibility to the truth, you must see that the original content gets onto the transcript.[14]

Punctuation

Punctuating and creating sentences so that you do not misrepresent the meaning is another challenge. Joyce described her method: she uses "nonstandard punctuation, with few commas, semicolons, and even periods, to convey the flavor of Sarah's expressivity—her rapid discourse and run-together phrases and sentences."[15] Short sentences, sentence fragments, and run-on sentences are the way human beings talk. Do not try to force them into standard written English.

Certain usages of punctuation marks are fairly standard in oral history. Use the three points of an ellipsis and a period to show that the sentence remains unfinished. Look at this example:

SMITH: There's nothing more I can say, I mean. . . .

Use a comma to show there was a brief pause, as in this example:

SMITH: In those days people didn't talk about such, didn't discuss, such things.[16]

Use a dash to indicate an interruption in thought:

ROSS: As a child, I used to make hats out of oak leaves—those big old oaks had beautiful leaves—and fastened the daisies on the leaves with broom straws.[17]

A dash is often necessary to make the sentence understandable. In *Oral History From Tape to Type*, Cullom Davis, Kathryn Back, and Kay MacLean gave this example of the way using the dash instead of the comma can clarify meaning:

I told Mr. Boardman, "You know, Mr. Smith, both of the two brothers and their father before them, had an undertaking shop right down on Fifth and Capitol.

I told Mr. Boardman, "You know, Mr. Smith—both of the two brothers and their father before them—had an undertaking shop right down on Fifth and Capitol.[18]

Special Problems in Transcribing

Do you include all the "uh-huhs" and "hmms"? Yes, definitely, if the speaker was troubled, because these may indicate hesitation. If this is just his or her normal speech pattern, then leave enough in to show the pattern but not so many that the speaker's meaning is obscured. J. A. Progler, in his article for the *Oral History Review* on choices in editing, advises first typing an absolutely verbatim account and then deciding which "ums" to leave out. He shows how he types out the verbatim transcript and then its "next distillation." For publication he does still another distillation: Here I present the verbatim transcription and the version for readers.

Verbatim Transcription

HILLER: Uh, well that was written in um, that was written in um, oh by the way, I should mention with the illiac, eh subsequent to the illiac suite we did some, we did some um, programming of um, of um, score composition, in other words how to lay out an actual score with musical notation and I went um, uh to a um, fellow in denver colorado his name was um, um, um, he was a composer, and he devised this thing . . . . (my ellipses)[19]

Distillation 3

HILLER: Subsequent to the Iliac Suite we did some programming of score composition. In other words, how to lay out an actual score with musical notation, and I went to a fellow in Denver, Colorado, he was a composer and he devised this thing. . . . (my ellipses)[20]

(Progler has gone through a second distillation, which I do not show, in which he still leaves out capital letters at the beginning of the sentence and most punctuation.) This narrator, Dr. Lejaren Hiller, is a composer and computer music specialist. The verbatim transcript with all of the "ums" does not correctly represent him; on the other hand, he had just suffered a serious illness that had made remembering difficult. Progler was right to delete some of the "ums" for purposes of offering the interview to the public, but it reads too smoothly to give the reader an indication of the difficulty Hiller was having.

There are "crutch" words and phrases that speakers use over and over again. Sometimes you can leave some of them out if you include enough to indicate the speech habit. "Well" is one, "you know" is another. Look at this example in which the transcriber has rightly left in every word:

QUESTION: Did you try to stop the argument?
ANSWER: Well, I couldn't do. . . . Well, but it wasn't, don't you know, any of my business. No. I didn't try.[21]

Here the repetition of "well" is not just a speech pattern; the speaker is troubled about admitting something.

Sometimes the narrator will begin a sentence, stop, begin again. Do you leave in the false starts? Almost always that is appropriate because the false starts indicate the way the narrator is thinking through the topic as he or she speaks. Look at this example: "I would say yes, we were all—I would have to say I think we were all in it together. It was a group cause."[22] The speaker hesitates, phrases the answer a little differently, and in fact qualifies the statement he originally intended.

The following example may look like a meaningless false start, but it is a meaningful beginning to a story. Notice the way the first use of punctuation misleads the reader, while the second correctly conveys the narrator's meaning: "I will tell you a story from the past now."

Well, that goes back—my first bitter experience with John Lewis goes back to 1917.

Well, that goes back. My first bitter experience with John Lewis goes back to 1917.[23]

Advice to date in manuals has been to leave out a false start if it conveys nothing significant. Keeping to the goal of reproducing the actual speech as closely as possible on the verbatim transcript, I include the false starts almost always. An exception would occur when a narrator stutters or just has a habit of starting a sentence several times: Leave in enough to indicate this speech pattern, but you may not have to leave in every sound if this makes the reading almost impossible or obscures the meaning. Allen rightly makes this distinction: A stutter or a cough (and, I add, habitual repetition of a phrase) is not significant to meaning and therefore may be deleted. Her rule of thumb in making this kind of judgment is helpful: "The only alterations ventured by a transcriber or an editor in creating a transcript should be those that enhance the reader's awareness of what was actually said."[24]

If there is a moment in the interview where the narrator has motioned you to turn the machine off, in parentheses write: "Taping stopped at narrator's request." When there is an interruption, indicate that and the kind of interruption if it makes a difference. Here are two examples, one of which requires an explanation to the reader who will want to know why there was a change in conversation: In one, the narrator lets the dog out; in the other, the man's wife enters the room.

JONES: Did I tell you about the time I . . . (interruption). The time I was sent to the southern part of the peninsula?
SMITH: Yes, I did go to Japan when I was on leave. I had a . . . (interruption when wife enters the room). What else did you want to know about combat duty?[25]

Underline words that the narrator has emphasized. When there are audible clues on the tape or you remember or have written down notes about the nonverbal gestures, write them in parentheses. For example, the sound of pounding can be heard on tape, and the interviewer has indicated that the narrator frowned at the same time:

JONES: He was lying! (Frowns and pounds the table.)

Or, there is a distinct change in the voice:

BROWN: I loved him. (Speaks softly.)

As you transcribe, there will be times when, try as you might to understand, the words are just not audible. Leave a space on the transcript and pencil in "inaudible." It may be that the narrator or someone else more familiar with the regional speech can help you out.

If the narrator consistently mispronounces a word, then spell it as it sounds and indicate in a footnote on the transcript what term is being referred to. For example, "The narrator here says 'sadistics,' which is her substitute for 'statistics.' " Last names needed to identify a person mentioned in the conversation are placed in brackets. If you need to clarify something, place the clarification in brackets. Here is the way Davis, Back, and MacLean suggest doing this:

Original transcript:

We were on this strike fighting against an imposition that the coal company had imposed upon us where the loaders would add their loads 275 more pounds for the ton. . . .

Edited version:

We were on this strike fighting against an imposition that the coal company had imposed upon us where the loaders would [have to] add [to] their loads 275 more pounds for the ton. . . .[26]

The rule is that any word an editor adds must be in brackets.

At the end of the transcribing process, listen to the tape once again as you read the transcription, word for word. Give close attention to word order. This is the careful checking for accuracy that makes the transcription a worthwhile research tool.

Return of the Transcript to the Narrator

If you, as a historian, make a transcript, you should return it to the narrator for corrections. And ethnographers who plan to use direct quotations to illustrate points must be sure the phrasing is correctly transcribed. In any case, the researcher does not want to work with a faulty transcription. Inevitably you miss something, and this final check may save the narrator and yourself much trouble later. (If you are a social science researcher whose project does not require deposit of the transcripts in archives or if you are looking only for data to be coded and used in the aggregate, then you may not need to return the transcript. But carefully check the transcription word for word as you listen to the tape.)

Allen gives an example of a faulty transcription from a project when the narrator was talking about the first time that he met Chief Justice Fred M. Vinson:

My first meeting with Fred was at the Woodland Auditorium Convention [Lexington, Kentucky] and my first observation of him was when Ben Johnson and Billy Klair and some of the rest of them agreed to be for Happy [A. B. Chandler] for lieutenant governor when the fool was nominated, and I think he was nominated in 1931. . . .[27]

The narrator was actually speaking of Ruby Laffoon. The narrator might have gone into print as having called Happy Chandler a fool if the transcription had not been checked. In this case, the interviewer and editor caught the error before the transcription went to the narrator, but it is just such a mistake that could cause everyone a lot of grief.[28]

Beyond that, there is an ethical issue here: When you commit something oral to print and deposit it in archives so that it becomes available to the public, the narrator has a right to see what has happened to her or his words. Everybody knows the taped version is an informal conversation: There is something about print that gives it a formality taped sound does not have. Therefore, there has been a change and the narrator has a right to see what you have done.

When you send the tape and transcript to the narrator, make it clear that you expect that the narrator will not delete material or change meaning. In this accompanying letter, say something like, "I want to be sure this is an accurate representation of your words. Please check to see whether I have misunderstood a word or have spelled a name or term incorrectly." Explain that this transcript should be as close to spoken words as you can make it. Remind the narrator that speech is different from written dialogue. You might even include a page from another transcript if you have the release form for it to show what a final transcript looks like.

Most of the time, a few minor corrections will be made and the document returned to you. Occasionally, however, there is trouble. In *Effective Interviewing*, E. Culpepper Clark warned interviewers not to be surprised if the reaction is negative. He presented an excerpt from a letter he received:

> You cannot imagine the state of shock I was in after first reading your transcription. Truly, I've never liked to hear myself on tape, but. . . . What I do mind is sounding like a bumbling, illiterate. . . . In other words what I'm trying to say is that I'm revolted to the point of nausea about the whole tape. . . . Please endeavor to realize that I am not trying to be unkind or that I am pompous about my intellectual opinions. I can only be myself—honest and plain—very plain spoken.[29]

After all the explanation you give, you will still encounter narrators like Clark's who will change the transcript until all the punch is gone out of it and it is simply a dull bit of prose not even close to the actual taped dialogue. It is unethical for you to change the transcript back; but before you deposit it, place a note on it to warn readers that this is an edited document. Any words the narrator has inserted are placed in brackets; any deletions are indicated by placing a warning in brackets at the appropriate place on the manuscript.

Sometimes you have a project in which the narrator cannot read the transcript for one reason or another. There may be a family member who can read it to him or her as the tape is played. Or you may have to go back and do that. If a family member or someone not connected with the project does this, you will have to explain why a transcript is a rendition of spoken language, not intended to be in correct English or polished. Sometimes it is just not possible for the narrator to go over the transcript: As a last resort, try to get the narrator's permission for a knowledgeable person to listen to the tape and check the transcript.

Index the transcript and compile a master index to the collection in preparation for deposit in the archives. A face sheet or title page, a sheet such as you prepared for the tape that contains interviewer's comments, and a table of contents should accompany the transcript as well. Davis, Back, and MacLean suggest a preface also that introduces the narrator. Readers even 50 years from now will want to thank you. Finally, be sure to send the narrator a copy of the final version. (See Appendix E for samples of record-keeping sheets that can guide you in your endeavor.)

By now you are shaking your head over the time spent on an oral history project. The usual time required for transcribing an hour-long tape is 6 to 10 hours. Willa K. Baum, who directs the oral history office at the Bancroft Library, University of California at Berkeley, estimates that it takes a total of 63 hours to transcribe, audit, do final typing, proofread, visit and call the narrator (to get the corrected transcript back), write the letter of thanks, index the transcript, prepare the pages on the interview history (interviewer's comments) and gather all documents such as the release form.[30] The cost of transcribing alone if you hire a transcriber will be about $10 per hour; for a 60-minute tape requiring 10 hours' work, the bill will be $100.

Considering the expense of money and time, you probably will not transcribe all the tapes in your collection. Decide on priorities: The tape that has little of interest to the general public, contains long segments blitzed by electrical interference, or is very general and not especially informative may not need to be transcribed. And you may not want to transcribe all of a tape: If there is a long section that is irrelevant, leave it out but note that on the transcription in parentheses, such as the one below.

(Portion not transcribed that consists of interruption caused by the passing of a heavy truck and ensuing conversation on noise level in neighborhood.)

It is also possible that certain segments are so intensely personal that the narrator does not want them transcribed or that you feel that, in so doing, you would cause the narrator pain. Indicate on the transcription the general topic not transcribed.

(Here the narrator, Lizzie Borden, requests that the taped segment concerning events involving her parents be sealed.)

Publication of Oral Histories

I have stressed here the necessity of making the transcript as close to a verbatim account as you can. For the publication of life stories, editors often want to "clean up" the language. For their book *Women of Crisis*, Robert and Jane Coles presented their interviews with working-class women, using standard English. Oral historian Sherry Thomas described her reaction to reading the book by admitting that she read 30 or 40 pages before she realized the narrator was not a university-educated white woman but a black itinerant farm worker. She felt that the way the authors had transcribed the language "took away the reality of the woman's experience."[31]

Thomas insisted that almost nobody carefully puts in all the "g's" at the end of a word. When you do that, and add prepositions to make the sentence read smoothly, you change the feeling of the personality of the speaker and obscure his or her reality.[32] After transcribing the words of black sharecropper Ned Cobb for the book *All God's Dangers: The Life of Nate Shaw*, Theodore Rosengarten said that he spelled the words the way they sounded to him. Certainly, he retained the rhythm of the sentences and the grammar that the narrator used. Listen to this example as you read out loud:

> That teached me fair that a white man always wants a nigger in pref-
> erence to a white man to work on his place. How come that? How
> come it for God's sake? He don't want no damn white man on his
> place. He gets a nigger, that's his glory. He can do that nigger just like
> he wants to and that nigger better not say nothin against his rulins.[33]

Editors also rearrange the parts of the transcripts so that all of the discussion on one topic goes together and all of the discussion on another topic is placed together. The very questions asked, which would help the reader to approach the document critically, are omit-ted. Studs Terkel, a journalist who has written several oral histories, including *Hard Times: An Oral History of the Great Depression*,[34] reacted to a question about his editing practices put to him by Ronald Grele, who heads Columbia University's oral history program:

GRELE: [The narrators] respond to you—they respond to the questions
  you ask and by eliminating your questions, aren't you somehow
  obscuring the relationship that evolves there?
TERKEL: No, because it isn't me. See, two things are involved: How do
  you get the truth about—again truth or fact—about the person.
  You've got to get it out. Sometimes my questions might intrude in
  print. I don't need it. Sometimes it's needed.[35]

In the preface to *All God's Dangers,* Theodore Rosengarten ex-plained his method of selecting and rearranging passages and omit-ting his questions so that the narrative is presented unbroken:

> In editing the transcripts of our recordings I sometimes had to choose among multiple versions of the same story; other times, I combined parts of one version with another for the sake of clarity and complete-ness. Stories that seemed remote from Shaw's personal development I left out entirely. By giving precedence to stories with historical inter-est or literary merit I trust I haven't misrepresented him.
>
> Besides this hazardous selection process, my editing consisted of arranging Shaw's stories in a way that does justice both to their occur-rence in time and his sequence of recollection. I tried, within the limits of a general chronology, to preserve the affinities between stories. For memory recalls kindred events and people and is not constrained by the calendar.[36]

Here two experts talking about leaving things out and rearrang-ing are obviously troubled about doing so. Rosengarten is especially sensitive to the distortion that can come about by placing together stories for which the narrator had a different association in mind. These published versions of in-depth interviews can be regarded as highly edited primary sources, as a second step removed from the taped interview, the original primary source (the transcript is the first step removed). Certainly both writers have made available to the public worlds of experience we might never have known but for their work. They have presented others' words in a narrative form so compelling that we are caught up in these worlds.

Did they not do what was necessary to accomplish this? Yes, but there are degrees of tampering. For me personally, as both historian and general reader, I prefer the least possible tampering with the primary source even in the published version. The editor is saying to the reader: Here are the words of this narrator. But they are not the narrator's words if the editor has changed them. I acknowledge the necessity of arranging segments of the taped memoir so that the narrative flows; I am much less accepting of a change in someone's words. At least, in the preface to a book based on taped interviews, the author owes readers an explanation of the editing policy and information about location and accessibility of the original primary sources.

Last, as you write for publication, you will need to footnote the oral history interviews correctly. The *Chicago Manual of Style* advises including names of narrator and interviewer, date and place of the interview, where the tape or transcript is located.[37] However, the footnote or endnote also should have tape side number, tape counter number, or transcript page number:

> Amy Smith Hunt [pseud.], interview by John Jones, Carrboro, North Carolina, 16 June 1976, Tape recording 1:360. Southern Oral History Collection, The University of North Carolina, Chapel Hill, North Carolina.

Or another version:

> Amy Smith Hunt [pseud.], oral history interview with John Jones, Carrboro, North Carolina, 16 June 1976, 1:360. Southern Oral History Collection, The University of North Carolina, Chapel Hill, North Carolina.

For the transcription:

> Amy Smith Hunt [pseud.], transcription of the interview by John Jones, Carrboro, North Carolina, 16 June 1976, p. 23. Southern Oral History Collection, The University of North Carolina, Chapel Hill, North Carolina.

The second citation can be shortened:

> Hunt, taped interview, 1:230.

Or

> Hunt, oral history, 1:230.
> Hunt, transcription, p. 24.

The *Oral History Review* and *International Journal of Oral History* footnote differently from the *Chicago Manual* and from each other: The important thing is to include the information the reader needs to know.

Sharing Information

You have put much work into a project, having made sure that the project has a wider significance than just one person's or one local group's interests. By depositing the collection of tapes in a library or in archives, you can make sure your research continues to be useful even though your own work has come to an end. We are not isolated human beings: The endeavor we undertake to understand human experience is a common one. We need all the help we can get from others, and we give all the help we can. Sometimes the historian has been compared to the detective, which suggests an individual working alone. But the comparison obscures the "full spectrum of criminal investigation" that goes on; for a historical question, it is the work of many investigators over generations that builds the needed evidence.[38]

Now researchers in other disciplines also recognize the importance of making their data available to others. Data from classic studies such as William Foote Whyte's *Street Corner Society* have been placed in archives and made accessible.[39] And granting agencies are beginning to require research data in social science projects to be deposited for other scholars' use.

In searching for a "home" for a collection, try to find out what kind of security system it has. Are tapes that are sealed in whole or in part, according to the narrator's wishes, likely to remain locked up? Are there adequate provisions for public access to the collection? For example, will these tapes appear in the library catalogs? Are there machines in good condition for the public to play the tapes? Will the institution make a copy available to the public, preserving the original? Does the curator understand the value of an oral history collection? Is the curator willing to bind the transcripts and to provide adequate means for preserving these documents?

An important consideration in deciding where to deposit a collection of tapes is the kind of storage facility available for the tapes. Kevin Mulroy, at the Getty Center for the History of Art and the Humanities, advises that the climate in the storage room should remain at about 60 degrees Fahrenheit, plus or minus 5 degrees, with a relative humidity of 40%, plus or minus 10%. If there are drastic changes in temperature or humidity, the tape may swell or shrink. This causes stress on the tape and affects the sound. Of course, tapes should not be placed next to heaters, but they also should not be left in direct sunlight or even artificial light lest there be enough heat to damage them. Tapes should not be stored close to conduits, electric motors, transformers, and other sources of magnetic energy. The storage and playback sites should be kept as dust-free as possible, and no food particles or cigarette ash should be allowed to come in contact with the tapes.[40]

The plastic containers in which cassette tapes come offer good protection. When they are placed in storage, avoid using metal shelving unless the metal has been grounded first. Wooden shelves are safer.[41]

With these recommendations in mind, you can talk over with the curator the environment in which the tapes will be maintained and judge whether this is a good place to put them.[42]

Discuss with the curator ways to publicize the collection's existence and availability. A library or archive that has funds to publish a guide to its oral history collections is providing a very useful bibliographic tool for the public. A copy of such a guide should be copyrighted, and another should be sent to the offices of the *Oral History Review* for inclusion in its bibliography of published collections. It will then be picked up in the next edition of the *Oral History Index*, last published in 1990 by the Meckler Corporation.[43] State and local historical associations should receive notice of the collection, whether or not there is a publication. Finally, you may wish to speak at meetings of local and state historical associations and other professional meetings to let the public know what the project was about and what is contained in the collection. Like an artist, you can now put your brush down, step back and survey the picture, and truly say, "Finished."

Summary

Look at the interview critically for your purposes and for others who will listen to the tape or read the transcript in the future. Everyone will benefit from knowledge of the usefulness and limitations of the document. Try to corroborate the information on tape with other sources. Listen for inconsistencies within the narration. Point out testimony that is not firsthand. Explain how the interpersonal relations and the interviewer's skills affected the interview. Also consider how the current situation and the narrator's purposes influence the way the story is presented.

To enable you and other listeners to retrieve information easily, index each tape and prepare a master index to the collection. In transcribing, strive for a readable text as close to the oral testimony as possible. Listen and check the transcript again; then send it to the narrator to check. If you publish an interview, inform the reader about the editorial guidelines you have followed and the archives where the original verbatim transcript can be read.

Take care in choosing the place where the tapes will be deposited. Will the collection be adequately publicized? Will the public have easy access to the information? Are storage conditions such that tapes and transcriptions will be preserved? Does the curator understand the value of an oral history collection and will he or she make a commitment to honor the narrator's wishes about sealing a tape or portions of it? Having put the archives to these tests and satisfied yourself that this is a safe place, you can deposit the collection.

Notes

1. John Lofland and Lynn H. Lofland, *Analyzing Social Settings: A Guide to Qualitative Observation and Analysis* (Belmont, Calif.: Wadsworth, 1984), 135.

2. Patrick B. Mullen, *Listening to Old Voices: Folklore, Life Stories, and the Elderly* (Urbana: University of Illinois Press, 1992), 238-240, 256-259.

3. Miles F. Shore, "Biography in the 1980's," *Journal of Interdisciplinary History* 12, no. 1 (Spring 1981): 89-113; see pp. 96-103.

4. David Mandelbaum, "The Study of Life History: Gandhi," *Current Anthropology* 14, no. 3 (1973): 177-206. Discussed in L. L. Langness and Gelya Frank, *Lives: An Anthropological Approach to Biography* (Novato, Calif.: Chandler & Sharp, 1981), 71-72.

5. Langness and Frank, Chapter 3, *Lives*, pp. 63-86.

6. Sara Alpern, Joyce Antler, Elisabeth Israels Perry, and Ingrid Winther Scobie, eds., *The Challenge of Feminist Biography: Writing the Lives of Modern American Women* (Urbana: University of Illinois Press, 1992). See also Lawrence C. Watson and Maria-Barbara Watson-Franke, *Interpreting Life Histories: An Anthropological Inquiry* (New Brunswick, N.J.: Rutgers University Press, 1985), 161-184.

7. Alessandro Portelli, "Peculiarities of Oral History," *History Workshop Journal* 12 (Autumn 1981): 96-107; see p. 100.

8. Ronald Grele, "Listen to Their Voices: Two Case Histories in the Interpretation of Oral History Interviews," *Oral History* (Spring 1979): 33-42.

9. Leonard Schatzman and Anselm L. Strauss, *Field Research: Strategies for a Natural Sociology* (Englewood Cliffs, N.J.: Prentice-Hall, 1973), 110.

10. Ibid., 114.

11. Norman Denzin, *The Research Act: A Theoretical Introduction to Sociological Methods* (Englewood Cliffs, N.J.: Prentice Hall, 1989), 195-199. Denzin presents a brief overview of approaches and discusses problems in the analysis of life histories. Cited

works are Kimball Young, *Personality and Problems of Adjustment* (New York: Appleton, Century, Crofts, 1952), and L. L. Langness, *Life History in Anthropological Science* (New York: Holt, Rinehart & Winston, 1965). See especially Kimball Young, *Personality,* pp. 303-311, 320-322, 687-693.

12. David King Dunaway, "Transcription: Shadow or Reality," *Oral History Review* 12 (1984): 113-117; see p. 116.

13. Rosemary O. Joyce, *A Woman's Place: The Life History of a Rural Ohio Grandmother* (Columbus: Ohio State University Press, 1983), 10.

14. Susan Emily Allen, "Resisting the Editorial Ego: Editing Oral History," *Oral History Review* 10 (1982): 33-45; see p. 35.

15. Joyce, *A Woman's Place,* 20.

16. Valerie Yow (listed as Valerie Quinney) and Linda Wood, *How to Find Out by Asking: A Guide to Oral History in Rhode Island* (Providence, R.I.: State Board of Education, 1979); see p. 28.

17. Ibid.

18. Cullom Davis, Kathryn Back, and Kay MacLean, *Oral History From Tape to Type* (Chicago: American Library Association, 1977), 53.

19. J. A. Progler, "Choices in Editing Oral History: The Distillation of Dr. Hiller," *Oral History Review* 19, nos. 1-2 (Spring-Fall 1991): 1-16; see p. 6.

20. Ibid., 8.

21. Davis et al., *From Tape to Type,* 53.

22. Ibid., 51.

23. Ibid., 51-52.

24. Allen, "Resisting the Editorial Ego," 35.

25. Yow and Wood, *How to Find Out by Asking,* 28.

26. Davis et al., *From Tape to Type,* 55.

27. Allen, "Resisting the Editorial Ego," 38-39.

28. Ibid.

29. E. Culpepper Clark, "The Oral History Interview," in *Effective Interviewing,* ed. Alexander Toler (Springfield, Ill.: Charles C Thomas, 1985), 191.

30. Willa K. Baum, *Transcribing and Editing Oral History* (Nashville, Tenn.: American Association for State and Local History, 1977), 18-19.

31. Sherry Thomas, "Digging Beneath the Surface: Oral History Techniques," *Frontiers* 8, no. 1 (1983): 52.

32. Ibid.

33. Theodore Rosengarten, *All God's Dangers: The Life of Nate Shaw* (New York: Avon, 1974), 511.

34. Studs Terkel, *Hard Times: An Oral History of the Great Depression* (New York: Avon, 1970).

35. Ronald Grele, ed., *Envelopes of Sound: The Art of Oral History* (Greenword Publishing, 1992), 36.

36. Rosengarten, *All God's Dangers,* xxiv.

37. *The Chicago Manual of Style* (13th ed.) (Chicago: University of Chicago Press, 1982); see p. 468.

38. G. S. Cause, "Collingwood's Detective Image of the Historian," in *Reassessing Collingwood,* ed. George H. Nadel (Middletown, Conn.: Wesleyan University, 1990), 57-77; see p. 77.

39. William Foote Whyte, "In Defense of *Street Corner Society*," *Journal of Contemporary Ethnography* 21, no. 1 (April 1992): 52-68.

40. Kevin Mulroy, "Preserving Oral History Interviews on Tape: Curatorial Techniques and Management Procedures," *International Journal of Oral History* 7, no. 3 (November 1986): 190-193.

41. Ibid., 192.

42. Ibid., 193.

43. *Oral History Index* (Westport, Conn.: Meckler Corporation, 1990).

Recommended Reading

Preparation of Tapes and Transcripts

Allen, Susan Emily. "Resisting the Editorial Ego: Editing Oral History," *Oral History Review* 10 (1982): 33-45. This is the single most valuable article for information on problems in transcribing.

Baum, Willa K. *Transcribing and Editing Oral History.* Nashville, Tenn.: American Association for State and Local History, 1977. This has long been the most informative book on transcribing and remains a useful book to consult.

Davis, Cullom, Kathryn Back, and Kay MacLean. *Oral History: From Tape to Type.* Chicago: American Library Association, 1977. Chapter 3, "Processing Oral History," has information on transcribing and auditing. The authors permit rather more editing than some current practitioners would sanction, but there is still much that is useful in this book, especially models for record keeping.

Dunaway, David King. "Transcription: Shadow or Reality," *Oral History Review* 12 (1984): 113-117. The author presents a thought-provoking discussion on the relationship of transcription to tape.

Moss, William. *Oral History Program Manual.* New York: Praeger, 1974. This is one of the first comprehensive guides, and it is still useful.

Mulroy, Kevin. "Preserving Oral History Interviews on Tape: Curatorial Techniques and Management Procedures," *International Journal of Oral History* 7, no. 3 (November 1986): 189-197. This is an informative account of how to store and manage an oral history collection.

APPENDIX A

Sample Interview Guide:
Workers at Wurlitzer, World War II

I. Biographical Information

1. Birth, birthplace
2. Father's name; mother's maiden name; siblings
3. Birthplace: father, mother
4. Father's work; mother's work
5. Narrator's education
6. Family of origin: special remembrances such as a Christmas day, a family vacation, Sundays, birthdays
7. Family of origin: cultural life (favorite books, radio programs, church experience)
8. Chores as an adolescent, favorite social events as an adolescent
9. Marriage (date, spouse, where met)
10. Children (names, date of birth)
11. Work before the war

II. Work at Wurlitzer: Beginning Employment

1. Why did you go to work at Wurlitzer?
2. When did you begin work there?
3. In what department did you first work?
4. What shift did you work? How many hours? Overtime?
5. What did you do on your first job there?
6. Did you have prior training or special skills?
7. (If no) How did you train? How long did it take to learn your job? Who trained you?
8. Explain how you did your first job.
9. What did you like about it? Anything you worried about?

III. Production During the War

1. Would you explain what you did in your longest-held job in the plant during the war?
2. How did your work change in the conversion to war production from peacetime production?
3. How did you feel about this different way of working?
4. What was made in your department? In other sections on that floor? Do you know what was made on other floors?
5. Did employees usually know what was going on in other departments? How did they know?
6. What happened to the glider (or bat bomb, or glider wings, or army cots, or TDRI) after it was finished?
7. How was the finished glider transported?
8. Were the parts inspected? By whom? What happened to rejects? Were there repercussions for the workers?
9. Were there quotas? Were they met? What happened if the quota was not met?
10. Did there seem to be a shortage of workers? (If yes) How was this shortage dealt with?
11. How much time was allowed to do the job? Who set the time limits? How did workers handle this?
12. Were you ever aware of a shortage of materials?

IV. Organization of Work

1. Were any skills from prewar production useful in war production?
2. How were workers organized in the plant—did you have a foreman? What was his main job? Superintendent? How often did you see him in the plant? Director? Any contact with him?
3. How many workers were you working with?
4. Did you work with women?
5. What kinds of work did women do in the plant before the war?
6. What kinds of work did women do during the war?
7. Were women assigned to jobs that required long training?
8. Were women seen as bringing special skills to the job?
9. Were women clustered in certain areas of the plant?
10. Were men and women working together on tasks? Do you know of men who refused to work with women or minority groups?
11. Were there any women supervisors?

12. Were there things about the work situation that stand out in your mind that you would like to talk about?

V. Work Community

1. Did you have family members working in the plant? Did family members help each other get jobs?
2. Did you see your fellow workers outside of work?
3. What nationalities and minorities worked at the plant? Did they tend to work together? Socialize together?
4. What were the company-sponsored social activities?
5. Were you involved in company-sponsored activities? Separate activities for men and women?
6. How were new workers coming in treated? Were new male workers treated differently than new female workers?
7. Was there a special place where employees could take breaks and talk to each other? (If yes, were there separate places for foremen? For men and women?)
8. Did co-workers help each other out?
9. Did you make friends working in the plant? Would you tell me how this happened?
10. Did you ever observe incidents of unfairness? Did you ever observe incidents of real helpfulness and kindness?
11. Were there any celebrations at work for birthdays or anniversaries? What did foremen and superintendents think about this?
12. Did most workers attend the company-sponsored events for work awards or war victories?
13. How did people react to war news? Deaths from the war? How did management react? What effect did the good or bad news have on work morale?
14. Were there any social events or places in town that workers went to regularly?
15. Did you feel your income during the war was better than it had been during peacetime? (If so, any special things you did with extra money?)
16. How was your family life affected by the hours you put in at Wurlitzer?
17. Did your spouse also work? Where? Did this necessitate a new way of getting work done in the home?
18. How did you get to work?

VI. Motivation to Work at Wurlitzer During the War

1. Were you ever asked to do special things for the war effort at Wurlitzer?

2. Did management do anything to make people feel a part of the war effort?

3. Were you aware of absenteeism during the 1940s? (If no or yes) How do you account for that situation?

4. What, if anything, did management do to inspire workers to work harder?

5. Were you there in 1944 when the company received the Army/Navy E Award? What happened? How did you feel about the award? Do you recall things people said about it?

6. What were the things about defense work that impressed you? Anything that worried you?

7. At the time, were you thinking about safety on the job? Any company publicity about this? Did you consider possible health hazards in this kind of work? Any talk in the plant about this?

VII. Security

1. How would you describe security precautions in the plant before the war? After the conversion to war production?

2. How were you made aware of security?

3. Were you in a section that dealt with more sensitive production?

4. Were you aware of being closely watched? By whom, do you think? Were explanations given?

5. Were you given any information about cooperating in searches? Were you searched? How did you feel about that? Were searches a frequent occurrence?

6. Did security precautions differ according to what was made in the section?

7. Were you aware of any group that was watched more closely or excluded from sensitive projects?

8. Did you know of German-Americans working in the plant? How were they treated?

9. Who were the guards? How were they chosen? How did you feel about these individuals?

VIII. *Labor Relations*

1. What would you say was the Wurlitzer Corporation management's attitude toward the workers?
2. How did you yourself get along with the managers and the superintendents, directors, chief engineers? (If narrator was promoted to this category later, ask how many contacts he or she might have continued with line workers and what kind.)
3. How often did workers get raises? What would a worker have to do to get a raise?
4. How was a personal disagreement between a boss and a worker dealt with?
5. What were the workers' complaints? How were they dealt with by management?
6. Were there things the management could have done for the workers? Anything you would have especially liked? Why?
7. Was there talk of starting a union? When? How did you hear?
8. What did you observe as workers' reactions to the possibility of forming a union? Management's reactions?
9. How was unionization portrayed by management? How about the newspapers?
10. What steps were taken to form a union?
11. Why do you think unionization did not take place?
12. Were workers' attitudes about working at Wurlitzer different during the war than they had been before?

IX. *Wurlitzer After the War*

1. When did you leave Wurlitzer? Why?
2. What changes in production that started during the war persisted in peacetime? How did those changes affect your job?
3. Did you know people who were laid off immediately after the war? Did they find other jobs? What happened to them?
4. What did you do during the time you were waiting to go back to work?
5. Did returning veterans get their jobs back?
6. Did many women remain in the work force at Wurlitzer?
7. Did workers' attitudes change at Wurlitzer after the war?

Women-Only Questions

1. Were there any differences in working conditions for men and women?
2. At Wurlitzer, was there equal pay for equal work?
3. Did employment benefits for women differ from those offered to men?
4. Were there any incidents in which women were treated differently from their male co-workers by foremen?
5. What requirements were there concerning clothing to wear on the job? Did men also have special clothing requirements?
6. Did you feel that you had skills that came in handy when you were working in the plant?
7. Did a man train you for the job? What were men's attitudes about training a woman?
8. Did you ever hear male employees talking about having women in the plant? What kinds of things did they say?
9. How were you treated by male co-workers in the plant?
10. How did you feel about being able to do the work? Did you see changes in your attitude about the work as time went on? Did you start thinking about yourself in a different way? (Did this job make you want to work?)
11. What were the satisfying things about working at Wurlitzer? Hard things about the job?
12. Did you hope to continue working in this position after the war? Was it a job that would lead to the future?
13. What changes in your own life did the war bring for you?
14. Did women at Wurlitzer ever go places together after work? Visit on weekends? Celebrate birthdays?
15. Were most of your women co-workers from the same age group?
16. What shift did you prefer? Why?

I'd like to ask you now about ways you managed to work full time and care for a family.

17. Were there any child care services provided by the plant? Any social services? Nurse? Cot to lie down on?
18. Who took care of your children while you worked? How did you feel about being separated from them?

19. Were superintendents understanding about absences when a child or spouse or parent was sick? Do you remember any specific incidents?

20. Did you have help with cooking? Cleaning? Child care? Shopping?

21. Would you describe a typical workday during the war years?

22. Was your husband working in DeKalb? How did your husband feel about your working? How did your parents feel about your working? Your children?

23. Was the money you earned yours to do with as you liked? Did the money go into a general family fund? How were decisions made about spending money?

24. What kinds of things did you buy as a result of your having an income?

25. When the war was over, was there pressure for you to quit your job and return home?

26. How did your life change after the war was over?

27. If you could re-live an experience at work during the war years, what would that be?

28. If you could re-live an experience in the family during the war years, what would that be?

APPENDIX B

Principles and Standards
of the Oral History Association

The Oral History Association promotes oral history as a method of gathering and preserving historical information through recorded interviews with participants in past events and ways of life. It encourages those who produce and use oral history to recognize certain principles, rights, and obligations for the creation of source material that is authentic, useful, and reliable. These include obligations to the interviewee, to the profession, and to the public, as well as mutual obligations between sponsoring organizations and interviewers.

Oral history interviews are conducted by people with a range of affiliations and sponsorship for a variety of purposes: to create archival records, for individual research, for community and institutional projects, and for publications and media productions. While these principles and standards provide a general framework for guiding professional conduct, their application may vary according to the nature of specific oral history projects. Regardless of the purpose of the interviews, oral history should be conducted in the spirit of critical inquiry and social responsibility, and with a recognition of the interactive and subjective nature of the enterprise.

Responsibility to Interviewees

1. Interviewees should be informed of the purposes and procedures of oral history in general and of the aims and anticipated uses of the particular projects to which they are making their contribution.
2. Interviewees should be informed of the mutual rights in the oral history process, such as editing, access restrictions, copyrights, prior use, royalties, and the expected disposition and dissemination of all forms of the record.
3. Interviewees should be informed that they will be asked to sign a legal release. Interviews should remain confidential until interviewees have given permission for their use.

4. Interviewers should guard against making promises to interviewees that they may not be able to fulfill, such as guarantees of publication and control over future uses of interviews after they have been made public.

5. Interviews should be conducted in accord with any prior agreements made with the interviewee, and such preferences and agreements should be documented for the record.

6. Interviewers should work to achieve a balance between the objectives of the project and the perspectives of the interviewees. They should be sensitive to the diversity of social and cultural experiences, and to the implications of race, gender, class, ethnicity, age, religion, and sexual orientation. They should encourage interviewees to respond in their own style and language, and to address issues that reflect their concerns. Interviewers should fully explore all appropriate areas of inquiry with the interviewee and not be satisfied with superficial responses.

7. Interviewers should guard against possible exploitation of interviewees and be sensitive to the ways in which their interviews might be used. Interviewers must respect the right of the interviewee to refuse to discuss certain subjects, to restrict access to the interview, or under extreme circumstances even to choose anonymity. Interviewers should clearly explain these options to all interviewees.

Responsibility to the Public and to the Profession

1. Oral historians have a responsibility to maintain the highest professional standards in the conduct of their work and to uphold the standards of the various disciplines and professions with which they are affiliated.

2. In recognition of the importance of oral history to an understanding of the past and of the cost and effort involved, interviewers and interviewees should mutually strive to record candid information of lasting value and to make that information accessible.

3. Interviewees should be selected on the basis of the relevance of their experiences to the subject at hand.

4. Interviewers should possess interviewing skills as well as professional competence or experience with the subject at hand.

5. Regardless of the specific interests of the project, interviewers should attempt to extend the inquiry beyond the specific focus of the project to create as complete a record as possible for the benefit of others.

6. Interviewers should strive to prompt informative dialogue through challenging and perceptive inquiry. They should be grounded in the background of the persons being interviewed and, when possible, should

carefully research appropriate documents and secondary sources related to subjects about which the interviewees can speak.

7. Interviewers should make every effort to record their interviews. They
   should provide complete documentation of their preparation and
   methods, including the circumstances of the interviews. Interviewers,
   and when possible interviewees, should review and evaluate their interviews and any transcriptions made from them.

8. With the permission of the interviewees, interviewers should arrange to
   deposit their interviews in an archival repository that is capable of both
   preserving the interviews and eventually making them available for
   general use. Interviewers should provide basic information about the
   interviews, including project goals, sponsorship, and funding. Prefer-
   ably, interviewers should work with repositories prior to the project to
   determine necessary legal arrangements. If interviewers arrange to re-
   tain first use of the interviews, it should be only for a reasonable time
   prior to public use.

9. Interviewers should be sensitive to the communities from which they
   have collected their oral histories, taking care not to reinforce thought-
   less stereotypes or to bring undue notoriety to the communities. They
   should take every effort to make the interviews accessible to the communities.

10. Oral history interviews should be used and cited with the same care and
    standards applied to other historical sources. Users have a responsibility
    to retain the integrity of the interviewee's voice, neither misrepresenting
    the interviewee's words nor taking them out of context.

11. Sources of funding or sponsorship of oral history projects should be
    made public in all exhibits, media presentations, or publications that
    result from the projects.

12. Interviewers and oral history programs should conscientiously con-
    sider how they might share with interviewees and their communities
    the rewards and recognition that might result from their work.

Responsibility for Sponsoring and Archival Institutions

1. Institutions sponsoring and maintaining oral history archives have a
   responsibility to interviewees, interviewers, the profession, and the
   public to maintain the highest professional and ethical standards in the
   creation and archival preservation of oral history interviews.

2. Subject to conditions that interviewees set, sponsoring institutions (or
   individual collectors) have an obligation to prepare and preserve easily
   usable records; to keep accurate records of the creation and processing
   of each interview; to identify, index, and catalog interviews; and to

make known the existence of the interviews when they are open for research.

3. With the parameters of their missions and resources, archival institutions should collect interviews generated by independent researchers and assist interviewers with the necessary legal agreements.

4. Sponsoring institutions should train interviewers, explaining the objectives of the program to them, informing them of all ethical and legal considerations governing an interview, and making clear to interviewers what their obligations are to the program and to the interviewees.

5. Interviewers and interviewees should receive appropriate acknowledgment for their work in all forms of citation or usage.

Oral History Evaluation Guidelines

Program/Project Guidelines

Purposes and Objectives

a. Are the purposes clearly set forth? How realistic are they?

b. What factors demonstrate a significant need for the project?

c. What is the research design? How clear and realistic is it?

d. Are the terms, conditions, and objectives of funding clearly made known to judge the potential effect of such funding on the scholarly integrity of the project? Is the allocation of funds adequate to allow the project goals to be accomplished?

e. How do institutional relationships affect the purposes and objectives?

Selection of Interviewers and Interviewees

a. In what ways are the interviewers and interviewees appropriate (or inappropriate) to the purposes and objectives?

b. What are the significant omissions and why were they omitted?

Records and Provenance

a. What are the policies and provisions for maintaining a record of the provenance of interviews? Are they adequate? What can be done to improve them?

b. How are records, policies, and procedures made known to interviewers, interviewees, staff, and users?

c. How does the system of records enhance the usefulness of the interviews and safeguard the rights of those involved?

Availability of Materials

a. How accurate and specific is the publicizing of the interviews?
b. How is the information about interviews directed to likely users?
c. How have the interviews been used?

Finding Aids

a. What is the overall design for finding aids?
b. Are the finding aids adequate and appropriate?
c. How available are the finding aids?

Management, Qualifications, and Training

a. How effective is the management of the program/project?
b. What provisions are there for supervision and staff review?
c. What are the qualifications for staff positions?
d. What are the provisions for systematic and effective training?

What improvements could be made in the management of the program/project?

Ethical/Legal Guidelines

What procedures are followed to assure that interviewers/programs recognize and honor their responsibility to the interviewees? Specifically, what procedures are used to assure that:

a. the interviewee is made fully aware of the goals and objectives of the oral history program/project?
b. the interviewee is made fully aware of the various stages of the program/project and the nature of his/her participation at each stage?
c. the interviewee is given the opportunity to respond to questions as freely as possible and is not subjected to stereotyped assumptions based on race, ethnicity, gender, class, or any other social/cultural characteristic?

d. the interviewee understands his/her right to refuse to discuss certain subjects, to seal portions of the interview, or in extremely sensitive circumstances even to choose to remain anonymous?

e. the interviewee is fully informed about the potential uses to which the material may be put, including deposit of the interviews in a repository; publication in books, articles, newspapers, or magazines; and all forms of public programming?

f. the interviewee is provided a full and easily comprehensible explanation of her/his legal rights before being asked to sign a contract or deed of gift transferring rights, title, and interest in the audio and/or visual tape(s) and transcript(s) to an administering authority or individual; and, whenever possible, the interviewee is consulted about all subsequent use of the material?

g. all prior agreements made with the interviewee are honored?

h. the interviewee is fully informed about the potential for and disposition of royalties that might accrue from the use of her/his interview, including all forms of public programming?

i. the interview and any other related materials will remain confidential until the interviewee has released their contents for use?

j. care is taken when making public all material relating to the interview?

What procedures are followed to assure that interviewers/programs recognize and honor their responsibilities to the profession? Specifically, what procedures assure that:

a. the interviewer has considered the potential for public programming and research use of the interviews, and has endeavored to prevent any exploitation of or harm to interviewees?

b. the interviewer is well trained and will conduct his/her interview in a professional manner?

c. the interview is well grounded in the background of the subject(s) to be discussed?

d. the interview will be conducted in a spirit of critical inquiry and that efforts will be made to provide as complete a historical record as possible?

e. the interviewees are selected on the basis of the relevance of their experience to the subject at hand and that an appropriate crosssection of interviewees is selected for any particular project?

f. the interview materials, including tapes, transcripts, agreements, and documentation of the interview process, will be placed in a repository after a reasonable period of time, subject to the agreements made with the interviewee, and that the depository will administer their use in accordance with those agreements?

g. the methodologies of the program/project, as well as its goals and objectives, are available for the general public to evaluate?

h. the interview materials have been properly catalogued, including appropriate acknowledgment and credit to the interviewer, and that their availability for research use is made known?

What procedures are followed to assure that interviewers and programs are aware of their mutual responsibilities and obligations? Specifically, what procedures are followed to assure that:

a. the interviewers are made aware of the program goals and are fully informed of ethical and legal considerations?

b. interviewers are fully informed of all tasks they are expected to complete in an oral history project?

c. interviewers are made fully aware of their obligations to the oral history program/sponsoring institution, regardless of their own personal interest in a program/project?

d. programs/sponsoring institutions treat their interviewers equitably, including the establishment of provisions for appropriate compensation and acknowledgment for all products resulting from their work, and support for fieldwork practices consistent with professional standards whenever there is a conflict between the parties to the interview?

e. interviewers are fully informed of their legal rights and of their responsibilities to both the interviewee and to the sponsoring institution?

What procedures are followed to assure that interviewers and programs recognize and honor their responsibilities to the community/public? Specifically, what procedures assure that:

a. the oral history materials, and all works created from them, will be available and accessible to the community that participated in the project?

b. sources of extramural funding and sponsorship are clearly noted for each interview or project?

c. the interviewer and project endeavor not to impose their own values on the community being studied?

d. all tapes and transcripts will not be used in an unethical manner?

Tape/Transcript Processing Guidelines

Information About the Participants

   a. Are the names of both the interviewer and interviewee clearly indicated on the tape/abstract/transcript and in catalog materials?

   b. Is there adequate biographical information about both interviewer and interviewee? Where can it be found?

Interview Information

   a. Are the tapes, transcripts, time indices, abstracts, and other materials presented for use identified as to the project/program of which they are a part?

   b. Are the date and place of the interview indicated on the tape, transcript, time index, and abstract, and in appropriate catalog material?

   c. Are there interviewer's statements about the preparation for or circumstances of the interviews? Where? Are they generally available to researchers? How are the rights of the interviewees protected against improper use of such commentaries?

   d. Are there records of contracts between the program and the interviewee? How detailed are they? Are they available to researchers? If so, with what safeguards for individual rights and privacy?

Interview Tape Information

   a. Is the complete master tape preserved? Are there one or more duplicate copies?

   b. If the original or any duplicate has been edited, rearranged, cut, or spliced in any way, is there a record of that action, including whom and when and for what purposes the action was taken?

   c. Do the tape label and appropriate catalog materials show the recording speed, level, and length of the interview? If videotaped, do the tape label and appropriate catalog information show the format (e.g., U-Matic, VHS, 8mm, etc.), and scanning system, and clearly indicate the tracks on which the audio and time code have been recorded?

   d. In the absence of transcripts, are there suitable finding aids to give users access to information on tapes? What form do they take? Is there a record of who prepares these finding aids?

   e. Are researchers permitted to listen to or view the tapes? Are there any restrictions on the use of tapes?

Interview Transcript Information

a. Is the transcript an accurate record of the tape? Is a careful record kept of each step of processing the transcript, including who transcribed, audited, edited, retyped, and proofread the transcripts in final copy?

b. Are the nature and extent of changes in the transcript from the original tape made known to the user?

c. What finding aids have been prepared for the transcript? Are they suitable and adequate? How could they be improved?

d. Are there any restrictions on access to or use of the transcripts? Are they clearly noted?

e. Are there any photo materials or other supporting documents for the interview? Do they enhance and supplement the text?

f. If videotaped, does the transcript contain time references and annotations describing the complementary visuals on the videotape?

Interview Content Guidelines

Does the content of each interview and the cumulative content of the whole collection contribute to accomplishing the objectives of the project/program?

a. In what particulars does each interview or the whole collection succeed or fall short?

b. Do audio and visual tapes in the collection avoid redundancy and supplement one another in interview content and focus?

In what ways does the program/project contribute to historical understanding?

a. In what particulars does each interview or the whole collection succeed or fall short of such contribution?

b. To what extent does the material add fresh information, fill gaps in the existing record, and/or provide fresh insights and perspectives?

c. To what extent is the information reliable and valid? Is it eyewitness or hearsay evidence? How well and in what manner does it meet internal and external tests of corroboration, and explication of contradictions?

d. What is the relationship of the interview information to existing documentation and historiography?

e. How does the texture of the interview impart detail, richness, and flavor to the historical record?

f. What is the basic nature of the information contributed? Is it facts, perceptions, interpretations, judgments, or attitudes, and how does each contribute to understanding?

g. Are the scope, volume, and (where appropriate) the representativeness of the population interviewed appropriate and sufficient to the purpose? Is there enough testimony to validate the evidence without passing the point of diminishing returns? How appropriate is the quantity to the purposes of the study?

h. How do the form and structure of the interviews contribute to making the content information understandable?

i. If videotaped, does the interview capture unique "visual information"?

j. Does the visual element complement and/or supplement the verbal information? Has the interview captured interaction with the visual environment, processes, objects, or other individuals?

Interview Conduct Guidelines

Use of Other Sources

a. Is the oral history technique the best means of acquiring the information? If not, what other sources exist? Has the interviewer used them, and has he/she sought to preserve them if necessary?

b. Has the interviewer made an effort to consult other relevant oral histories?

c. Is the interview technique of value in supplementing existing sources?

d. Do videotaped interviews complement, not duplicate, existing stills or moving visual images?

Interviewer Preparation

a. Is the interviewer well informed about the subjects under discussion?

b. Are the primary and secondary sources used in preparation for the interview adequate?

Interviewee Selection and Orientation

a. Does the interviewee seem appropriate to the subjects discussed?

b. Does the interviewee understand and respond to the interview purposes?

c. Has the interviewee prepared for the interview and assisted in the process?

d. If a group interview, have composition and group dynamics been considered in selecting participants?

Interviewer-Interviewee Relations

a. Do interviewer and interviewee motivate each other toward interview objectives?

b. Is there a balance between empathy and analytical judgment in the interview?

c. If videotaped, is the interviewer/interviewee relationship maintained despite the presence of a technical crew? Did the technical personnel understand the nature of a videotaped oral history interview, as opposed to a scripted production?

Technique and Adaptive Skills

a. In what ways does the interview show that the interviewer has used skills appropriate to . . .

—the interviewee's condition (health, memory, mental alertness, ability to communicate, time schedule, etc.)?

—the interview conditions (disruptions and interruptions, equipment problems, extraneous participants, etc.)?

b. What evidence is there that the interviewer has . . .

—thoroughly explored pertinent lines of thought?

—made an effort to identify sources of information?

—employed critical challenges when needed?

—thoroughly explored the potential of the visual environment, if videotaped?

c. Has the program/project used recording equipment and tapes which are appropriate to the purposes of the work and use of the material? Are the recordings of good quality? How could they be improved?

d. If videotaped, are lighting composition, camera work, and sound of good quality?

e. In the balance between content and technical quality, is the technical quality good without subordinating the interview process?

Perspective

  a. Do the biases of the interviewer interfere with or influence the responses of the interviewee?

  b. What information is available that may inform the users of any prior or separate relationship to the interviewer to the interviewee?

Historical Contribution

  a. Does the interviewer pursue the inquiry with historical integrity?

  b. Do other purposes being served by the interview enrich or diminish quality?

  c. What does the interview contribute to the larger context of historical knowledge and understanding?

Independent/Unaffiliated Researcher Guidelines

Creation and Use of Interviews

  a. Has the independent/unaffiliated researcher followed the guidelines for obtaining interviews as suggested in the Program/Project Guideline section?

  b. Have proper citation and documentation been provided in works created (books, articles, audio-visual productions, or other public presentations) to inform users of the work as to interviews used and permanent location of the interviews?

  c. Do works created include an explanation of the interview project, including editorial procedures?

  d. Has the independent/unaffiliated researcher provided for the deposit of the works created in an appropriate repository?

Transfer of Interviews to Archival Repository

  a. Has the independent/unaffiliated researcher properly obtained the agreement of the repository prior to making representations about the disposition of the interviews?

  b. Is the transfer consistent with agreements or understandings with interviewers? Were legal agreements obtained from interviewees?

  c. Has the researcher provided the repository with adequate descriptions of the creation of the interviews and the project?

  d. What is the technical quality of the recorded interviews? Are the interviews transcribed, abstracted, or indexed, and, if so, what is the quality?

Educator and Student Guidelines

Has the educator:

a. become familiar with the "Oral History Evaluation Guidelines" and conveyed their substance to the student?

b. ensured that each student is properly prepared before going into the community to conduct oral history interviews?

c. become knowledgeable of the literature, techniques, and processes of oral history, so that the best possible instruction can be presented to the student?

d. worked with other professionals and organizations to provide the best oral history experience for the student?

e. considered that the project may merit preservation and worked with other professionals and repositories to preserve and disseminate these collected materials?

f. shown willingness to share his/her expertise with other educators, associations, and organizations?

Has the student:

a. become thoroughly familiar with the techniques and processes of oral history interviewing and development of research using oral history interviews?

b. explained to the interviewee the purpose of the interview and how it will be used?

c. treated the interviewee with respect?

d. signed a receipt for and returned any materials borrowed from the interviewee?

e. obtained a signed legal release for the interview?

f. kept his/her word about oral or written promises made to the interviewees?

g. given proper credit (oral or written) when using oral testimony, and used material in context?

APPENDIX C

Sample Face Sheet

UNIVERSITY OF RHODE ISLAND
STATE ORAL HISTORY PROGRAM: HISTORY OF HERA

Oral History Review
with
NATALIE KAMPEN

by Valerie Yow
The Hera Gallery, Wakefield, Rhode Island
July 18, 1988

SOURCE: Samples are used with permission from Alexandra Broches and Natalie Kampen.

Sample Information Sheet

UNIVERSITY OF RHODE ISLAND

STATE ORAL HISTORY PROJECT: HISTORY OF HERA GALLERY

General topic of interview: The making of an art historian. The intellectual ferment in South County in the early seventies. The place of Hera Gallery in the history of South County and in the lives of its founders.

NARRATOR: NATALIE KAMPEN   INTERVIEWER: VALERIE YOW

DATE: July 18, 1988   PLACE: Hera Gallery
                                                          Wakefield, Rhode Island

PERSONAL DATA
Birthdate: 1944
Spouse: (divorced)
Occupation: college professor of art history

BIOGRAPHY

Natalie Kampen, at the time of this oral history recording, had just finished teaching at one university and was getting ready to take a new position as a director of Women's Studies at another. She had come to the community in 1969 with a master's degree in Art History. During her years of teaching art history in the state, she had finished her Ph.D. in art history and built a distinguished record of research and publication. Not a member of the Hera Gallery, she was, nevertheless, a consistent supporter and close friend to founding members. Her marriage had just ended at the time of this recording and the interview catches her on the point of a new career in administration and a new personal life.

INTERVIEWER'S COMMENTS

This recording by a very perceptive, articulate observer is invaluable for information on the intellectual ferment among women in South County during the seventies. While there is little specific on the founding of Hera, the intellectual climate which made that possible is explained here. This testimony is straight forward; the point of view is that of a feminist art historian. Natalie Kampen's involvement continues to be that of supporter and consultant to the gallery; and therefore she does not choose the role of noninvolved observer, but openly states her allegiance to the gallery and championship of women in the field of art. The candor of the interview may be in part a characteristic of the narrator's personality, in part a result of the preexisting friendship and trust between narrator and interviewer.

Sample Index (first page)

UNIVERSITY OF RHODE ISLAND

STATE ORAL HISTORY PROGRAM: HISTORY OF HERA

NARRATOR: NATALIE KAMPEN   INTERVIEWER: VALERIE YOW

Place: Hera Gallery   No. of tapes: 1
          Wakefield, Rhode Island   No. of sides: 2
                                        Length of tape: 60 minutes
Date: July 18, 1988

Initials, Side, Counter Number			TOPIC OF DISCUSSION
NK	1	002	Introduction
NK	1	008	Birthplace and birthdate Philadelphia, 1944
NK	1	010	Growing up place Philadelphia suburb
NK	1	012	Parents' work Father trained in ancient history, but worked as a certified accountant. Mother, an art and architectural historian.
NK	1	015	Siblings Sister, 3½ years younger. She is married and teaches neurophysiology at a medical school.
NK	1	020	Art education in childhood She was regarded as a promising child artist and was given art lessons. At fifteen or sixteen, she went to an art school in Philadelphia eight hours a day during one summer. She found out she did not want to do art as a full-time occupation.
NK	1	032	Ambition in childhood Her mother, a graduate student then in art history, took her to a lecture about art history. Natalie fell in love with art history. The lecture, given by Frederick Hart, was on paintings from the Italian Renaissance. The slides were so beautiful and the language was so vivid that she remembers the lecture almost word for word. She saw for the first time the "connection between the beautiful object and the beautiful question."

APPENDIX D

Sample First Page of a
Tape Collection's Master Index

Oral History of the Hera Gallery, Wakefield, Rhode Island

MASTER INDEX

Please note: the first number after the name of the oral history is the side number; the second number refers to the tape counter number.

ADMINISTRATION AT HERA (See also Coordinator at Hera)
Broches 2: 379. Gutchen 2: 191. Richman 2: 319; 3: 060, 339.

ADMINISTRATIVE ASSISTANT AT HERA
Bodin 1: 240. Chabot 1: 288. Richman 3: 060. Waterston 1: 053; 2: 266.

ADMISSIONS PROCESS AT HERA (See also Men and Hera, Admissions)
Barnett 2: 280. Chabot 1: 221; 2: 035. Greene 1: 311. Hackett 2: 119. Jahn 2: 138. Killilea 2: 298. Malik 1: 522. Powers 2: 020, 034.

ART AND ART HISTORY WOMEN'S GROUP
Christofferson 1: 225. Kampen 1: 360. Killilea 2: 025. Richman 2: 241.

ART DEPARTMENT, UNIVERSITY OF RHODE ISLAND
Christofferson 1: 075, 330. Cutting 1: 075, 097, 109. Gelles 1: 088. Greene 1: 060, 075, 095, 108, 485. Gutchen 1: 417. Hackett 1: 148, 188, 295, 330; 2, 285. Jahn 1: 271, 305, 326. Kampen 1: 532. Malik 1: 177, 188. Pagh 2: 042, 150. Powers 1: 572. Richman 1: 320. Rohm 1: 340, 360, 405, 454, 609.

ART EDUCATION BEGINNING IN ADULTHOOD
Barnett 1: 018. Gelles 1: 099, 110, 163. Greene 1: 060, 108, 124. Gutchen 1: 409, 417. Hackett 1: 092,148, 188, 330. Killilea 1: 158, 165, 181, 219. Malik 1: 160. Pagh 1: 112, 293. Richman 1: 212.

ART EDUCATION IN CHILDHOOD
Bodin 1: 062. Bornstein 1: 202. Broches 1: 064. Cutting 1: 061. Gutchen 1: 086, 115. Hackett 1: 056. Jahn 1: 064, 122. Kampen 1: 020. Killilea 1: 069. Richman 1: 065. Rohm 1: 021. Waterston 1: 153.

SOURCE: Used with permission from Alexandra Broches and Natalie Kampen.

APPENDIX E

Model Record-Keeping Sheets

You will need a log for registering the tapes and a form for recording information in more detail about each narrator's interviews. Here are some ways of keeping records. Sample 1 is based on that shown in *Oral History From Tape to Type*, by Cullom Davis, Kathryn Back, and Kay MacLean (Chicago: American Library Association, 1977), which I have modified.

Sample 1   Interview Data Sheet

NARRATOR: ADDRESS:

TELEPHONE: BIRTHDATE: BIRTHPLACE:

INTERVIEWER: PLACE OF INTERVIEW:

	Date	Total Time	Collateral Materials	Indexed
Introductory letter				
Telephone call				
Preliminary visit				
Interview 1				
Interview 2				
Interview 3				
Interview 4				
Release form returned				

Tapes received	_____	Proofread	_____
Labeled	_____	Corrected	_____
Collateral materials returned	_____	Indexed	_____
Transcribing begun	_____	Table of contents	_____
Number of pages	_____	Transcription photocopied	_____
Total time	_____	Tape duplicated	_____
Editing	_____	Thank you letter	_____
Returned to narrator	_____	Tape and transcript deposited	_____
Received from narrator	_____		
Reread by	_____	Duplicated tape and transcript sent to narrator	_____
Final typing	_____		

Problems: _____

Special considerations: _____

Sample 2 is a master log for the project. As you accumulate tapes, you need to know at a glance which ones have been processed, what remains to be done for others.

MASTER LOG FOR PROJECT														
Interviews Completed	Date	Release form signed	Tape indexed	Copy of tape sent to narrator	Transcription begun	Transcription completed	Transcription sent to narrator	Transcription returned	Transcription corrected	Transcription retyped	Proofreading final	Table of contents	Transcription sent to narrator	Deposited in archives

APPENDIX F

Sample Release Forms

The following sample release forms both for narrator and for interviewer are from the University of Rhode Island and the University of Maine. They illustrate the range of complexity in forms of releases.

I _____ hereby give to the University of Rhode Island this taped life history and grant the university the right to make it available to the public for such educational purposes as the archivist or Director of Oral History Program judges worthwhile.

NARRATOR _____

ADDRESS _____

_____

DATE _____

INTERVIEWER _____

ADDRESS _____

_____

DATE _____

RESTRICTIONS _____

_____

_____

NORTHEAST ARCHIVES OF FOLKLORE AND ORAL HISTORY
South Stevens Hall
University of Maine
Orono, Maine 04473

In consideration of the work the Northeast Archives of Folklore and Oral History is doing to collect and preserve material of value for the study of ways of life past and present in the New England–Maritime area, I would like to deposit with them for their use the items represented by the accession number given below.

This tape or tapes and the accompanying transcript are the result of one or more recorded, voluntary interviews with me. Any reader should bear in mind that he is reading a transcript of my spoken, not my written, word and that the tape, not the transcript, is the primary document.

It is understood that the Northeast Archives of Folklore and Oral History will, at the discretion of the Director, allow qualified scholars to listen to the tapes and read the transcript and use them in connection with their research or for other educational purposes of a university. It is further understood no copies of the tapes or transcript will be made and nothing may be used from them in any published form without the written permission of the Director.

Signed: _____

Date: _____

Understood and Agreed to:

Interviewer: _____   Date: _____

Director: _____   Date: _____

Accession number: _____

From Edward D. Ives, *The Tape-Recorded Interview: A Manual for Field Workers in Folklore and Oral History* (Knoxville, Tenn.: University of Tennessee Press, 1974, appendix). Used by permission. Ives advises that this their standard release form, the one used 95% of the time.

Interviewer Agreement

NORTHEAST ARCHIVES OF FOLKLORE AND ORAL HISTORY
South Stevens Hall
University of Maine
Orono, Maine 04473

<u>Interviewer Agreement</u>

I, _____ , in view of the historical
        (Interviewer: type or print)
and scholarly value of the information contained in the interview(s) with

_____

(Interviewee(s): type or print)

and as designated as accession number _____, knowingly and volun-
tarily permit the Northeast Archives of Folklore and Oral History the full
use of this information, the tapes and transcripts and all other material in
this accession, and hereby grant and assign to the Northeast Archives of
Folklore and Oral History all rights of every kind pertaining to this information, whether or not such rights are now known, recognized, or contem-
plated, except for such restrictions as are specified below.

_____
       (Date)

                         _____
                            (Interviewer's signature)

Restrictions:

Understood and agreed to: _____
                                   (Director)

                         _____
                                    (Date)

From Edward D. Ives, *The Tape-Recorded Interview: A Manual for Field Workers in Folklore and Oral History* (Knoxville, Tenn.: University of Tennessee Press, 1974, appendix). Used by permission.

Deed of Gift for Deposit in Archives

UNIVERSITY OF RHODE ISLAND
KINGSTON • R.I. 02881

University Library

DEED OF GIFT

The following material is hereby presented as a gift to the University of
Rhode Island Library, with the understanding that it shall be cared for in a
manner which will, in the judgment of the University, best provide for its
physical preservation and at the same time make it available to properly
qualified research scholars and students.

Dated this _____ day of _____ 19 _____

Signature _____

Address _____

The University of Rhode Island hereby accepts and acknowledges the gift
to the University of Rhode Island Library of the collection described below
and agrees to administer it in accordance with its established policies.

Dated this _____ day of _____ 19 _____

Accepted by: _____
              Signature

_____
      Title

Description of Collection: _____

_____

_____

Name of Collection: _____

Author Index

Subject Index

American Anthropological Association, 89
American Historical Association, 89
American Psychological Association, 89
American Sociological Association, 89
Anonymity, 92, 93, 94, 95, 109
Archives, selection for deposit of oral histories, 240-241
Artifacts: used to stimulate interest in family history, 197, 204-205; used to stimulate memory, 74
Autobiography: distinguished from life history, 169, 170; retrospective accounts in, 172

Bias: in biography, unconscious fulfillment of needs, 177, 178; negative attitude toward narrator, 178-179; researcher's, 7, 32, 33, 76, 110, 136, 157, 158, 168, 177-180; testing for bias, 180
Biography: distinguished from life history, 169; means of unconscious fulfillment of biographer's needs, 177, 178
Biography and oral history: constructing interview guide for, 186-187; constructing the self in, 169, 170, 172, 173, 179; conveying the whole person, 178-179; initial contact with subject, 170; interviewing subject's associates and enemies, 181, 182; legal difficulties in biographical research, 184; negative attitude toward narrators in researching biography, 178; places in which to record, 171; representativeness of the life, 185; resisting inclination to judge, 179; testing for interviewer's bias, 180

Chicago Manual of Style, 237
Collaboration in oral history research, 33
Commissioned research: checks, 98-99, 108; commissioners'expectations, 157-161; community review, 99; contracts in, 105, 110; pressure on researcher, 100, 110; setting up a board, 160; truth in, 157, 158. *See also* Community studies; Work community
Communication: gender and, 129-134; nonverbal, 76-77
Community studies: choice of narrators, 149, 150; commissioned, 157-161; educating the community 146, 147, 149, 158; ethnic communities, special considerations, 151-153; interview guide, 147, 148, 150-151; neighborhood histories, 153-155; preparation for interviewing, 144, 145; structuring the interview guide, 150. *See also* Commissioned research; Work communities
Confidentiality, 93-95, 202
Conjoint interviews, 58, 92, 108, 110, 198-199
Constructing the self: in autobiography and oral history, 169, 170, 172, 173, 179
Content analysis of oral history: common themes and symbols, 224; concepts from clinical psychology, 223; folklorists' approach, 223; life stage approach, 225; parameters of individual life, 224; recurring concepts, 224-225
Contracts: in commissioned research, 105, 110; in recording and writing biography, 185
Copyright, 84-86, 109
Copyright Act of 1976, 84-85
Cost-benefit analysis, 91

About the Author

Valerie Raleigh Yow received her M.A. and Ph.D. in history from the University of Wisconsin. She trained in oral history methodology at the University of North Carolina's Southern Oral History Program. In addition, she studied adult development at the Harvard Graduate School of Education and psychology at Boston College.

With sociologist Hugh Brinton and social historian Brent Glass, she carried out her first oral history project, "Families of Carrboro," in 1974-1975, concentrating on interviewing women millworkers. She trained interviewers and interviewed in the project on the history of women clerical workers in Rhode Island, sponsored by their national organization, Nine-to-Five. She has been Associate Director of the State Oral History Project in Rhode Island and a member of the History Department at the University of Rhode Island, as well as a faculty member at Northern Illinois University in DeKalb.

Among her public history publications are *Patient Care: A History of Butler Hospital, 1957-1993* (forthcoming), *Hera: A Women's Art Cooperative, 1974-1989* (1990), *The Adventures of Saving a Historical House: The Gurler Heritage Association* (1991), and *Bryant College: The First One Hundred and Twenty-Five Years* (1988). Other publications based on oral history include "Women Clerical Workers" in Charles Stephenson and Robert Asher (Eds.), *Life and Labor* (1986); "Childhood in a Southern Mill Village" in *International Journal of Oral History* (Spring 1983); "Farm to Mill Village: Two Lives," in Marc Miller (Ed.), *Working Lives* (1981); and *How to Find Out by Asking: A Guide to Oral History in Rhode Island*, with Linda Wood (1979).

Dr. Yow has served as consultant on numerous oral history projects and has delivered papers at annual conferences of the Oral History Association and the American Association for the History of Medicine. She is an independent scholar living in Chapel Hill, North Carolina, where she researches and writes histories and conducts a practice in psychotherapy.